The Sociology of
Luigi Sturzo

The Sociology of
Luigi Sturzo

by Nicholas S. Timasheff

Professor Emeritus of Sociology
Fordham University

HELICON PRESS   *Baltimore—Dublin*

Helicon Press, Inc.
1120 N. Calvert St., Baltimore 2, Maryland

Helicon Limited
Dublin, Ireland

Library of Congress Catalog Card Number 62-18772

Copyright © 1962 by Nicholas S. Timasheff
All Rights Reserved

First edition

PRINTED IN THE UNITED STATES OF AMERICA
BY GARAMOND PRESS, BALTIMORE, MARYLAND

Contents

Introduction

It is commonly taken for granted that Vilfredo Pareto's *"General Treatise on Sociology"*[1] was the only first class work produced in the twentieth century by Italian Sociology. However, the main contention of this volume is that the name of Don Luigi Sturzo will be similarly remembered in the annals of sociology as long as there is interest in the historical development of the science founded by August Comte.

While Pareto's work contributes a great deal to sociology, his primary occupation was that of an economist, and he is frequently remembered in that role. Sturzo is best known as a prominent actor on the political scene of his native country, and is frequently remembered as the man who led a movement of Catholic social reform. Neither classically capitalist nor traditionally socialist, his movement attempted to combine Christian tradition with some of the rising elements of modern culture and to bring about a mutual revivification and ennoblement of both forces.[2] He felt that this program could not be accomplished without a thorough reform of modern social structures, and that such a reform would have to include the elimination of the wage system as a correlate of "the deproletarization of the proletariat."

Endowed with the qualities of an outstanding leader and with the gifts of a powerful propagandist, Sturzo used the spoken and written word as a strong weapon in his struggle toward the realization of a social ideal. The actor on the political scene was moved from within by the reflective thinker and the serious scholar. His directions and

[1] Published in 1915, simultaneously in Italian and French; English translation, under the title *Mind and Society*, 4 vols., 1936.
[2] Cf. R. Pollock, "L'uomonella società e nella storia" in Sturzo's *Del Metodo Sociologica*.

suggestions were based not on a superficial expediency but were from the beginning illumined by a vision of society which was both real and pragmatic.

Historical circumstances granted Sturzo a period of more than twenty years in exile in which to employ his ebullient energies and vigorous talents in research and writing. During these years, his thought shifted from a primarily political emphasis, enriched by a philosophical background, to a more reflective and scholarly concern with the living issues of the social reality that confronted him. This period saw the maturation of his sociological views and their expression in several sociological treatises. His sociology thus combines reflective thinking with a real awareness of society, both sharpened and refined by political action, effort, and struggle. It is the sociology of a participant observer who has reflected upon his experience. Of course, there are many other sociologists who have been keen observers, but these have commonly had limited and peaceful fields of observation. Sturzo's sociology is the result of an active participation and struggle for social and political ideals.

This kind of sociology should have aroused a great deal of attention, but it remained almost unnoticed, as the survey of the literature on Sturzo's sociological work in Chapter VIII will show. The reasons for this discrepancy between the inner value of his work and the extent of its influence are manifold and complicated. In his native Italy, his work was not noticed perhaps chiefly because it was the work of a political exile published in foreign languages; in America, his treatment was considered incommensurate with the "positivist" type of sociology predominant at the time of publication of his major works; in those European countries where sociology was cultivated, the various political conditions made the absorption of new ideas like Sturzo's untimely and unfavorable. These factors, however, are all descriptions of circumstances external to the value of Sturzo's work.

Perhaps the main internal reason for the indifference to Sturzo's sociology was its philosophical and even theological background. Many thought that it was only a disguised treatise on theology along the lines of Thomist philosophy. It is the contention of this volume that the philosophical and theological aspects of Sturzo's treatises may be removed like scaffolds are removed after the completion of a building, and that what remains is a magnificent contribution to sociology in its modern meaning, an empiric science of society. The problems posed by this viewpoint will be discussed in Chapter II and again in Chapter IX.

The order of arrangement of this volume follows logically from the foregoing preliminary remarks. It begins with a chapter devoted to "the man and his work." There follow five chapters (II–VI) each devoted to Sturzo's contribution to one of the major problems of sociological theory, namely: 1) what science is sociology; 2) what is society and what is its relationship with the individual; 3) are there sociological laws and eventually what is their nature; 4) what are the basic traits of society looked at from the static (morphological, structural) viewpoint; and 5) what does it mean that society is dynamic? Three concluding chapters (VII–IX) are devoted to the relationship of Sturzo's sociology with other sociological theories, viewed in three perspectives: 1) how did he appraise other sociological theories; 2) how has his theory been appraised by those scholars who have become familiar with his theory; and 3) in the general stream of sociological thought, what place should be assigned to Sturzo's "new sociology" as he himself calls it.

Note on References and Abbreviations

STURZO's WORKS are referred to in the text (in parentheses). If the page number is not preceded by any letter, the reference is to *Inner Laws*. (A table of concordance with the Italian version, *Società*, appears in Appendix I). Other works of Don Luigi Sturzo are referred to by using code letters, namely:

B—"La sociologia a la sua collegamento con le diverse scienze," in *Bollettino di sociologia dell' Instituto L. Sturzo*, No. 1, 1956.

C. & S.—*Church and State.*

G. M.—*Les guerres modernes et la pensée catholique*, Montreal, 1942.

H—"History and Philosophy," in *Thought*, March 1946.

I. C.—*The International Community and the Right of War*, London, 1929.

Inf.—"The Influence of Social Facts on Ethical Concepts," in *Thought*, March 1945.

L.—*Sociologia storicista* (Introductory lecture delivered at the beginning of the course on historicist sociology in 1958/9 and published by the Instituto Luigi Sturzo).

M—*Del metodo sociologico; riposta ai critici.* Milano-Bergamo, 1950.

N—*Nationalism and Internationalism*, New York, 1946.

P. M.—"Politique et morale," in *Cahiers de la nouvelle journée*, No. 40, Paris 1938.

S. P.—*Spiritual Problems of Our Time*, New York, 1945.

T. L.—*True Life* (La vera vita), New York, 1943.

References to works of other authors appear in footnotes except in the case when the work referred to is discussed in the same section of the text; in this case page references are preceded by the letter p.

Some of the works of Pitirim A. Sorokin are quoted so often that their titles (both in the text and in footnotes) are replaced by code letters. They are:

SCP–*Society, Culture, Personality,* New York, 1947.
SCD–*Social and Cultural Dynamics,* 4 vols., New York, 1937-41.
CST–*Contemporary Sociological Theories,* New York, 1928.

References to the present author's *Sociological Theory, its nature and growth,* 2nd edition, New York, 1957, are made by using the code letters ST.

Finally, the following abbreviations have been used in reference to a few periodicals:

ACSR–American Catholic Sociological Review.
AJS–American Journal of Sociology.
ASR–American Sociological Review.

❁ ❁ ❁

Direct quotations from Sturzo's work have been made in the following way. Whenever a work has been published only in English (English version being a translation of an unpublished Italian MS), or has appeared in English in addition to an Italian or French version, the English text had been used as the basis; however, the sentences have been simplified by omitting all words irrelevant in the given context (. . .); the sequence of words has sometimes been altered; finally, the text has been eventually clarified by introducing additional words omitted in Sturzo's elliptic sentences [   ]. In a few cases, the reasons for alterations have been explained in footnotes. If more serious alterations were necessary, Sturzo's ideas have been rephrased; the corresponding sentences appear without quotation marks, but still with references to the pages of Sturzo's works.

Whenever a work is available only in Italian or French, the present author has offered his own translation, in quotation marks if it is close to the original, but without them if the text renders only the meaning, but not the words of the master.

CHAPTER I /

The Man and his Work

The Man and His Work

1. *A biographical sketch*[1]

"TO UNDERSTAND Sturzo the sociologist, one has to understand Sturzo the man," says Paul Furfey,[2] one of his greatest admirers. "The personality and experience of Sturzo are reflected in his sociology. He is a philosopher, a poet and a statesman, and these vocations have left an important imprint on his theoretical work. As a philosopher, he has felt the necessity of synthesis; as a poet, he is endowed with a peculiar vision which conduces him directly, by a kind of intuition, to the kernel of a complex problem. As a statesman, he has acquired a vast experience which is not granted to the majority of the sociologists."[3] This statement succinctly indicates the desirability of opening this study of Sturzo's sociology with a biographical sketch.

Luigi Sturzo was born Nov. 26, 1871, in a family belonging to the lower but ancient Sicilian nobility. His place of birth was Caltagirone, a town then famous for its ruins of Greek temples, now an industrial center and the heart of a fertile agricultural district. From his early youth, Luigi displayed an inclination for the priesthood; this was significant in a family in which another son, Luigi's elder brother, later became a bishop. Luigi Sturzo was trained for the priesthood

---

[1] This section has been written mainly on the background of Sturzo's "My Political Vocation," *Commonweal*, vol. 34, Sept. 29, 1941, and of scattered statements in Sturzo's *Del Metodo*. For secondary sources P. Furfey's paper "La sociologia di Luigi Sturzo" in Sturzo's *Del Metodo* (pp. 125-69), A. Robert Caponigri's "Don Luigi Sturzo," *Review of Politics*, vol. 14 (1952), and M. Moos' "Don Luigi Sturzo, Christian and Democrat," in *American Political Science Review*, 39 (1945) have also been amply used. Special references are made only with respect to statements appearing in other sources.

[2] P. Furfey, *op. cit.*, p. 125.

[3] *Ibid.*, pp. 129-30.

first in Caltagirone and later in Catania. During his early years of
training, young Sturzo had already developed an unusual variety of
interests. He organized literary and musical circles and even composed a kind of lyrical drama. Before completing his studies, he
organized a diocesan committee and several cooperative societies. He
was ordained a priest in 1894. Initially he had planned to embrace
an academic career and to cultivate Thomist philosophy. He went to
Rome to study at the Angelicum and the Gregorian University,
dividing his time among theology, philosophy and sociology. During
these years of academic study, Sturzo was strongly influenced by G.
Toniolo[4]; for a while, he seemed inclined to modernism, but he remained uncompromising in his theology.

The 1890's were years of great political and social tensions and a
man of Sturzo's temperament could not remain out of the main
stream. He was both fascinated by *Rerum Novarum* (1891), and
disappointed by its rather cool reception. He found fertile ground
for reflection and action in his immediate environment. On Holy
Saturday, 1895, while assisting a parish priest on his visitation of the
homes of his parishioners, he was horrified by the people's incredible
misery and squalor. He became so ill after this visit that for several
days he could not bring himself to eat. For a while, he put aside his
books on theology and philosophy and began to study what the
socialists and the philanthropists had to say about the conditions of
the laboring masses.

In 1897, while on a vacation in Sicily, he witnessed an attempted
revolt of peasants and workers and its brutal repression by the government. As soon as he had completed his studies in Rome, he returned to Sicily. Having made the firm decision not only to study
(as he had originally planned) but also to act, he never swayed from
that decision, filling the long years that the Lord granted him with
relentless activity and intensive thought.

His activities were diversified; he taught philosophy and sociology
at the Caltagirone seminary, he founded a weekly newspaper in his
native town, *Il Croce di Costantino,* and in Palermo, he helped to
start *Il Sole,* a daily paper whose objective was to spell out the details
of his social ideals.

He began very early to participate actively in the municipal life of

4 See below section 3, p. 17 ff.

his region. To begin with, he became a municipal councillor in his native town. In 1905, at the insistence of Christian Democrats, he let himself be elected mayor of Caltagirone, despite the general directive to Catholics not to occupy political positions in the new realm (*Non Expedit*, 1874); however, at that time the position of the Vatican had already been somewhat mollified, and, in practice, municipal offices were exempted from the prohibition. He held the position of mayor until 1920, and by no means nominally; he tried to inculcate new life into the municipal self-government and succeeded rather well in this design.

Almost immediately upon his return to Sicily, Sturzo started to organize the youth, the peasants and the workers into professional associations. In connection with this line of his activity, he fought government orders disbanding Catholic and Socialist workers' organizations. On one occasion, he directed a strike of 80,000 rural workers who were demanding the improvement of labor conditions. In 1902, he joined the association of Italian municipalities, formed one year earlier in Milan. In 1915, he was elected its vice-president.

He published articles and pamphlets and two books on the social problems of the time, and was very proud when, in 1923 Vilfredo Pareto approved his *Indirizzi Politici e Riforma Locale* saying that, of course, the book was a scientific work, and not simply a statement of political views.

In 1915, when Italy joined the Western powers in their war against Austria (and later against Germany), Sturzo moved to Rome, where he was very soon elected secretary general of the *Giunta direttive dell' azione catolica*. He founded an institution for the care of war orphans, and actively participated in the organization of the Union of Christian Workers, which very soon counted 2,100,000 members—more than a similar socialist organization.

However, it was during the troublesome years of 1919-22 that Sturzo rose to the stature of a first class political figure on the national level. The Austro-Italian armistice was signed on Nov. 4, 1918; on Nov. 17th, in Milan, Sturzo delivered a major address on the problems of postwar reconstruction. On Nov. 23rd, he gathered in Rome with a group of friends. On January 18, 1919, the Populist Party was founded, and enjoyed an immediate success. At the November, 1919, elections, the Party won one fifth of the seats in the Chamber of

Deputies. To understand its rapid success, says Sturzo, one must realize that the Catholic social movement had developed uninterruptedly during the preceding years of crisis (N. 111). He defined the party—his party—as the formation of a political and economic center between the socialists-communists on the one hand, and the liberals expressing the views of bourgeois radicals on the other (N. 114). Alas, as it usually happens, too rapid growth was later on dissipated by a conspicuous lack of homogeneity; this weakness showed up during the years of contest with the Fascists, and appeared again in the Christian Democratic Party of De Gasperi, the postwar successor of the Populist Party.

Let us take a closer look at the glorious formative days. The formation of a party striving for the realization of Christian principles in society presented some difficulty because, at that time, the *Non Expedit* was still in force. However, the formation of the party had been preceded by a talk between Don Sturzo and Cardinal Gasparri, who had assured the former that the attitude of the Holy See would be benevolent[5] and that the *Non Expedit* would soon be revoked. The revocation came in November 1919.

The initial success of the Populist Party brought great influence to its leader and inspirer; but, since he had never been a member of the parliament, he could not become a member of the cabinet, much less the Prime Minister. Some political theorists have reproached him for not having seized the opportunity to form a cabinet, which might have prevented the Fascist march on Rome.[6] But it is doubtful whether Sturzo ever had this opportunity. Shortly before the ascent to power of the Fascists, Sturzo invited the Socialists to form a coalition cabinet, but, ignoring the danger, the socialists declined. They foolishly supported the general strike of July and August, 1922; which so frightened the Italian bourgeoisie that they opened the gates of Rome to the Fascists.

In the beginning of the Fascist era, Sturzo allowed two members of his party to accept ministerial positions under Mussolini, but they were to act as individuals, not as representatives of the Populists. The hope that the Fascists would show moderation was soon frustrated,

[5] Details are told in Carlo Sforza, *Contemporary Italy* (1944), p. 257, on the basis of Sturzo's personal communication.
[6] H. Finer, *Mussolini's Italy*, 1936, p. 135.

and Sturzo's party went over into opposition (April 1923). Under an obscure threat of reprisals against the Church in the event that Mussolini's government were overthrown by the Parliament, Sturzo left the leadership of the party and retired to the monastery of Monte Cassino. After a short while, he left Italy. His party was disbanded by royal decree in November of 1926.

He resided first in London, but in 1940, he moved to the United States, where he remained until 1946. These years of exile, so fruitful with respect to theoretical work (see below section 4), were also years of continuous action. Sturzo fought continuously, by spoken and written word, for the freedom of his country. When he resumed the studies he had interrupted by years of intensive participation in national politics, he found himself enriched by the political experiences he had accumulated. He says himself that this participation in political action could not but help him to understand theories and facts with more feeling of reality, and helped him to formulate with more precision the sociological theory that had always been one of the main concerns of his life (G. M. 27).

After the end of the second world war, Sturzo returned to his beloved Italy. By that time he had become too old to take up an active part in the political life of his country. However he was granted a lifelong seat in the Italian Senate, although he paid only rare visits to that assembly. He made a remarkable speech in February 1954 which—it is almost incredible, but is true—was his first formal parliamentary address. It might be summarized like this:

Freedom must be total, but attempts to achieve it are complicated by three factors: the fear of freedom, the inferiority complex *versus* the Marxian doctrine, and the vested interests of the governmental bureaucracy. Two concepts face each other. One of them is intervention on the part of the State, leading to State socialism. The other is freedom, leading to civil and social cooperation. "I am for freedom," said Sturzo. "Freedom is participation in power; but power presupposes property, initiative, risk. Such is the law of history."[7]

A few days later as a consequence of this speech, Premier Scelba appointed Sturzo to head a commission to investigate the network of government agencies dealing with industry.[8] Scelba's cabinet soon

[7] *Time*, March 8, 1954, p. 36.
[8] *Ibid.*, March 29, 1954, p. 26.

disintegrated, and no further development along the lines suggested by Sturzo's commission seems to have taken place.

Nevertheless, as he had done in exile, Sturzo continued to work as a political theorist and as a theoretical sociologist. His postwar papers on political issues will probably form at least two volumes of his *Opera Omnia*. In 1954, he prepared a report to the convention of the International Institute of Sociology (Baune, France, Sept. 1926) in which he summarized and in certain respects advanced the formulation of his sociological ideas. In 1956, he delivered an introductory lecture to a course on historicist sociology, given at the Instituto Luigi Sturzo in Rome. The Institute was founded in 1947 and has undertaken the publication of Sturzo's *Opera Omnia*, projected in approximately twenty volumes, of which, at the time of this writing, six have appeared.

Until early in 1959, reports from visitors to Rome about Don Sturzo's physical health encouraged the hope that he would live to 90 and perhaps longer. Alas, this hope has been frustrated; on August 8, 1959, in his 88th year, the great Italian master passed away in the Convent of the Canossian Sisters where he had been living since his return to Italy. During his last sickness, he was visited by Premier A. Segni and by many other Italian leaders. Pope John XXIII sent a special apostolic benediction and frequent messages, tributes to the great and beneficial role which the deceased had played in the political, social and cultural life of his fatherland.

2. The historical background

Although Sturzo's political activity is outside the compass of this volume, a summary of its goals must be offered to make some aspects of his sociology understandable. The principles which guided his activity (for he was a man of principle, never yielding on questions of ultimate value) were traced on the configuration of Italy's political and social life as he experienced it in the earlier years of his career. The situation at that time was dominated by the victory of the *Risorgimento,* a movement to bring new life to a country with a proud past, but a country which had experienced cultural retrogression as a result of several centuries of alien domination.

The greatest achievement of the *Risorgimento* was the political unification of Italy (1859, 1860, 1866, 1870). But since the new kingdom had absorbed the Pontifical State, an estrangement had developed between State and Church even though the overwhelming majority of the population were, at that time, fervent Catholics. As a reaction to the loss of her secular power, the Church responded with the *Non Expedit* (1874), which prohibited Catholics from occupying positions in any branch of the government. The State reacted by becoming thoroughly secular and bureaucratic, which in turn caused it to lose contact with the spiritual life of its people.

The conflict might have been resolved in three ways. There were those who dreamed of the return to the *status quo ante;* but too many thought that a return to the past was obviously out of the question. There were those who wanted Italy simply to persist in the policies engendered by the *Risorgimento;* such was the position of the majority of the politicians, and of a large number of intellectuals. But there were also those who sought a third way—not a middle way tantamount to compromise, but a new and vital way, a creative combination of the best elements of the new and of the past.

This way was suggested by the Christian democrats. The movement began in the 40's and 50's, almost simultaneously in France (Frederic Ozanam) and in Italy (Ventura and Serbat). The name "Christian Democracy" was adopted during the first few years after the appearance of the *Rerum Novarum* which many felt had opened truly new horizons (N. 95-6, 108).

But for a long time Christian democracy was considered more a pious dream than a practical reality. It was Sturzo who gave it flesh and blood, and tried to show by example, the feasibility and practicality of the many devices required if its goal of harmonizing Catholicism with political democracy and advanced economic and social reforms were to be realized.

Some thought that Sturzo's ideas about social reform were so advanced that they accused him of being a socialist in clerical garb. Of course, he never was. He emphasized the legitimacy and even the necessity of private as well as public property. In accordance with the social encyclicals, he fostered the formation of vocational corporations, and through them, he hoped to harmonize the activity of those who participated in the many particular branches of economic endeavor. He asserted the "right of organization" as one of the natural rights of man. He believed that Italy would remain a predominantly agricultural country for some time, and therefore insisted on far reaching agrarian reforms. Guided by Sturzo, the Populist Party issued its own challenge to property and privilege, a limited challenge indeed, but delivered in the name of the landless and small-holding peasants crying out for additional acres of land.[9] In the name of industrial workers, the Populist Party demanded not total transfiguration, but an amelioration, by orderly steps, of the productive organization of Italy.

Moreover, Sturzo advocated regional decentralization in the framework of the unitary State. Finally, in the tradition of the *monarchomachi*, he recognized the right of revolt, i.e. the right of active resistance against political power under certain conditions and for moral reasons. "In general, it is the right of all those who are called to cooperate in an unjust war to refuse political obedience." *A propos* of the invasion of Albania (1939), he admonished his compatriots, from exile, to defy the Fascists "even if we must go to the catacombs."[10]

These words illustrate how the individual points of Sturzo's programs were well adjusted to the particular conditions of Italy's political life. They are important indices though not absolutely necessary for the understanding of some aspects of his theoretical views. Witness these somewhat amended words of one of his sincere admirers; "His life-long effort to draw the Catholic Church into the orbit of political and social democracy will outlive his importance as an Italian political leader."[11]

3. *A scientific autobiography*

Once stated, ideas can become detached from their originators and begin to live a life of their own in the ideational realm of culture (in contradistinction to its material, esthetic and behavioral realms). In other words, the will of their originators does not control for all time how ideas will be interpreted and used. For example, it is difficult to see how Kant could have foreseen what is known today as neo-Kantianism.

[9] J. S. Sprigge, *The Development of Modern Italy* (1944), p. 180.
[10] Moos, *op. cit.*, pp. 287-9.
[11] *Ibid.*, p. 292.

Nevertheless, the explorer and interpreter of a system of ideas having originated in a master mind would be remiss if he did not make use of available knowledge about the genesis of ideas in the mind of their author. If one holds that ideas are engendered by filiation, opposition and combination, then, relative to an author under study, these processes should be established. Such knowledge can be very helpful in clarifying obscure points in the author's work and also in the arrangement of his ideas in a dynamic system.

Very often, painstaking efforts are necessary to reconstruct the genesis and gradual development of an author's ideas. With Don Sturzo, the task is simplified because in the first chapter of his treatise on *Method,* he offers a kind of scientific autobiography. The lines of ideational advances which he narrates there can serve as a map in charting the general considerations about "the intellectual climate" in which they arose, i.e. the climate of the Italian *post-Risorgimento,* and the particular propositions forming Sturzo's sociological theory. This narration, with the elimination of theoretical and polemical digressions (which will be discussed in later chapters of this book) and the addition of some comments, will now be offered to the reader as an historical introduction to the rather complex system of sometimes highly abstract ideas forming Sturzo's sociology. Sturzo's narration stops at the early thirties, but, by then, his sociological thought had almost been formulated in its final shape. For this reason, bringing the story up to date does not present too much difficulty.

In 1898, Sturzo had just returned to Caltagirone and had begun to lecture on philosophy, and also very soon thereafter, on sociology. Socialism was then one of the important interests of the Italian social scientists; among them were Arturo Labriola who was interested philosophically; Benedetto Croce, who had recently detached himself from an interest in Marxism; and Giovanni Toniolo, Sturzo's beloved teacher, who had opposed to socialism the idea of the corporative organization of labor. This partially explains why Sturzo's earliest scientific endeavor was to write about socialism from the philosophical point of view. But these early influences brought him far away from what was being debated at the time; so Sturzo chose for concrete study the professional organization of the workers. As a result, in 1901 he published his first volume, dedicated to Toniolo and entitled *L'organizzazione di classe e le Unioni professionali* (Roma 1901). The work enjoyed a certain success, and Toniolo encouraged Sturzo to devote himself to further studies of a similar character. But Sturzo was still engaged in philosophical meditation and therefore sought for a philosophical solution of the "social problem"—a term which, in those days, was current in Europe to connote the problem of the relationship between the classes in capitalist society. So Sturzo's next work was *Lotta di classe legge di progresso* (Roma 1902; reprinted in 1906 in *Sintesi Sociali*). The thesis of this work was based on a twofold version of historical process; first, the view that the road of humanity toward progress was struggle; and second, the view that historical struggle is concentrated in class struggle (a statement dangerously close to the central theme of Marxism). But the study was more philosophical than historical and was based on a Christian spiritualistic conception of history rather than upon a Marxian materialistic conception. In the course of this study Sturzo discovered an idea which in his later works appears as the law of immanence-transcendence. On the other hand, when completing this study, Sturzo began to experience the debility of social studies fed only by philosophical theory. This was a decisive step in the development of his thought system, and rather unexpected on the part of a Catholic priest well trained in philosophy. This peculiarity of Sturzo's mentality has often escaped the attention of his critics with the consequence that they have sometimes discussed his statements in a perspective explicitly rejected by him. We shall frequently meet this situation in Chapter VIII, devoted to the study of Sturzo's dialogues with his critics.

Armed with the basic insights he acquired in his early writing, Sturzo turned his attention to the origin of socialism in the works of its immediate predecessors, St. Simon and Karl Marx. This study was never published, and Sturzo shifted his attention to the impact of Marxism on scientific thought, political life and labor organization since the middle of the 19th century. But the field proved to be too vast; moreover, a serious sickness interfered with the study; most important, however, was the fact that, about that time, events drew Sturzo into the midst of politics, both local and national (cf. Section 1). Sturzo began to be obsessed by the task of investigating "social reality" and of discerning the influence of ideas on social facts. Perhaps, by a kind of delayed action, this phase of Sturzo's meditations resulted, in 1945, in the publication of one of his most important collections of essays, entitled *Spiritual Problems of Our Time*.

For Sturzo himself, the immediate result of his new line of investigation was, in his own words—the decision not to consider philosophical theories about society as absolute schemes, but to look at them in their historical context, as reflections of the environments in which they were generated and as germs of further theories and applications. Thus Sturzo's historicism was generated; this is what Sturzo says himself. An investigator of his thought might add that, at that moment, Sturzo had a vision of the sociology of knowledge, then present in germ in the works of Marx and Durkheim, and later to be unfolded by Karl Mannheim.[12]

Sturzo continues his narration by relating that, when he arrived at the conclusion about the relativity of philosophical theories, he was afraid he might succumb to relativism; but he held firmly to the principles of Christian philosophy, and combined them with the historicist tendency of his work. The principal theme of his study was still concerned with socialism, not as a particular phenomenon of industrial society, but as a fundamental tendency displayed by masses in all epochs from antiquity to our day.

With regard to political implications, two theories prevailed at that time, the liberal (improvement through free play of social forces) and the Marxian (liberation through class struggle and victory of the proletariat). The Christian philosophers could easily criticize both of them but were themselves unable to present a theory acceptable to scholars and which could simultaneously provoke enthusiasm in the laboring masses. Traditional providentialism applied both to the Church and the State (the latter always governed by the upper and middle classes) found the spirit of liberty repugnant and was unable to solve the social problems of the time. The Christian Democrats suggested interventionism as a social duty of the ruling classes. The presence of liberalism, the doctrine of class struggle, providentialism, and interventionism called for a unified theory of society which could

[12] K. Mannheim, *Ideology and Utopia*, published first in English (1936) and later on in the author's native German (1952).

animate all these movements. A new theory was needed as a frame of reference for the facts under study, and it would have to make a new beginning where the other theories had abandoned the search. It was obvious that advancement called for men to struggle. But the reduction of struggle to a single economic factor was contrary both to human mentality and to the complexity of the human spirit and was felt to be unsupported by historical evidence. In that regard, acknowledges Sturzo, his early view that class struggle was *the* law of progress had to be superseded by a more general doctrine.

So, continuing study and research, reading stimulating works like those of Georges Sorel and Mosca, Max Weber and Pareto, Sturzo arrived at the thesis that in every society, large or small, primitive or advanced, there gradually arise, in organization and culture, two camps, the conservative and the progressive. In no society are such opposing forces absent. For Sturzo, this was the point of departure in his search for the fundamental laws which could shed light on the phenomenon of socialism; later on, this proposition became one of the basic laws in Sturzo's sociology.

Furthermore, Sturzo found that the polarization of forces into conservative and progressive camps did not necessarily result in antagonistic struggle; these forces could collaborate, and could even be integrated into higher units, political or ecclesiastic. These observations were confirmed by historical data and incited him to introduce into sociological study the commonly neglected element of freedom, both individual and collective.

There arose the necessity of finding out how it came to be that the margin of liberty was more extensive for certain categories of people (e.g. universitarians in the late Middle Age, humanists and artists during the Renaissance, the burghers of the free cities and the guilds of artisans) while for other classes, liberty was relatively more restricted. During the semi-liberal period of the early 19th century, political liberty was conquered by and for the bourgeoisie, but the state of the laboring classes deteriorated.

To solve the problem, Sturzo returned to the study of antagonistic groups. The conflict of interests of the possessing and the non-possessing classes he found to have been caused by the impermeability of the class structure, that is, the absence of normal ways of ascent to the status of an entrepreneur for a member of the labor class. This fact, says Sturzo, was not an economic fact, as then commonly assumed, but a fact both political and social.

His attention was then directed to the study of the relationship between the political (ruling) and the possessing class. The study resulted in establishing the sociologically relevant fact that between the private interest of the possessing class and the public interest of those in power there prevails the principle of mutual help to maintain, for both, the social positions attained. Sturzo expressed these ideas in an essay entitled "Possession and Power" later on published in the volume entitled *Politics and Morality*. The problem, he says, deserves more sociological study.

The sociological law of duality, or of the division of society into a conservative and a progressive camp, extended to all the phases of social life, seemed to Sturzo to open the way for the entire elimination of the residues of historical materialism. But, as first formulated, the law seemed to point to a kind of flux of eventful activities without consistency or general trend. These considerations led Sturzo to the conclusion that the forces tend to become crystallized in groups, associations and institutions and in this way to form diarchies of power. The term was already commonly used to designate State-Church relations, but he extended it to other social situations.

The idea of finding an element of unification in society preoccupied Sturzo, despite his opposition to philosophical monism. At that time he had not yet discovered that the unifying tendency exists also on the highest level. (He later presented this view in *True Life*.) But Sturzo had already found in history indications of a tendency of unified structures to disintegrate, under the impact of a plurality of centrifugal forces, and that the social process does not stop there; it always returns to duality, then proceeds to unification, and so on.

The formulation of a law giving to this dynamism a non-deterministic meaning took many months of research and meditation. To achieve this goal, Sturzo had to remove any deterministic character from the concept of progress. He substituted the notion of process for progress, and the notion of development for evolution.[13] Finally, Sturzo concluded that there was no specific difference between the activity of a single individual and that of individuals united in society,

---

[13] He obviously did not know that this had been done in 1903 by Charles Ellwood, whose work remained almost unnoticed.

since both were moved by reason and instinct, striving for ideals and succumbing to passions, fluctuating between generosity and malevolence.

Thus, Sturzo reached one of the central ideas of his sociology: the only true agent of society is the individual man as he is associated with other men for the accomplishment of definite purposes. Thereby Sturzo rejected the idea of society as a *tertium quid,* a third entity above two or more interacting individuals, and rejected with it the idea that the State, the family, the class or the religious group act of themselves or can determine men to act from above.

In making these decisive advances toward his own sociological theory, Sturzo did not want to lose the advantages he had gained in the company of such positivists as Durkheim or of those idealistic sociologists who followed the Hegelian scheme. He contributed to the study of them and in so doing, discovered their essential weaknesses (see Chapter VII).

Sturzo then began to investigate the problem of conditioning on which the positivist sociologists laid great emphasis, attributing to it the power of an extra-human force, and determining *per se* human actions. Sturzo's historical research brought him to other conclusions. He found that conditioning may be physical, historical and social; but the constant fact is that man either adapts himself to this conditioning, or evades it. Although he cannot act without being conditioned, he nevertheless finds in himself an impulsion to overcome a given situation, which strengthens his efforts toward the attainment of his goals. Consequently, he concluded that these two principles regulate human activity: 1) the inner principle of rationality, which pushes man toward the good and the true and gives him the faculty of determining himself; and 2) the external principle of conditioning. Both principles oblige men to act in union with others, since otherwise their ends cannot be attained. Outside society, man is doomed.

Having come so far, Sturzo had placed at his own disposal several firmly established foundations on which to construct a sociological theory. The most important were these: 1) society is tantamount to the coexistence of individuals cooperating toward the realization of common goals; 2) human action is directed by rationality and limited (and at the same time stimulated) by conditioning; 3) neither principle is a mechanical determinant of action; man preserves a sufficient margin of initiative and the ability of experimentation[14]; 4) through dynamism based on initiative and experimentation a tendency is generated by which every society passes from plurality to duality toward unification and then multiplies again to plurality.

Sturzo next investigated the coordinating relation between the rational element in human action and the historico-social tendency toward unification. In the absence of such coordination, society would seem to consist only of the blind actions of extra-human dialectics exhibiting no intelligible patterns or trends. Yet he was sure that society did not lack an animating finality which held together the associations of men. In other words, he felt that the dialectical cycle from plurality to duality to unity and then to plurality again was not an aimless process. Experience shows that society is finalistic: men act to obtain goods, real or alleged, which they feel are worth while being fought for. Of course, every one can err, whether by ignorance or passion, and so can associated men. Rationality, the guiding star of action, can be temporarily hidden behind clouds of pseudo-rationality or irrationality; and yet it eventually reëmerges in its role of the guiding star of individual and collective action. The victory of rationality in history seemed to Sturzo quite evident. From this he derived the proposition that human progress is due to rationality. But since neither truth nor goodness determine an individual in each of his actions, the movement from irrationality or pseudo-rationality to increasing rationality is not always linear, not always progressive, and not without setbacks.

These considerations brought Sturzo to the study of collective consciousness. He distinguished between deliberate and instinctive actions and therefore between explicit and implicit finality. Holding that both of these go into the formation of ends and goals he concluded that there can be no organized society unless its ends and goals are consciously willed by the members. Consciousness is so necessary to animate society that without it one could not speak of a true society. Sturzo became so convinced of these ideas at that time (1932) that they have since become the key to his sociological theory, which culminates in the proposition that the determining factor of every society is inter-individual or collective consciousness. At bottom, this is merely a formula connoting the fact that society is the con-

[14] Sturzo probably means behavior commonly called "trial and error."

sciousness of each of us reflected in each other in the mutual process of actualizing common ends. The family, the friendship group, the social class, the school, the nationality, the religious association are the diverse modes through which individuals contact each other. A man who rejects these contacts, or is unaware of their value, is unable to reproduce the mind of others in himself and consequently, cannot join in the ends of life in common.

These ideas were revealed to the public in 1935 when his *Essai de sociologie* appeared.[15] The first chapter of this book was first published as an article in *Revue Internationale de Sociologie*,[16] and provoked objections. The editor of the *Revue* added a note to Sturzo's paper expressing his disagreement with Sturzo's assertion that there are no animal societies, since the animals lack consciousness. Sturzo was certain that the editor was wrong: he asserted that sheer sexual union, the formation of herds, the division of functions (as among bees and ants) are not sufficient bases on which to form societies. On the other hand, he asserted that in whatever manner we study society, the conclusion emerges that those societies are more stable, efficacious and progressive whose members have consciousness of it, of its nature and of its ends. This is true of all types of societies, beginning with the family. This is evident in many instances, as for example in the submission of men to civil authority, one of the most startling facts of social life. The conviction that it must be so—that the citizens must obey civil authority—is derived from reason and experience; submission is a voluntary act. Obviously, if submission were only individual, and not collective, it would lack meaning and social value.

Sturzo continued the demonstration of this proposition, citing the example of the formation of collective consciousness in the United States in the attempts to create organized international communities, especially the League of Nations and the United Nations. On this point, he terminates his scientific autobiography, apparently because, having assigned this key roll to collective consciousness in his sociological theory, Sturzo's "new sociology" was ready for its systematic formulation.

[15] Published in English under the title *The Inner Laws of Society: A New Sociology* (1943); in Italian, as *Società, Sua Natura e Leggi* (1949).

[16] "Le concretisme de la société," *Revue Internationale de Sociologie*, vol. 40 (1934), pp. 149-164. The editor's note mentioned in the text appears on p. 155.

4. A survey of major works

As already noted, this new sociology was formulated for the first time in the *Essai de sociologie* (1935). All the basic theorems he had arrived at during the long years of preparation (from around 1900 to 1932) and briefly reported above, are found in the *Essai* with many valuable additions.

The book begins with an Introduction which, in the English version, has been given separate pagination; this is a concise and therefore difficult essay on historicism in sociology, expressing Sturzo's views on the relationship between history, philosophy and sociology as well as his conviction that data of Christian revelation, concerning themselves with the historical process, form an integral part of sociology. The body of the treatise is divided into two parts; Part One is devoted to "Sociality, Forms, Concretization and Historicity"; Part Two deals with "The Synthesis of Sociality." The latter includes a chapter (XI) in which the general theory of duality is applied to the modern State, especially to the totalitarian State. The chapter is illuminating, but stands midway between sociology and political science.

During the 25 years which followed the publication of the *Essai*, Sturzo continued to work in the field of sociological theory. His *True Life*[17] offered substantial clarification on two subjects—what sort of science is sociology and what is history—including a detailed exposition of the thesis that the study of the impact of the supernatural on human society can and must be made an integral part of sociology.

In 1950, Sturzo published, in his native tongue, a long essay on *Sociological Method* followed by a rejoinder to his critics and accompanied by a translation, from English into Italian, of two papers, one by Father Paul Furfey and another by Robert Pollock. Both in the essay and in the rejoinder, Sturzo explained a number of misunderstandings which his basic treatise (*Essai de sociologie—Inner Laws of Society—Società*) had caused. It seems that major original work is often misunderstood and even occasionally distorted by other cultivators of the same scientific field. Sturzo did not escape this unpleasant aftermath of publication.

No major sociological work by Sturzo has appeared since. But be-

---

[17] Italian version *Vera Vita*, 1947.

fore the appearance of *Essai de sociologie* and also later on Sturzo published several volumes of sociological relevancy. They are 1) *The International Community and the Right of War* (1930); 2) *Church and State*[18]; 3) *Politique et moralité* (Paris, 1938); 4) *Les guerres modernes et la pensée catholique* (Montreal, 1942); 5) *Spiritual Problems of Our Time* (New York, 1945) and 6) *Nationalism and Internationalism* (New York, 1946).

With the exception of *Church and State*, which is a splendid monograph on the historical development of one of the major problems affecting Western society from the days of early Christianity right on up to the present time, these volumes are collections of essays on various subjects, some theological, others definitely not. A short survey of their sociologically relevant parts will be now offered.

The volume entitled *International Community and the Right of War* is particularly interesting because it was written before Sturzo reached the conclusion that individual-social consciousness was the key concept of sociology. The first part of the book contains a short but well rounded theory of society, treating the international community as one typical specimen. Most of the basic concepts used in *Inner Laws* are already present, especially those of rationality and of sociological laws. A law of "sociality-individuality" (not reappearing in *Inner Laws* or *Method*) is treated with some detail and is declared to be the fundamental law of every form of human society. According to Sturzo, "the more individuals increase in conscious personality, the fuller the development of their associative quality and forces" (I. C. 44). But, since social consciousness is not yet there, society is interpreted approximately along the lines of relationism (not to be confused with relativism). "The concept of human society implies the existence of relations. Human society is neither more nor less than the expression of human relations, of the relative coexistence of men" (*ibid*. 36). Some concepts, especially those of law, force, power and autonomy are defined and correlated in clearer terms than in *Inner Laws*.

The major part of the volume is devoted to war, as a right (real or alleged), so that the perspective of the treatment is not so much sociological as political and philosophical. When discussing the

[18] First published in German, Augsburg, 1932; English translation, 1939; Italian version, 1959.

causes of war, Sturzo affirms the concept of sociological laws and makes these important statements: "Common sense admits two facts as indisputable: first, the cosmos (including humanity) has its laws; second, social order is necessary so that humanity, by observing its laws, may fulfill its own needs" (*ibid.* 143).

The treatise *Church and State* must be briefly examined, although contrary to Sturzo's assertion, it is less a sociological work than an historical one. It does not explore society as a whole, that is, before it is analyzed into such compartments as the religious, political, legal, educational and so on. Two of these compartments, the political and the religious, he confronts in a most brilliant and impartial way, proceeding step by step, placing the unique and non-recurring aspects in the forefront. It is true that the work is permeated by one of Sturzo's predilected sociological ideas, the one he calls the law of duality-unification. But, just as a good historical work must necessarily make use of a sociological framework either explicitly or implicitly, so, according to Sturzo, true sociology must make use of a great deal of historical material. The study of the duality expressed in the terms Church and State provided Sturzo with particularly illustrative material which must have helped him a great deal in the construction of his sociological theory on the subject. However this does not make that work sociological; otherwise any good historical work could be claimed by the sociologists.

The volume entitled *Politique et moralité* opens with a chapter entitled "Possession and Power" (5-18). He formulates the main problem as follows: how can possession and power be rendered innocuous, still more, be made instruments of goodness (in the meaning of reconstructing society in closer approximation to certain ideals)? The problem is obviously one of politics and morality, but in answering it, Sturzo makes a number of sociologically relevant statements, to be reported in the chapters that follow. Toward the end of the volume, Sturzo asserts the right of revolt against unjust orders of the government (129-54) briefly referred to in the biographical sketch above. Throughout the discussion it is less the sociologist than the political thinker and vigorous actor on the political scene who is speaking.

The volume *Les guerres modernes et la pensée catholique* is a collection of essays. The first, concerning Sturzo's political vocation, is the translation of a paper which appeared first in English.[19] Since this essay contains an extensive contribution to the author's biography, frequent reference to it was made in the opening section of this chapter. The essay which belongs properly to the field of Sociology is entitled "Democracy, Authority, and Liberty." Although Sturzo had discussed the problem of Liberty-Authority in *Inner Laws* (Chapter VIII), the treatment in *Les Guerres* offers additional insights into the problem, since it probes into the relationship between force, power, and authority, (vs. law, force, and power in *International Community*).

In *Spiritual Problems of Our Time* (1945) only the first chapter, "The Present," belongs to the field of sociological inquiry. The rest of the volume is devoted to the "Inner Morality of Art," "The Problem of Knowledge and the Intuition of God," and "The Quest of the Good," which are actually ethical, epistemological and theological problems. But the chapter singled out is a beautiful expression of Sturzo's idea that historicism is the best possible approach to sociology. The present is treated in relation to the past and the future, on both the individual and social levels, which are shown to be inseparable. He says, for example, "We feel ourselves parts of a whole, living elements of a life surpassing the individuals" (S.P. 4).

The last of the semi-sociological books by Sturzo is his *Nationalism and Internationalism*. It consists of an introduction and nine essays, some of which are devoted to specific historical situations, in which only scattered statements of sociological relevance can be found (e.g. "The Roman Question," "The State, The Unions, and the Liberal Party," and "The Postwar International Crisis"). But some of the other essays offer valuable contributions to the treasury of Sturzo's sociological thought, as, for example, the first essay, concerned with the concept of the nation (mentioned only briefly in the *Inner Laws*). Here the nation is analyzed thoroughly, is contrasted to the State, and is similarly contrasted to the religious association and "any kind of voluntary society to be freely solved and dissolved." He also emphasizes the importance of contrast between one nation and other nations (N. 4, 13, 16). He assigns a sociological place between the family and the state to the nation (*ibid.* 23). The abstract conception of nationalism is illustrated by sketches of British, American and French nationalism. This is followed by a discussion of the relation-

[19] In *Commonweal*, quoted in note 1.

ship between nation and war. A long essay, devoted to Empire and imperialism, goes significantly farther than the statements found in the basic sociological treatises of Sturzo where Imperialism was not as clearly distinguished from nationalism (*ibid.* 239-240). In the essay on the international community, the idea is presented that nationalism is an historically rooted factor, while internationalism is an ideal to be realized (*ibid.* 304).

The above survey, without pretending to be complete, shows that some of Sturzo's sociological ideas have been expressed in his semi-sociological works. Naturally, these additions and clarifications will be given due consideration in successive chapters of this volume devoted to a systematic presentation of Sturzo's sociology.

In the course of the years not surveyed in his scientific autobiography (that is, after 1932) Sturzo published a number of sociologically important articles. Two of them, "History and Philosophy"[20] and "The Influences of Social Facts on Ethical Conceptions"[21] deserve special attention.

5. *The sixteen theses*

A last step remains to be made before embarking on the systematic presentation of Sturzo's sociology. This is the reproduction of several summaries of his sociology lately made by Sturzo himself.

The first is contained in the concluding chapter of his essay on sociological method. There, Sturzo offers sixteen "theses," similar in form to those offered by scholars of former times. They are reproduced here in translation, with some abridgment of theses Nos. 13-16 which are accompanied by rather lengthy statements explaining and developing them beyond the thesis form.

1. The proper object of sociology is the study of society in the concrete, in its various forms, development and dynamism. The study of society in the abstract may be the domain of philosophy, ethics, jurisprudence, anthropology, economics, politics or other sciences, but not of sociology.

2. To acquire a correct knowledge of society in the concrete, one must study the historical process which is the temporal dimension in which society develops through the centuries.

[20] *Thought,* March 1946.
[21] *Thought,* March 1945.

3. Society must be studied primarily from the aspect of individual-collective consciousness where sociality [the associative aspect of human consciousness] is concretized into forms, organs, institutions, syntheses, all created, developed, destroyed and renovated by man in society.

4. To know well and evaluate the rhythm of social dynamics and its effectiveness, one must study the two motives of conservation and reform which animate social groups and create among men contrasts of interests and classes, people and nations, cultural and ecclesiastical groups.

5. Since society in the concrete is nothing but the realization of the associative activities of men, the investigator of society must have complete knowledge of man and of theories concerning him. This is essential for finding out the right methods of sociological investigation. No analytical study of social phenomena can be consistent and serious without a complete and realistic knowledge of society in the concrete.

6. One cannot conceive of society in the concrete, i.e. the associated activities of men, without knowing the inner laws of the associative nature of men, which could be called sociological laws. One must avoid attributing to sociology laws extraneous to it.

7. The search for sociological laws is a delicate task because of the lack of scientific tradition and of rigorous methods. It is advisable not to attribute a definitive character to sociological laws before sufficient verification, but to treat them as working hypotheses or lines of orientation until, on the basis of consensus among scholars, we can either retain them as true or reject them.

8. Sociological laws are always laws of action in society, while conditioning is regulated not by sociological laws, but by physical or historical laws, according to the nature of conditioning.

9. The study of the conditioning of men in society is an integral part of sociology. This conditioning must not be identified with deterministic causality, but should be treated as a conditional and indetermined complex which man acknowledges, specifies and realizes.

10. The facts and data of the existence of men in society, past and present, form the material of sociological study. But it is impossible to utilize them scientifically without the study of facts in their complexity, with the motives behind them, and the traits which individualize

each and make them distinct from all other facts apparently similar.

11. For the study of social causation, the pure fact abstracted from reality lacks any significance, since every social fact is the product of a long series of antecedents which have made it possible. Social causation, a rather equivocal term, is not determinative; a social fact cannot be imputed to a unique efficient cause which would not be the will of individual men having generated the social fact.

12. The application of statistics to social facts does not prove anything, since it puts under one denominator facts which are apparently similar but in actuality are qualitatively different. It can be used only as a preliminary ascertainment of facts. One must avoid drawing any scientific conclusion on the basis of pretended similarity and alleged frequency.

13. Sociological comparisons derived from history tend to deviate far from the correct interpretation of a particular reality. This is true of the study of civilizations and of social forms (such as the family, the State, religion). The comparative study of civilizations has the value of an illustration and serves to deepen the understanding of the facts compared, provided that each is kept in its context, and for each civilization laws are found permitting a systematic sociological study of the facts.

14. A sociologist who is able to find the laws of the civilization into which he was born and lives is not enabled thereby to interpret completely another civilization. Such a sociologist will always remain an observer from the outside, unable to penetrate the spirit of what he observes.

15. To whatever civilization a sociologist belongs, he cannot avoid studying religious phenomena and the penetration of the supernatural into history and therefore into society. Modern scientism and naturalism have induced the sociologists bluntly to accept postulates from the outside.

16. If one believes that the study of historical societies can yield elements common to all societies, past and present, but confines himself to this stage of research, he will perhaps present a morphological description of various societies, or a philosophical systematization concerning itself with social facts, but will not produce a scientific work in sociology.

6. *Two further summaries*

During the last years of his life, Sturzo had two opportunities to summarize his sociological views, first, in a paper addressed to the 1954 session of the International Institute of Sociology, and second, in an inaugural lecture at the Don Luigi Sturzo Institute in Rome (in 1958). He no longer used the technique of "theses" as he had done in the *Metodo*. But it is possible to excerpt from the two summaries several theses representing the latest available formulation of Sturzo's "New Sociology." Combining the two summaries, the theses might be formulated as follows:

1. Humanity is crystallized in innumerable human nuclei. Each human nucleus is a society in the concrete.

2. Society in the concrete has two dimensions, the structural and the temporal. The two are integrated in the fact that society is mobile, is a process. Both dimensions are essential: if society had no structure, it could not move and live; but a society deprived of movement could not exist.

3. Society, in the meaning above, is not a reality different from the individuals composing it. Therefore, the social sciences must start from the premise that man is both individual and social. Man in society must be studied both in his inter-individual activities and in the framework of the development of society.

4. Society is not determined by external facts, but is self-determining. It conditions the individuals both from the inside and from the outside.

5. Sociology is the study of society in its structural and processual (dynamic) aspects.

6. In social dynamics, one finds, over and above the associative instinct, the tendency to embody rationality. However it is difficult to find an adequate study of the social functions of rationality in modern sociology.

7. The idea of goodness, which is one of the major manifestations of rationality, passes from individualistic through social into associative conceptions, that is, the associative component of individual consciousness.

8. To understand and analyze society, the sociologist cannot ignore the historical action of the divine in our life. The need of an absolute

orientation is a necessary prerequisite of social stability and is therefore one of the most noteworthy aspects of social life.

9. Each particular branch of science, including sociology, must have its particular method. The best method to be applied in sociology is the historical one.

10. The reduction of sociology to a philosophy of history or of society is wrong; such hybrids are fruitless. Sociology does not and should not surreptitiously incorporate philosophical or theological propositions. In any case, the author's (i.e. Sturzo's) work has been completed without resorting to metasociological premises.

The study of the genesis of Sturzo's sociological theory, as narrated by himself and supplemented by a brief analysis of his works not covered by the narrations, as well as by two sets of theses just offered, should be considered by the reader as an introduction to the systematic presentation of Sturzo's work. In the following chapters (II to VI), his sociology will be analyzed topic by topic and in much more detail than in this chapter. Of course, this procedure will involve some repetition, since the theses form the very backbone of his theory. But some repetition is perhaps the best possible way to accomplish this volume's objective, that is, conveying to the reader some insight into the richness and originality of the contribution of the great Italian master.

CHAPTER II /

What Science is Sociology?

What Science is Sociology?

EVERY SCIENTIFIC study must begin with an explicit or implicit circumscription of its scope. Sociology cannot escape this rule; it must begin by answering the question—what science is sociology? The answer must be two-dimensional since it must define first the portion of reality to be studied and then the perspective of the study, the point of view from which it will be carried out.[1]

Therefore, the analytical study of Sturzo's sociological theory must begin with establishing his answer to this double question. This must be done despite his *boutade* that he does not want to discuss whether sociology *is* a science (XI). In actuality his works are full of statements on this subject.

1. *"Integral sociology"*

The scope of sociology, as viewed by Sturzo, is quite unusual: it includes "the study of the laws of social structure in the light of the contribution of the supernatural, with its transforming influx" (T. 16). This inclusion, he says, does not mean any departure from the scientific rigor of sociology (M. 36). On the contrary, this step *must* be taken, "since there is not one society for the sociologist and another for the theologian, but only one which interests all the scholars" (M. 15-16). It is not a case of theology but of true sociology when the supernatural is studied in its sociological implications (T. 11). In this way, sociology becomes "integral" (T. 16-17).

The vast majority of sociologists, on the contrary, do not introduce into their science propositions based on revelation. Explicitly or

[1] N. S. Timasheff, *ST.*, pp. 9-10.

implicitly, they consider that their science is empiric. An empiric science is based on observations and is limited to logical inference and eventually theory construction on that basis, while, as fully acknowledged by Sturzo, the supernatural is knowable only through revelation (T. 27, 218-9). Even philosophy, he says, does not give us "the fact of the supernatural, which does not exist in nature and which therefore cannot be proved by reason" (H. 59).

Only a few Catholic sociologists would endorse Sturzo's expansion of the field. Paul H. Furfey, though asserting that there is no logical reason why sociologists could not borrow facts and postulates from supra-empiric sciences such as metaphysics and theology, still warns against the broad use of such procedures because "supra-empirical assertions are usually very controversial"[2] and suggests a distinction between sociology in the narrow sense, which would be a purely empiric science, and sociology in the broad sense, taking in whatever supra-empirical postulates that might prove necessary or useful for the fullest possible interpretation of society.[3] He acknowledges however that the empiric method "is most characteristic of sociological science."[4]

One may assume that Sorokin occupies a position close to that of Sturzo. In the last chapter of his *Sociocultural Causality, Space, and Time* he declares himself to be a member of "the integralist school of sociology"[5] relying not only on "the truth of the senses," the backbone of empiricism, but also on the "truth of reason" (which, he acknowledges, has always been employed even by the most empirical, most behaviorist, and most mechanicist theorists in the field),[6] and finally "the truth of faith," i.e. knowledge based on a supersensory, superrational, metalogical act of intuition.[7] He is quite right when asserting that the construction of a theory always involves intuition, i.e. an irreducible creative effort.[8] But "the truth of faith" in this meaning is

[2] *Scope and Method of Sociology*, 1953, p. 145.
[3] *Ibid.*, p. 40.
[4] In his contribution to Sturzo's *Del Metodo Sociologico*, p. 168.
[5] *Sociocultural Causality, Space and Time*, 1941, pp. 226-37, especially 233.
[6] *Ibid.*, p. 227.
[7] P. A. Sorokin, *SCD*, 1941, vol. IV, Chap. XVI, and the "Supra-conscious in Man's Mental Structure, Creativity and Cognition," *Scritti di Sociologia e Politica* in onore di L. Sturzo, vol. III, pp. 387-446.
[8] N. S. Timasheff, *ST.*, pp. 9-10.

by no means the same thing as the introduction into sociology of propositions the content of which is based on revelation, in other words, of propositions acknowledged to be true *ratione auctoritate*. So, despite the community of terms used by Sorokin and Sturzo, their integral sociologies are quite different. Sorokin's integralist sociology still remains within the compass of empirical sociology, since the propositions reached by him or anybody else by intuition are subject to the empirical procedure of verification by facts, while the interpretation of facts derived from revelation, by the very nature of the latter, does not allow of such verification.

2. The definition of sociology

The gulf between Sturzo's conception of sociology and the one now prevailing among the sociologists is deep. This is so despite the surprising fact that Sturzo's formal definition of sociology does not differ substantially from those offered by empiric sociologists. Sturzo is eager to emphasize this lack of difference; his works, he says, are works on sociology in the sense commonly given to the term in Europe, namely "a theory of society and the factors which constitute it and give it life and development (H. 53-4)," or, still simpler, the study of "men in society" (M. 39). At another place, he defines sociology as "a study of society as it is in the concrete, its origin, structure, form, character, process, with the aim of discovering the inner laws which are bound up with its very nature" (T. 2-3). In still other words, sociology is a study of society "in its synthetizing factors" (XI). This definition, as well as the preceding one, does not differ very much from Sorokin's widely accepted formula emphasizing the study of the generic traits of social phenomena in contradistinction to those which are particular to their individual classes.[9] Nor does it differ significantly from the formula derived by Paul H. Furfey from a sample of 81 of the definitions he found in recent works.[10]

It is noteworthy that in his *Inaugural Lecture* Sturzo comes close to the formula accepted by many contemporary sociologists of the so-called "structural-functional school"[11]: according to him, sociology is

[9] *CST*, 928, pp. 506 (note 2) and 760-1.
[10] *Scope and Method*, p. 139.
[11] Consisting of T. Parsons and his followers.

the study of society in its structural and processual aspect (L. 8); "processual" may be interpreted as identical with "dynamic" and even "functional" in the "weak" meaning of the term given to it by the members of that school.[12]

Throughout Sturzo's work, he emphasizes that sociology is the study of society in the concrete. Although the full meaning of this proposition will be discussed later on, at this place it is sufficient to say that emphasis on the concrete is made to distinguish sociology: 1) from a study of society in the abstract as "a metaphysical entity"; 2) from what are commonly called "the special social sciences," as for example, economics, government, jurisprudence, etc.[13]; and 3) from sociological specialties, such as "studies of ecology, race relations and all the studies of differential distributions of social phenomena in time and space on the basis of statistics." Philosophers, says Sturzo, "will search in society for universal reason, apply the four causes. Moralists, economists, educators will look at society from their own points of view" (M. 38). But the study of sociological phenomena "must reveal the proper characteristics of society" (M. 40). He accuses modern sociologists of having neglected "to study society *in se*, and having addicted themselves to the study of specialties without attention to the whole" (M. 27). "The sociologist," says Sturzo, "must look at society sociologically, in its concreteness and complexity. In concrete society, one finds merged politics and economics, morals and religion, ethnography and history. . . . It is one thing to study partial social facts, and another to study society in its existential and historical complexity, in its morphology and dynamics" (M. 37).

It should be noted that Sturzo's indictment against the inclination of modern sociologists to gather partial and unrelated facts was made a quarter of a century ago, before the "back-to-theory" movement started in this country, and sociology revived in Europe after a long period of anabiosis. On the other hand, one has to consider that the field of study delimited by Sturzo corresponds to what we would now call general sociology, the central core of sociology which unifies and gives meaning to its special fields.[14]

[12] Cf. *ST.*, p. 222.
[13] These sciences are often called "the concrete social sciences" while for Sturzo *they* are abstract and *sociology* is concrete.
[14] N. S. Timasheff, *ST.*, p. 310 and P. A. Sorokin, cf. the subtitle of *SCP.*

Despite the almost complete concordance of Sturzo's definition of the scope of sociology with common opinion prevailing in that science, the gulf between Sturzo's integral sociology and the dominant type of sociology remains. It is there because the dominant type of sociology is based on the assumption that sociology is an empiric science, while Sturzo's sociology is not.

But Sturzo not only rejects the limitation of sociology to the empirical study of society. As seen from the initial quotations (Section 1), he believes that sociology as he understands it is the only true sociology. "If others like to give the name of sociology to the study of analytical elements of society . . . nobody can prohibit them from doing so. But nobody," he says, "can prevent me from calling such studies pseudo-sociology" (M. 67). The full understanding of his position requires an exposition of his rather complicated views on the relations between philosophy, history and sociology. Evidently the study of this triangular relationship must begin by fixing the three points between which lines (corresponding to relations) are to be drawn.

3. *Philosophy, History, Sociology*

Philosophy is defined by Sturzo as "rational knowledge of reality through its ultimate causes" (H. 48). Since philosophy is knowledge gained by reason, it stops at the threshold of the supernatural, which is knowable only through revelation. Philosophy is a thought system which discerns the laws of thought and action and arranges them into a rational system (XXX). Offering such a statement it seems obvious that Sturzo has in mind only that part of reality which is related to human affairs; one might be tempted to use the term "social philosophy" but this would go against Sturzo's denial of the possibility of partial philosophies (see below). As knowledge of reality through its ultimate causes, philosophy is oriented to *total* reality; this is not stated explicitly, but may be derived from Sturzo's treatment of philosophy as a more general and comprehensive theory than, say, the theory of society.

History, according to Sturzo, is a term used in three meanings. First, it is the course of events or, more exactly, the human process, which evokes the idea of succession, of the difference between a before and an after (XXIV). "History means the stream of associative life, the struggle for the formation of a peculiar existence, the march of progress" (S. P. 4).

Second, history is a systematic and rational exposition of the events forming the process, so far as they are known. Of course, not all the events have to appear in that exposition (T. 199). "History is made of events that concern not this or that family, or economic craft or trade group, class or tribe . . . but the part of the population . . . which has gained consciousness of the [group's] personality over and above domestic and economic contingencies" (T. 205). In that meaning, the history of an epoch or civilization is always in the making, because the "rational orientation in which the known events are interpreted and systematized varies with the different epochs, cultures and philosophical systems" (XXVII).

Third, history is the consciousness on the part of a determined group as such. It is an important ingredient of group tradition (we would say, culture).

The three meanings are closely interrelated. The events forming the human process (1) are "historicized" or rationally interpreted, (2) and this product becomes the material of history in the meaning of tradition (3) (XXVIII).

The third point of our triangle is sociology. Sturzo's definition of sociology as well as his emphasis on the study of society in the concrete has already been reported. The latter idea must now be developed.

Insistence on sociology as the study of society in the concrete leads Sturzo to oppose "abstractionism" rather violently. Sturzo states that it is time to abandon abstractionism, which he believes is based on deterministic interpretations of collective activity (T. 9). Abstractionism means an interpretation of concrete reality which prescinds from its essential factors and their concrete syntheses, and then ascribes reality to the result of this logical operation. Society must be taken in its living nature and not reduced to conceptual hypostases (T. 10). He begins his *Inner Laws* with the statement that "society in general is merely an abstract concept. Society . . . in the concrete consists of individuals cooperating . . . for common ends (T. 10). In the concrete, we do not find society, but societies, in the plural. A single society of all men is an abstract conception" (T. 19). Almost every contemporary sociologist would agree with these statements; in con-tradistinction, earlier sociologists believed in the evolution of a *single* human society.

On many occasions, Sturzo attacks abstractionism, or the tendency to replace the real facts of society by abstract thought models. "We must avoid," he says, "the analysis of social phenomena without pene-trating into reality" (M. 41) which is immediately given to us before analysis and is complex and concrete.

But he does not deny the validity and value of abstraction. "We in no sense renounce the quest for what, beyond all phenomena and all material structure, will prove to be a specific, definitive and original element of society, embracing all social forms" (8). If we use the word rationality as we use the word sociality, it is because we are proceeding *analytically,* presenting human faculties in their abstract-edness.[15] Only by means of ideas and logical symbols can we lay hold of *concrete reality* in its being and operation (11). "My critics," says Sturzo, "will never find anything else than sociality (a very abstract concept indeed) as a *universal* term *abstracted* from reality" (11). "All analysis means abstraction, under the aspects of forms, values, social structures" (30). The study of such forms and structures con-stitutes the bulk of Sturzo's *Inner Laws.*

Moreover, although firmly convinced that man is free, Sturzo con-siders that it is a mistake to deny the existence of historical or socio-logical laws (258). "Ours is a sociological vision," he says, "of laws derived from human nature, from its rationality, from its mode of action, from its social effectiveness" (*ibid.*). Of course, these laws are not the same kind as those expressing the mechanical determina-tion of physical phenomena (cf. Chap. IV). Comte had already em-phasized the flexibility of social laws, and in contemporary sociology, social laws are often constructed in the form of statements about the probability of specified developments (among them, human behaviors) in specified situations.[16] Sturzo's laws are evidently of the same type. *But statements of this type are abstractions by their very nature.*

There is no doubt: while rejecting "abstractionism" in the meaning

---

[15] The two terms, sociality and rationality, play a major part in Sturzo's sociological theory. They will be discussed in later chapters. Throughout the paragraph, the italics are mine (N.T.).

[16] N. S. Timasheff, *ST.*, p. 180.

explained, Sturzo nevertheless recognizes the validity of analysis resulting in abstraction. But, in his opinion, sociology should not stop at that point. Analysis should be followed by the "study of social syntheses and their factors in their concreteness and in the dialectic of human process." He prefers this approach because it "carries to the heart of reality . . . since there is no living reality which is not at once concreteness and process, that is history, while the findings of analytical procedures" remain lifeless "like the elements of a dissected corpse."

There can hardly be any objection against the demand that analysis be followed by synthesis. It is also true that synthesis is often badly neglected. The reason is obvious: the methodology of analysis, in many sciences, now in sociology too, has been worked out in detail; one who has carefully studied this methodology can perform useful analytical work. But synthesis, above the level of inductive inference from analytically established facts, requires a creative effort; however the ability of creative effort is a rare gift—it is conspicuously present in Sturzo's work and conspicuous by its absence in the works of quite a few contributors to sociology.

But Sturzo goes further. He demands that synthesis be *complete*. For synthesis, it is necessary to embrace all human manifestations and all social forms in their concrete configurations (T. 7). In other words, he wants to concentrate study on the "total social phenomenon," to use a term favored by several contemporary French sociologists.[17] For Sturzo, the total social phenomenon includes the impact of the supernatural on the natural (T. 4); *ergo*, the supernatural cannot be put aside, or else, instead of a living society, one describes a "dissected corpse."

By insisting on complete syntheses, Sturzo exposes his theory to the same objection which recently has been made against the views of Gurvitch, who, like Sturzo, is inclined to concentrate on the study of the concrete. The objection states that, by concentrating on concrete syntheses, no room is left for a general theory which, by its very nature, deals only with what is recurring.[18] Sturzo foresees this ob-

---

[17] Marcel Mauss, *Anthropologie et Sociologie*, 1950, pp. 274 ff. and 303-4, and G. Gurvitch, "Le concept de la structure sociale," *Cahiers Internationaux de Sociologie*, vol. 19, (1955), pp. 3-44.

[18] H. Janne, "Fonctions et Finalité," *ibid.*, vol. 16 (1954).

jection and bluntly states that he has not "tried to create a general sociology, as base for and connection between various special studies" (B. 8).

But in the same paper, he says: "The structure of social nuclei [social groups] and the dynamics of their relations is the proper matter of sociology" and acknowledges that he is "looking for common elements among social nuclei" (*ibid.*, 4 and 7). At another place, he says: "In such words [as order and defense] we must embrace *all* that every civilization, every historical situation . . . comprehends as order and defense" (53) . . . "We must and should study the morphology of society. We shall take society at a given point of the globe and at a given moment of historical [time] and shall examine it in the concrete, seeking for the constant elements it has in common with other societies, in other places and at other times" (T. 7).

Confronted by such statements, one cannot but say: Sturzo's sociology is based on the study of concrete societies, but strives to transcend them in order to arrive at generalized and abstract propositions on the levels of social morphology and dynamics.

4. *Relations between philosophy, history and sociology*

Now we can shift our attention to the relations corresponding to the triangle philosophy–history–sociology. Of the three sides of the triangle, Sturzo chooses for elaborate study the relationship between history and philosophy. It is of crucial importance for the solution of the problem before us, namely, the problem of the reason for Sturzo's belief that the study of the impact of the supernatural on society is not only scientifically warranted, but indispensable.

1. Having emphasized rationality in philosophy and in history (in its second meaning), Sturzo goes on to say that the two are convertible, since both, in different ways, have as their object the rationality which is realized in human events (XXX), so that "history, thus conceived, presents itself with all of the characteristics of philosophy" (XXIX). Nevertheless, the two are not identical. Philosophy and history are two ways of considering human activity "either systematizing ideas drawn from reality [including human actions] or systematizing reality in accordance with [philosophical] ideas" (XXX). "History is human thought as realized in activity. Philosophy is human activity interpreted by thought. Both represent actual and present knowledge"

(S. P. 10). History lives on the truths that philosophy offers and explains; philosophy derives its theories from history (H. 61).

Despite the tendency to see in philosophy and history two convertible ways of conceiving human activity, it is remarkable that Sturzo denies the possibility of a comprehensive philosophy of history. He reasons that nobody is able to "create a philosophy of history which would be exclusively historical and autonomous in the sense of being independent of philosophy *tout court*" (H. 52). This is true; but why could there be no philosophy of history derived from general philosophy? He who creates a philosophical system or accepts an existing one may apply it to the interpretation of the course of history, universal or particular, covering all ages or specified periods. Such have been the majority of the existing philosophies of history.

2. The relationship between philosophy and sociology is not well developed in Sturzo's work. He often asserts that his doctrine is not a philosophical one, emphasizing that it is neither a philosophy of history nor a social philosophy. In his address to the International Institute of Sociology (1954) he said: "Reducing sociology to a philosophy of society . . . is not our way. The matter is either philosophy or sociology; the hybrid is not fruitful" (B. 7). In other words, he denies the very possibility of social philosophy, evidently for the same reason as his rejection of the philosophy of history. In his *Inaugural Lecture* he says: "sociology does not theorize on philosophical theses, nor does it surreptitiously introduce philosophy or theology" (L. 13).

Nevertheless, according to him, the sociologist and every scientist must look for light in philosophy, in order not to fall into errors of a non-sociological sort. Sturzo believes that the philosopher has a kind of right to demand that the sociologist make use of philosophy as a guide in his thought (M. 107-8). On the other hand, the sociologist can offer a number of facts and laws to the philosophers which may be helpful in their speculations about man and society. In his polemics with Franz Mueller and Oesterle[19] he suggests that the philosophers ought to revise some of their positions in the light of sociological studies (M. 97, 108).

But the sociologist should not begin with a definite philosophical position as, for instance, the doctrine of free will. Using this doctrine as an example, Sturzo says that the sociologist must begin by estab-

[19] Summarized in Chap. VIII, sections 3 and 4.

lishing the *fact* of social evil and its consequences and then attempt to derive sociological laws therefrom. The doctrine of free will can serve only as a background for the arrangement of his findings and for extra-sociological verification (M. 108). Such procedures offer the sociologists the opportunity to deepen both philosophically and theologically the theoretical foundation of their doctrines, for without that foundation society is incomprehensible (M. 111).

3. Sturzo conceived that the relationship between sociology and history centers around the proposition that true sociology *must* be historicist. In a relatively late article he regretfully abandoned the term "historicist" because of the misunderstanding it provoked and the confusion which ensued (H. 54-5). But he did not change his mind about the referent corresponding to the symbol "historicist." It is absolutely necessary to introduce "the time dimension" into sociology. In earlier works, he had called it "the fourth dimension" (T. 3), but in later ones it is coordinated with the spatial or structural dimension (M. 60). In his last contribution, however, Sturzo returned to his predilected term—historicist sociology (L. 12).

While the idea of the time dimension is essential for Sturzo's sociology, it did not of course originate with him. Sociology was born under the time dimension: Comte's work concentrated on social dynamics (not statics) and to a large extent was a reasoned history of Western civilization. A number of works devoted to the history of civilization followed, among them those of Guizot, Buckle and Draper which were widely read. In sociology proper, Durkheim, "from his earliest to his latest works urged the closest *rapprochement* between sociology and history."[20] But the first quarter of the 20th century was inimical to what could be called historical sociology, mainly because at that time it was erroneously identified with the discarded doctrine of evolution. Later on, a reaction took place, and such monumental works as A. Weber's *Kulturgeschichte als Kultursoziologie* and, of course, Sorokin's *Social and Cultural Dynamics* appeared, both of them almost simultaneously with Sturzo's *Inner Laws*.

But Sturzo goes further than his predecessors or contemporaries. For Sturzo, historicist sociology is the *only* possible type of sociology. Sociology is either historicist, or it is not sociology at all. This is

[20] As convincingly shown by Robert N. Bellah, *ASR*, vol. 24 (1959), pp. 447 ff.

intimately related to his basic view that sociology is the science of society in the concrete. Of course, concrete society is given in time. It is not simply Italian, or American, or French society, but one of these societies in 1900, or 1950, and so on. As correctly emphasized by Sturzo, a concrete society cannot be fully understood without a knowledge of its past and of the way this past is reflected in the "collective consciousness" of the society under study.[21] In the sentence above, the word *fully* should be underlined. For Sturzo, only an adequate knowledge of concrete reality, a knowledge of the object from all relevant points of view, can be called full knowledge.

Unfortunately, Sturzo never explained what procedural steps comprise the historicist method. The following quotations contain approximately all that can be found on the subject. "When studying history, we start from the present, from the reality that forms our personal experience; we search in the past for the laws of formation and development and try to find the ideal for the future. . . . On this conception of human process . . . is based what we call the historical system" (XXVI). At the start we study social facts gathered from historical experience to arrive at the formulation of principles, social laws and hypotheses (M. 42). "History, not history of material facts, but their inner reason, their logic, connection, the metaphysics to which they give birth, enables us to learn the laws of our social nature" (T. 8). In this connection Sturzo speaks of *penetrating* the spirit of history (M. 37).

Sturzo gives some indications as to how one can penetrate this spirit by referring to his own work. "For long years," he says, "my principal care was to achieve a sociological interpretation of the structure and process of society derived from the experience of facts and their confrontation with theories which influenced them or have reflected them" (M. 109)—a statement hinting at what is known today as the sociology of knowledge. At another place he says: "my research has been of an historical and experimental character." For instance, on many occasions, he discovered the recurrence of "the duality of social forces." He then asked himself such questions as these: "Is this dualism derived from an inherent or superficial dualism? If it is permanent, how is it articulated and crystallized?" When

[21] In this chapter, we shall not discuss Sturzo's conception of collective consciousness; cf. chapters III and IX.

doing so, he says, he was working in the field of sociological interpretation of complex historical facts which, to be classified, must be
schematized and categorized (M. 98-9). During such a work, the
fear of falling into the aberration of aprioristic and fictitious constructs
decreases little by little when in rigorous scientific research, the same
data appeared in both contemporary and past configurations (M. 39).

Of course, historical facts have been explored by many sociologists.
"But very often," says Sturzo, "theories founded on a few historical
data tend to generalize the concrete facts and to deduce laws from
them. Yet such laws are often the abstract aspect of a concrete datum
[contemplated] not dynamically, but statically" (M. 42). In trying
to explain why this is, he says, "The comparative study of civilizations
has only a relative value and serves to deepen the understanding of
the facts compared, provided that each is maintained in its context
and that for each [civilization] laws are established permitting their
systematic sociological study" (M. 64-5).[22] The insistence on studying facts in their context approximates the methodological canon of
contemporary functionalists.

Inspection of Sturzo's work shows that most of the sociological
generalizations he affirmed were derived from his painstaking study
of historical facts. There is no doubt about his wide and deep historical erudition, best manifested in his *State and Church*. But neither in
his predominantly historical treatises nor in his purely sociological
ones did he explain *how* he derived these laws from historical data.
Evidently, Sturzo read these laws into the historical events he studied,
believing them to be the most adequate rationalization of the human
process, tantamount to "history in the second meaning." But, according to Sturzo, history in that second meaning is closely allied with
philosophy; it is the systematization of the past in accordance with
ideas which cannot but be philosophical. Consequently, Sturzo's
historicist sociology cannot but be permeated by philosophical ideas;
no need to say that the illumination comes from Christian philosophy
(cf. T. 13).

Just as Sturzo is not the only historicist sociologist, neither is he the

---

[22] Sturzo is fully aware that there has not been sufficient exploration of
the methodological problems he poses and points to the works of Blondel,
Maritain, Boyer and Petruzelli (without specifying them) as promising
beginnings (T. 223).

only philosophical one: to mention only some recent ones, the theories of the institutionalists[23] and of the phenomenologists are also deeply permeated by philosophical premises. The uniqueness of Sturzo's position is that it is both historical and philosophical.

5. Social philosophy and philosophical sociology

According to Sturzo, true sociology must be both historicist and philosophical. While historicism is explicitly emphasized, the thesis that sociology must be philosophical can be implied from some of the quotations offered above. For Sturzo, history and philosophy are almost interchangeable concepts; so that when sociology is historicist, it cannot fail to be philosophical by the same token. Of course, Sturzo says that his work is neither a specimen of social philosophy nor a philosophy of history. But social philosophy and philosophical sociology are not the same thing. The difference between the two is the very topic of this section.

First, we must return to the thesis stated at the very beginning of this chapter: for Sturzo, sociology must embrace the impact of revelation *qua* revelation on society. This statement is inevitable because the philosophy Sturzo uses in its interpretation of historical facts is Christian philosophy, more precisely, Thomistic philosophy.

However the full and unquestioned acceptance of a certain philosophy by an author does not logically demand that its propositions be introduced into the body of the discipline he cultivates. What really compels Sturzo to introduce into his sociology propositions known only from revelation is his axiomatic acceptance of the proposition that sociology must study social phenomena "in the concrete," meaning "in totality." If this proposition is accepted, then a believer like Sturzo cannot proceed differently.

Let us postpone for a moment a discussion of the validity of this thesis, but answer the question—what is the scientific nature of Sturzo's sociology, using the yardsticks prevailing among contemporary scholars. The result will be approximately this:

1. A certain portion of Sturzo's sociology is beyond the scope of sociology as an empiric science. The most obvious example of non-empiric statements is the formula found in the concluding section of

[23] Which he explicitly rejects; cf. chap. VII, sect. 6.

the Introduction to the *Inner Laws*, according to which, history proceeds from a transcendental (that is, an empirically unknowable)
cause through an immanent process toward a transcendental (again
empirically unknowable) end (XXX). The major part of *True Life*
is devoted to the interpretation of human society and history from
this point of view. This is obviously a philosophy of history (perhaps
of Augustinian inspiration) grounded in religion combined with a
social philosophy. The propositions forming that part of Sturzo's
work can neither be empirically proved nor refuted; they have no
meaning on the level of empiric science, although they are meaningful on the levels of philosophy and theology.

2. The vast majority of statements found in *Inner Laws, Method,*
and other works described as sociologically relevant in Chapter I of
this work, do not depend on the total acceptance of Sturzo's fundamental thesis about the entire historical process. Nevertheless they
are often permeated with a philosophical spirit, as evidenced by
statements quoted in the preceding section. But they are not deductively derived from philosophical propositions. They have been
arrived at on the basis of a knowledge of facts, which are partly
historical, but which are to a large extent facts known to every one
from his personal experience of life in society. Philosophy appears
rather as a guide or background for the arrangement of the findings.
This does not render it impossible that the particular propositions (if
empirically verified or made plausible) can play the part of building
blocks in an empirical thought system. In Sturzo's work they form a
sociological system of the philosophical type like those of the institutionalists and phenomenologists mentioned above, but they should not
be considered as a new specimen of social philosophy.

As stated above, there is a great difference between social philosophy and philosophical sociology. Social philosophy, like any special
philosophy, is the application of propositions contained in a general
philosophical system to the study of a particular segment of reality,
in this case, the social segment. The major part of Sturzo's work is
definitely not the result of this kind of thinking.

Philosophical sociology is characterized by a particularity in the
process of theory construction. Theory construction cannot be
effected simply by induction *à la* J. S. Mill or by any of the sophisticated procedures unfolded in contemporary treatises on research in

the social sciences. Theory requires a creative effort, based on thorough knowledge of facts and generalizations available in the chosen field, and meditation about them. Creative effort results in the formulation of a hypothesis or a set of hypotheses, forming a logical system, such that generalizations may be deductively derived from them. However, it must be emphasized that the generalizations must already have been there, arrived at by former induction or by earlier creative efforts of the theorist himself or by other scholars. If the hypothesis is verified—on the logical level—a theory is constructed which covers a segment of reality "explaining" the facts by reference to high level postulates.

The total personality of the theory constructor is involved in this creative effort, including his scientific and philosophical assumptions (the latter may be explicit or implicit). If the creator of a theory is strongly convinced of a philosophy, he will rely on it by necessity in his effort and make his theory explicit. Such is the case with the majority of propositions Sturzo offers.

The general procedure of testing a theory by confronting it with facts requires, in the specific case of a philosophical sociology, the removal of its supporting scaffolds (Spencer's expression). If this can be done without damaging the edifice of substantive propositions, the theory can be validated even though it is interwoven with philosophical considerations. It is the contention of this writer that a very large part of Sturzo's work can meet this test.

In practice, the difference between a social philosophy (declined by Sturzo) and philosophical sociology (the framework in which he operates) is this: In social philosophy, a proposition is validated by proving its conformity with the philosophical system in question, whether it be Christian, Kantian, Hegelian, Existentialist, and so on. In philosophical sociology, the proposition is validated by proving its conformity with facts. Sturzo's propositions (except those dealing with the impact of the supernatural) are always validated by reference to facts known to him from history or his participation in the turbulent social and political life of his time; moreover, in his work, scientific scepticism, so important for the advancement of science, is often salient, since he consistently points to the possibility that further investigations might modify or even destroy his theorems. This is in the spirit of science, in its empiric sense.

6. *Sturzo and empiric sociology*

The findings of the preceding section have been reached by applying the yardstick of empiric science to Sturzo's sociology. Sturzo does not deny the value of empiric science, yet he believes not only that the science of man and society cannot be constructed without introducing the supernatural into the field of sociological study, but that the supernatural ought to be used as the cornerstone. "I could not but bring into light what history . . . teaches us about Christianity. I started from no dogmatic preconception but from historical [data] which I interpreted from a strictly sociological viewpoint [in the meaning reported above]. My theory of historicist sociology obliged me to study the thesis of the supernatural in history. If society . . . is a mixture of natural and supernatural [elements], a naturalistic study . . . is simply analytical or falsified by the omission of essential data on social reality" (T. 13, 14; cf. H. 59).

The impact of Christianity on the history of mankind, especially on Western civilization (in the broad meaning which also covers the European East) is so conspicuous that it is acknowledged even by militant atheists. For instance, in 1939, turning to the New Religious Policy, the Communists issued a statement acknowledging that Christianity had been a progressive social force, since it recognized the dignity of "the abstract man" and proclaimed the equality of men independently of sex and status.[24] But Sturzo goes much further: he treats the supernatural character of the *source* of the progressive moment as one of the basic propositions of sociology. The major part of *True Life* (whose subtitle is *The Sociology of the Supernatural*) is devoted to the demonstration of this theorem.

In his *Inaugural Lecture*, Sturzo returns with vigor to his central thesis. There he says: "To understand and analyze society, the sociologist cannot ignore the insertion of the divine into our life. . . . The historical realization of the influence of religion varies in time and space. It may be infected by superstition, false tradition, wrong infiltrations, deviant theories, political complications and passions. . . . At the present time many are accustomed to look at religion as something which is going to disappear. But true history, well studied and objectively evaluated, presents the historization of the divine as a

[24] N. S. Timasheff, *Religion in Soviet Russia,* 1942, p. 114.

constant datum; sociology cannot but take this into account" (L. 10-11). He asserts that sociology does not surreptitiously introduce philosophy or theology, but he adds "If these *sciences*[25] have influenced the real social forces, sociology must take this into account" (L. 13).

In a debate with Sturzo, however, an empiric sociologist would say: The interpretation of history as the unfolding of supernatural forces in human society, is an interpretation based on revelation, not observation and inference therefrom. This interpretation is rejected by the non-believers; and the Christian interpretation is unacceptable to non-Christian believers. Sturzo himself says: "A Mohammedan or Hindu sociologist has the experience of [his] religion and of the environment in which he lives; hence he will present problems otherwise than a Christian sociologist, even if he does not go into religious and supernatural questions" (T. 20). If that is so, there must be as many sociologists as there are religions. Sturzo goes even further when he says that there *should* be as many sociologies as civilizations, a term which he uses in approximately the same meaning as Toynbee. This is so because a sociologist who can find the laws of the civilization in which he was born and is living is not thereby enabled to interpret correctly another civilization (M. 65), a statement analogous to Spengler's well known assertion of the impermeability of cultures (which, in his language, has the same meaning as civilization in Sturzo's work). Relative to former civilizations, continues Sturzo, the sociologist will always remain an observer from the outside, unable to penetrate the spirit.[26] Sociology as a science is a product of modern Western civilization, Christian in origin and later secularized; Hindu, Chinese, Japanese and other sociologists can produce only superficial imitations. Among Western sociologists, one without faith can hardly penetrate into the Christian ambit and produce a satisfactory sociology (*Ibid*).

If this is correct, there can be no general sociology,[27] an idea expressed by the young Max Weber, but implicitly rejected in his masterwork *Wirtschaft und Gesellschaft*. The impossibility of a gen-

[25] Italics mine (N.T.).

[26] The conclusion is inescapable: if the statement in the text is true, then historicist sociology is impossible.

[27] In the meaning of a sociology covering all civilizations and epochs.

eral sociology is explicitly asserted by Sturzo, despite the fact that he himself offers a system of general sociology.

But let us return to the imaginary debate between Sturzo and the empiric sociologist. The latter would say: The existence of a common universe of discourse is a functional requisite for the advancement of a field of knowledge. The empirical sociologist is not entitled to deny the supernatural, but he is entitled to assert that the supernatural does not belong to his province just as, according to Sturzo, it does not belong to the province of philosophy.

In his debate with the "positivists" (as Sturzo often calls the empiricists) Sturzo answers: "No science can escape the multiplicity of systems. A sociologist who accepts individual liberty writes differently from one who accepts social determination" (T. 11). This is true. Whenever a man of science expresses in words his ideas about reality he necessarily pays allegiance to one or another of the epistemological and ontological systems. The philosophically informed do this explicitly; those who are not so informed imply that they have no use for philosophy, without realizing that this statement manifests a definite philosophical position. Those who care for the emergence of a widely accepted universe of discourse in sociology (where it is badly needed), try to reduce their philosophical premises to the minimum, and to express their propositions in such a way that translation into the language of another theory is made possible. The majority of empiric sociologists state their views in terms of moderate realism and treat human decisions as "independent variables" without entering into a debate about free will vs. determinism. They can do so because the days when acceptance of the dogma of mechanical determination of "everything" are gone, even in natural science. In their own fields many contemporary physicists acknowledge the existence of areas of indeterminacy. A. H. Compton, a Nobel prize winner, says: "There is nothing known to physics that is inconsistent with a person exercising freedom."[28]

The limitation of sociology to empirically observable facts, inference from them and construction of adequate theories—eventually under philosophical influence—is a conscious and self-imposed limitation. By implication, the empirical sociologist is not entitled to ascribe

[28] A. H. Compton, "Science and Man's Freedom," *Atlantic Monthly*, October 1957, p. 75.

to himself "the position of true and sole interpreter of society." Unfortunately, this was actually done by the founding father of sociology, A. Comte, and continues to be asserted by all those who assume that there is no knowledge outside of empiric science. Such a position is justly attacked by Sturzo (T. 8). But it is by no means the position of all the empiric sociologists. Those who do not share this view concede that their knowledge is limited, but claim that what they are doing is, in principle, acceptable to all minds, independently of philosophical and religious differences.

The circumscription of a field of investigation is based on a decision of the investigator which, as a scientific decision, is free. Therefore, Sturzo is entitled to treat sociology in the boundaries he sets for himself; however, the "empiricists" are also entitled to circumscribe sociology as they do by the same principle. The problem, after all, is not one of truth *vs.* fallacy, but one of adequacy.

It is precisely this alleged adequacy of Sturzo's choice which may be questioned. He acknowledges the desirability of using the "commonly accepted methodological criteria" (one must suppose, first of all the existence of his fellow scientists) since otherwise one "detaches oneself from the community of thought and thus loses efficacy among the addressees of his writings" (M. 3). He qualifies this statement by asserting that every scholar has the right to adopt his particular methods. In still another writing, he states: "Every scientist creates his language and method, but he [should] make his writings communicable to others" (B. 7). In actuality, Sturzo goes far beyond his own boundaries. He expands sociology into an all-embracing theory of society, covering what is empirically knowable and what can be predicated of society philosophically and theologically. In this way he disrupts a universe of discourse about society on the empirical level, until the day when (if) all men acknowledge the truth of Christian revelation.

7. Is reduction of Sturzo's sociology to the empiric level possible?

Any presentation of Sturzo's theory of society, in the meaning above, minus its supernatural aspects, will run contrary to Sturzo's explicit statements. However let us not forget that ideas once expressed live on independently of their originators.

On the other hand, so long as Sturzo insists on the study of the impact of the supernatural on natural society, his sociology remains incommensurable with other, less ambitious, sociological theories. This will mean, in addition, that many of the brilliant insights of the great Italian scholar will not exert any influence on the development of sociology, considered as that vast field cultivated by men of different "civilizational," religious or philosophical backgrounds. It will remain simply alien to those who do not share Sturzo's ideas about the supernatural and its relationship to sociology.

In accordance with the findings of the preceding section, an effort will be made to distinguish the two parts of Sturzo's sociology by employing Paul Furfey's ideas of sociology in the narrow (empiric) sense and in the broad (integral) sense. The latter approach makes use of philosophical and theological terms and premises, while the former should be treated the way scientific generalizations are usually treated, as propositions to be factually confronted, systematized, and measured for consistency and universality; these propositions, by the way, need not be absolute; some may refer only to societies and cultures characterized by specified traits, but not necessarily those of time and space. Despite Sturzo's emphatic denial of the validity of a sociology limited to the empiric level (in contradistinction to the supernatural level), one can be encouraged in the enterprise just outlined by a number of his own statements.

First, he acknowledges the validity of theories which do not reach the top level of understanding. In one of his most important articles he says: "The theory of society and its laws [cannot] be regarded as definitive knowledge, since such theories can be reduced to another more general and comprehensive theory, namely philosophy" (H. 54). In other words an author may choose his own level of theorizing. If it is legitimate to choose the level of "integral sociology" as defined by Sturzo, it must be equally legitimate to choose another still lower level, that of empiric science, which, while not resulting in a definitive knowledge of reality in its complexity, nevertheless can claim to deal with the "total social phenomenon" minus revealed knowledge about the supernatural and its impact on human history.

Second, in Sturzo's writings the statement is made: "In the Church —in its human part—one finds multiple groups, dynamic duality, the unifying tendency" (M. 103), in other words, properties found in other social formations. But he believes that in addition to the human part, there is a Divine part in the Church; nevertheless one can see

from this that Sturzo does not doubt the validity of propositions true
only of the human part.

Third, Sturzo's "theory of society" (a term he uses himself) contains an interpretation of the meaning of history, i.e. a philosophy of
history. According to Sturzo himself, such an interpretation is only
possible in terms of transcendental principles (first causes) and of
transcendental ends (XXX). Yet, according to Sturzo, knowledge of
reality in terms of first causes belongs to the province of philosophy.
Ergo, it is outside the proper field of sociology.

Fourth, in his *Inaugural Lecture* Sturzo says: "Sociology is not a
science fit to confront the problem whether human reason can or
cannot solve the problem of mystery[29] or whether preternatural religion can or cannot violate the rights of reason. Society in the concrete historicizes such problems with all the scientific and cultural
consequences" (L. 11). We could continue: the historization of religious dogmas, that is, their acceptance into concrete cultures, is an
empiric fact that can and must be studied in sociology. But here
sociology stops, precisely because, as Sturzo himself acknowledges,
the confrontation of different religious views cannot be adequately
performed as a scientific function.

In the same lecture Sturzo says: "Among the most noteworthy
aspects of life there is the need of an absolute as an orientation and
as an element of stability; the sociologist cannot ignore that" (L. 12).
And so it is: a number of contemporary sociologists and cultural
anthropologists introduce orientations to higher values which give
men the motives to live and work as one of the functional prerequisites
of society and culture; but it does not follow therefrom that the
sociologist should check the objective validity of these orientations
and make one of them an ingredient part of his sociological system.
This task he leaves to others with the special competence to accomplish it.

Sociology, and every other generalizing empiric science (e.g., the
general theory of law) is really an explanation from the inside. In
other words, it is an explanation couched in terms of observations and
inferences made in the framework of the field. Incidental borrowing
of propositions from neighboring empiric sciences does not make it
necessary to resort to propositions explaining reality in its totality, as

[29] Probably in the meaning of mystical experience.

philosophy claims to do. Thus circumscribed, sociology may enter into compounds with social philosophy and the philosophy of history to form "social theory,"[30] or with economics and government, to form the compound, "the social sciences," or with psychology and cultural anthropology, to form the compound, "the behavioral sciences."[31] The multiplicity of possible compounds is an additional and strong argument in favor of limiting sociology to what is empirically knowable about society.

The *total* thought system of Sturzo about society cannot be translated into terms of an empirical science—the two are incommensurable. But from that total system one might separate a *portion* which would be commensurable with sociology, today a well established science. The question is—what would be the result—a "dissected corpse," according to Sturzo's own expression; or a system of propositions, both original and productive of new insights in the science of human behavior in society, where so many facts are accumulating, but where their intelligible and enlightening arrangement is so rare. This was the crucial question which posed itself before my mind when, in 1957, I started working on Sturzo's sociological theory. I came to the conclusion that by putting aside Sturzo's social philosophy, which deals with first causes and the ultimate ends of an "immanent process," i.e. the social and historical process, and by systematizing Sturzo's statements about the latter scattered through numerous sociological and semi-sociological works, one finds not a dissected corpse, but a self-contained and beautiful structure.

Although a systematic presentation of Sturzo's views detached from supernatural postulates cannot give a *complete* image of his theory of society, the less ambitious program of singling out and systematizing those of Sturzo's ideas which can be treated on the empiric level could contribute to the recognition of Sturzo as one of the great sociologists of the mid-twentieth century.

This expectation is the rationale for the way in which the following chapters are written.

[30] The term "social theory" has been used by W. I. Thomas and F. Znaniecki, *The Polish Peasant at Home and Abroad,* to designate the combination of sociology and social psychology.
[31] The term "behavioral sciences" is replaced by Furfey (*Scope,* p. 116) by the term "moral sciences" with the explanation that, in this context, moral is derived not from morals, but from mores.

CHAPTER III /

Society and the Individual

Society and the Individual

1. The formal definition of society

In MANY of the more recent sociological theories, primary consideration is given to the nature of culture, but in Sturzo's sociology, the questions "what is society?" and "what is the relation between society and the individual?" form the central problems. From Sturzo's point of view a more exact formulation of the first question would read "what is a concrete society?" Holding that the term "society" is often used too abstractly and with premature generality, Sturzo does not make the term coextensive with "humanity," which, in contradistinction to the international community, is not one concrete society, but several. Nor does he consider that short-lived interaction systems are societies, especially if they do not pursue common ends. Hence, there are several types of concrete societies, and Sturzo offers a list of examples, which, while not exhaustive, includes a family, a class, a city, a nation, a religion (meaning individuals who are bound together by adherence to a common denomination).

As a first approximation to a formal definition, one could say that Sturzo's term "society" connotes the same referent as the term "social group" in the schemes of many contemporary sociologists.[1] However, Sturzo was not satisfied with a definition based on the demonstration of a few instances, since this procedure imposes the burden of generalization on the addressee.[2] Like many sociologists, he offers not one but several formal definitions of a concrete society. One finds in his works

---

[1] Cf. my "Basic Concepts of Sociology," *AJS* 58 (1952), pp. 179-81.
[2] There are however cases when demonstration is the only means of conveying to another the meaning of a term. Cf. my "Definitions in the Social Sciences," *AJS* 53 (1947), pp. 204-9.

such statements as these: "Society is nothing other than the operative coexistence of individuals in an inexhaustive process" (T. 3). "A concrete society is the coexistence of individuals consciously cooperating for an end" (M. 75). "Society is nothing else than the realization of the associative activities of individual men" (M. 62). In an earlier work, written before his conversion to the thesis that consciousness lies at the root of all social phenomena, Sturzo wrote statements like these: "The generic concept of human society implies the existence of relations; man exists socially inasmuch as he is relative," i.e. inasmuch as relations between him and other men can be established. . . . "Human society is neither more nor less than the expression of human relations, of the relative coexistence of men" (I. C. 36).

However all of these statements are either incomplete definitions which do not juxtapose all the necessary and sufficient traits of a society, or "theorems," which predicate of a society properties not included in the definition.

A proposition containing an analytical definition lists those traits of an object sufficient and necessary for a verifying observation of that object. Following this method, Sturzo does offer one well developed analytical definition, according to which, a concrete society is observed whenever the following traits are co-present: 1) a plurality of individuals; 2) striving for common ends; 3) possessing collective consciousness; and 4) subject to a temporal process, beyond the limits of individual life (M. 75). Sturzo emphasizes the importance of this definition by addressing to his critics this rather rhetorical question: are there any other elements of a concrete society which could not be resolved into those just enumerated? (*ibid.*)

For Sturzo, the term "resolved" is not tantamount to "dissolved": resolution (or reduction, a term taken over by him from the physico-mathematical sciences, [300]) means reduction to those primary elements which permit no further resolution (8). In true science, such resolutions or reductions are indispensable.

To clarify his conception of a concrete society, Sturzo sometimes uses the device of the negative case. A woman and her assailant do not form a society because of the absence of common ends (M. 32). A plurality of men consisting on the one hand of a tyrant and a certain number of sycophants, and on the other hand, of a terrorized mass, does not form a "true" society, because of the absence of collective consciousness (181). A mother and a newly born baby form a society *in statu nascendi* because the mother knows in advance that collective consciousness will develop, although it is not yet fully there (M. 32).

Sometimes when Sturzo speaks of the traits of societies, he asserts that a certain plurality of men possessing some specified traits is not necessarily a "true" society. One may raise the question whether in so doing, Sturzo has not introduced normative (evaluative) elements into his definition, i.e. whether he means that a society which is not "true" is a poor society. The answer is negative. Although Sturzo never explicitly stated what the contrary to a true society would be, one may assume, by analogy with his treatment of rationality and pseudo-rationality (see Chap. VI) that the contrary would be a pseudo-society, a configuration bearing some of the traits of a true society. Had he chosen to formulate a definition of society which could include what we have termed a "pseudo-society," he would have been faced with the necessity of unfolding a very large number of propositions and theorems, covering every conceivable social object, which, in turn, would have made it impossible for him to formulate an "adequate theory" of society. In any case, he could not have developed *his* theory as it now stands.[3] The procedure is methodologically sound; at least, we can point out that it has been used by a large number of theoretical sociologists. But perhaps the terminology should be modified in order not to provoke misunderstandings.

2. The real definition of society

Since he is both theoretical and realistic, Sturzo cannot be satisfied with a formal analytical definition. The real problem is posed only after the formal definition has been stated; what does it really *mean*, not on the level of concepts, but on the level of reality, that a plurality of men endowed with the traits enumerated forms a concrete society?

As stated by Sorokin, three basic answers are possible to the general question of the reality of a society.[4] First: the individual is the prime reality while society is something derivative, or a mere sum of individuals. Second: society is the true and primary reality, while

[3] Cf. my "Definitions" *loc. cit., supra*, p. 204.
[4] P. A. Sorokin, *SCD*, II, pp. 262-3 (New York, 1937).

the individual is the derivative phenomenon. Third: society and the individual are inseparable and represent different aspects of the same reality. Since each of these three basic positions may appear in various modalities, they will be classed hereafter as sociological personalism, sociological collectivism, and sociological synthetism.[5]

Sturzo's theory belongs to the third class, the least represented in the history of social thought, but gaining momentum in our day. When Sturzo published his *Essai de sociologie* in 1935, sociological synthetism was represented only in singular works which commonly remained unnoticed (with the exception of Cooley, often cited, but rarely followed).

Sociological synthetism is characterized by Sorokin as the integration of the first and the second positions. According to the third position, both society and the individual are real; the individual is the singularized incarnation of the whole; society is the universalization of all individuals, permeating each of them; without it, the individual is impossible. The synthesis is achieved not mechanically, but intimately, mystically. This current, Sorokin said in 1937, still waits elaboration, and the particular theories of this class are often obscure because of the difficulty of articulating their terms in a synthesis.[6]

It is the contention of this chapter that Sturzo's theory of the relationship between society and the individual belongs to the class designated as "sociological synthetism," with a certain inclination toward personalism. It is another contention that Sturzo's work offers an original variety of social synthetism, giving it more depth, and bringing to it what Max Weber called *verstehen*.

As already stated, social synthetism is a synthesis of personalism and collectivism. On the level of ideas, a synthesis presupposes a thesis and an antithesis, a form of presentation which imposes itself on the investigator and is the more appropriate since Sturzo himself, without being an Hegelian, likes to use the term "dialectic."

1. Let us begin by collecting and confronting those of Sturzo's statements which, taken out of context, would compel the investigator to classify him with the personalists. "There is no such thing as a

---

[5] It must be emphasized that the sociological concepts in the text are not identical with the philosophical concepts nominalism-realism-conceptualism.

[6] Sorokin, *ibid.*, II, pp. 267-8. He uses the term harmonism to connote what is here called synthetism.

self-subsistent social entity outside individuals" (7). "Society is not an entity . . . outside and above the individuals" (XIV). "After all, society is a sum total of individuals" (*ibid.*), "an outcome of the activities of individuals and is implicit and potential in each of them" (XVI). "It is individual activity which grants vitality to values, efficacy to social groups" (157). "The associative tendency of men is not a product of blind forces, but of human freedom and responsibility" (T. 6). "The only consciousness in the concrete is, of course, that of individuals" (5). "Man is the active and effective cell of every social organization. It is man who thinks, wills, creates, reacts, perpetuates himself and dies" (M. 34). "Man's creative act . . . is nothing other than a continuous activity of mind and will. It is only this that produces the process we call history. . . . History is not extraneous to men, but purely human" (S. P. 8).

The personalistic component of Sturzo's analysis is also evident when he discusses particular types of societies (social groups). Thus, for instance, with respect to the family, he says: "The achievement of the ends of the family is imputable to the consorts and the children simultaneously; the ultimate term of the resolution of the family is its components" (T. 151; M. 86).

Sturzo vigorously attacks the tendency of ascribing the same capability of action and thought to collective forces and to living persons. When we come to speak of the State in ordinary conversation, we usually mean the ruling group, eventually the people. "When we pass from the level of journalism to that of sociological study, we must abandon such equivocal and inaccurate phraseologies and make clear of what collective forces we are speaking" (M. 51). When making such statements, Sturzo comes dangerously close to Max Weber who held in horror the "reification" of such concepts as the State. For him, the State was merely the probability that certain courses of action would take place under specified conditions; reality was confined to actors performing specified actions.[7] Now, Max Weber's theory is commonly and rightly classified as nominalist, corresponding to "personalist" in the terminology used here.

As is often the case, the thesis of an author becomes particularly clear when he attacks and tries to demolish its antithesis, a perform-

[7] Max Weber, *Theory of Social and Economic Organization*, (1947), p. 328; Cf. my *ST*, p. 179.

ance in which Sturzo excels. He never passes up the opportunity to refute Durkheim, whose treatment of collective consciousness as a mysterious entity standing above men and exerting irresistible constraint is abhorrent to Sturzo. For Sturzo, Enemy No. 2 is organicism, that is, the sociological theory built on the postulate that society is an organism, so that propositions about the latter can be used to describe the former. We shall examine Sturzo's criticism of the two theories in more detail in Chap. VII.

Sturzo's positive and critical statements in the personalistic (individualistic) style should not mislead us. One can say very definitely that he is not a personalist. He explicitly contrasts R. MacIver's individualistic definition of society as a network of social relations[8] with his own conception of society, and declares that MacIver's view is valid only on the descriptive or phenomenological level (M. 32), but is not a final explanation. Sturzo mentions that he studied and profited from Max Weber's contributions, but could not accept his treatment of society on the level of concepts (M. 111). Replying to his critics, Sturzo says that the idea of placing him among the nominalists (personalists) is ridiculous (M. 73), but in connection with his view that sociology and philosophy should not be mixed, he refuses, and rightly so, to treat the *sociological* problem of the reality of society on the *philosophical* level of the problem of the universals (M. 74). The misinterpretation that Sturzo's views are personalistic is similar to the tendency to classify Spencer among the individualists because of his laissez-faire position, which ignores the fact that Spencer identified society with an organism, thus placing himself among the sociological collectivists. Actually, although Spencer was both an individualist and a collectivist, he was not a sociological synthetist, because he never saw the inconsistency of holding both positions simultaneously and thus never tried to reconcile them.

2. However the decisive fact is that the "thesis" of personalism is held in balance by the "antithesis" of collectivism. Let us confront the corresponding statements.

After having emphasized that it is man who lives, thinks, wills, creates (as quoted above), Sturzo continues: "This man cannot act alone; he is part of an organization[9] which he himself forms and re-

[8] Sturzo quotes Robert MacIver, *Society, Its Structure and Change.*
[9] Sturzo actually says "organism" but means organization; see below.

forms, initiates and continues, both destroys and rebuilds" (M. 35).

"Our life is not an isolated, but an associative life. . . . We feel ourselves part of a whole, living elements in a life which surpasses the individual" (S.P. 3-4). "Society is self-determining, . . . conditioning the interior and the exterior of every individual operative in it" (L. 7). "Of course, every individual is a complete being, but he cannot express himself and unfold his personality safe of the concourse of others. . . . It would be a mistake to think that the individual will work in an extra-social human conditioning as though . . . there were no society at all. Without society, any human activity would be impossible. Society is always operating from the moment that there are individuals" (11-12). "Outside of society, man . . . would be cut from his historical past . . . and from the moral and material conquests of mankind. [He] would have to retrace by himself the experience of centuries" (162-3). "Every act of the individual . . . is in itself associative, implies inter-individual relationship" (XV). Sturzo goes so far as to assert that every thought, even before it is manifest, has an associative character; he argues that there could be no communication and hence no society without thought (XV). Of course, the argument is not quite convincing: from the proposition that society could not exist without thought it follows only that *some* thought must be associative. But, in the course of the present discussion, this does not matter. The propositions, as reported, make it evident that the collectivistic "antithesis" is quite strong in Sturzo's thought.

Just as it was possible to be misled by taking certain of his theses in isolation, so with the unfolding of his antitheses, Sturzo makes certain statements which could mislead the interpreter of his ideas. For example, he makes frequent use of the terms "social organism." "The organic factor in society," he says, "is so profound . . . that individuals are lost to sight. Even in highly individualistic society man is absorbed by the social organism, and if certain names of great men are registered by history . . . we catch only a glimpse of them" (M. 34). When speaking of organism, Paul Furfey correctly points out that Sturzo means organization,[10] so that his phrases should not be read as if Sturzo were a crypto-organicist. Perhaps a more adequate term would be "system," an idea to which we shall return in our last chapter.

[10] Paul Furfey, in M. 138.

Although Sturzo reenforces the personalistic component (the thesis) of his sociological synthetism by a vigorous refutation of collectivist conception of society (the antithesis), he offers no symmetrical counterpart to this method of discussion except for his refutation of those critics who accuse him of nominalism. Proceeding contrary to his usual procedure, he accepts the challenge in this case on the philosophical level. He asks the question—"where does sociality reside" and answers: "Only in associated individuals. It is actualized in every separate society. It has no other existence than notional" (M. 76). Since notional is synonymous with conceptual, this statement is clearly in the spirit of the conceptualistic solution of the philosophical problem of the reality of universals. But the lack of vigor in his rejoinder lends some support to the view that he is closer to personalism than to collectivism.

3. In a dialectical thought system, the thesis and antithesis are mere abstractions, one-sided presentations of one and then another aspect of a reality which can be grasped in totality only through the reunion or synthesis of what has been analytically separated. His synthesis is expressed in these propositions:

"Every concrete individuality is necessarily relative [expressed in relations] and associative, that is, exists in a plurality of individuals" (S.P. 4). "It is inexact to think of the individual as opposed to society" (5). "Human activity is at once individual and common. These two factors are so interwoven that it is hard to distinguish and impossible to separate them" (T. 199). "Society must be taken in its living nature and not reduced . . . to a mysterious being outside and above the individuals of whom it is composed" (T. 3). "Concrete society is the coexistence of individuals consciously cooperating toward a common end, and is not a reality distinct from the concrete individuals" (M. 75). "Society is not a *tertium quid* presupposing the single individual and coexisting individuals" (T. 3). "A cycle runs from the person to the collectivity and from the collectivity to the person, a cycle of inner thought finding outward expression, and of practical activity conceived and achieved" (301).

Now a crucial question may be posed—what comes first, society or the individual. "In the order of time," says Sturzo, "the question cannot be answered" (5), just because society and the individual are two ways of viewing the same reality. But "in the logical order, the individual comes first and society afterwards" (*ibid*). This is an important statement offering one more reason to consider that Sturzo's sociological synthetism is closer to personalism than to collectivism. Let us however note that the proposition is asserted to be true on the logical or conceptual level, which places it rather in the domain of philosophy than of sociology. After all, the question posed above is declared to have no answer, precisely because the individual taken as distinct from society is only an abstraction, just as society taken in itself, is an abstraction. In reality, there are only individuals in society (XIV).

3. *Individual-social consciousness*

A sociologist adhering to the synthetizing conception of society is faced with a difficult problem: what is the nature of the unity of society and the individual? For Sturzo this unity is rooted in the fact that man's consciousness is "individual–collective." "This is a primary datum," says Sturzo, "and in it one finds the key to the problem." In Sturzo's works, the term "individual-collective consciousness" is sometimes replaced by group consciousness, social consciousness, historical consciousness, and/or collective consciousness.

Sturzo does not explicitly discuss or explain consciousness as such. But it is evident that consciousness is not limited to perception and thought. "A state of consciousness," he says, "is a formation not only of the mind, but [also] of the free will" (178). "In the actuation of the associative tendency the individual will plays a large part" (12). But "the voluntary factor" does not constitute the original and irreducible principle of sociality. This is provided by the rational capacity of individuals to acquire consciousness of their associative nature (13).

In his early works, Sturzo places consciousness in the background and human relations in the forefront. For example, in the *International Community*, he said: "Every human society is nothing else than a relationship between individuals, in some way grouped together." He went on to say that the relationship may be close or loose, resulting in real [and] permanent [formations], or merely in temporary contacts, depending on whether its cause and type were permanent or temporal (I.C. 23). In this sense, society in general, apart from any particular form, is a necessary natural datum. This relative existence is not only physical, but rational and communicative. . . . Man gives the stamp of reason to the elements of his relative life; the most elementary needs of natural existence, insofar as they emerge in a social environment [are] rationalized, i.e., they take on a human character which is essentially rational (I.C. 36).

There is no contradiction between these statements in the relational style and those of the "psychologizing" type predominant in Sturzo's later works, namely: human relations are outward expressions of mental processes forming the changing content of human consciousnesses. Unfortunately Sturzo dropped this line of investigation altogether and did not coordinate it with the newly acquired insight that consciousness was the key to the problem.

Let us return to collective consciousness, which, as the reader will remember, forms the third of the four traits composing his analytical definition of society.[11]

Sturzo conceives of collective consciousness as the coalescence of specified elements of individual consciousnesses. The elements thus composed are not torn away from their roots, i.e. from the personalities of the individuals involved. Let us unfold these preliminary statements methodically and attempt to substantiate them by a confrontation with the master's own words.

1. In the consciousness of every individual one may analytically distinguish the individual or personal, and the collective or associative components (XVI). The personal component is *this man's* thought and will; it is the consciousness of the thinking subject, inasmuch as he relates it to himself, to his thoughts, aspirations and activities. By contrast, the collective component, centered around the instinct of association,[12] is formed of thoughts, aspirations, achievements of the individuals insofar as they are *related* to thoughts, aspirations, activities of *other human beings* forming a society with them (XVI, 4-5). It must be emphasized that the distinction is only analytical. "It is inexact to think of individual consciousness as opposed to collective consciousness [meaning here a society's own con-

---

[11] The first trait (plurality of individuals) is self-explanatory. The second trait (pursuit of common ends) will be discussed partly in the last section of this chapter, partly in Chapter VI. The fourth trait (temporal dimension) will be treated in the last section of this chapter.
[12] The term "instinct" should be replaced by "tendency."

sciousness]. The only consciousness . . . is that of the individuals, in which we may distinguish two component parts" (4-5).

2. Collective consciousness is first of all expressed in the conviction that each individual has or may have of belonging[13] in a certain fashion to others, as others belong to him, not only in the present moment, but also in the past, whence comes the today in which we live, and the future which is prepared into being in our today (4).

But it is more than that. There is communication of needs, language, affections (9). In other words there is communion[14] between the participants in collective consciousness, a consciousness of the society in which they live an active convergence [of ideas and activities]. In this sense, a concrete society is a community, a term pointing to the consciousness of its several members being in communion with each other (G. 10).[15] In a community, "one finds the bond of friendship which is a product of history lived in common, of cultural and spiritual affinity. . . . The whole edifice of social life is built on friendship (131-2)." "Through communion and friendship, the members of a community participate in ideas, sentiments, values and interests" (161). We could add to Sturzo's statements that the group members manifest their consciousness of belonging together when they utter the remarkable verbal symbol "we." Using "we," one asserts his identity with a larger social unit to which others also refer their identities. Using "we" to refer to each other, group members express the existence of group consciousness, the so-called "we-feeling." The unity of the group exists in the minds of the members whether it is observed or not by an investigator. This means that the unity is "real."

"True mental communion among the associated [men] . . . lighted by the ray of human reason" is identified by Sturzo with sociality (10), more exactly, with the concretization of sociality, i.e. of the associative tendency of men inherent in their nature. In Sturzo's

[13] Sturzo acknowledges the possibility that some individuals may not have the conviction of belonging; but he does not explain how one could interpret their membership in the group.

[14] Tantamount to the "we-feeling" of American sociology.

[15] Actually Sturzo defines community as the consciousness of group members of being in communion. But sometimes he speaks of community as a social group (especially when discussing the international community). This usage is more adequate than the one actually identifying communion and community.

sociological theory, sociality plays a large part; it is so closely related with social consciousness that it is sometimes identified with the continuous realization of social consciousness (13), presumably, through expression and action.

3. The real phenomena taking place in the associative component of individual consciousness include an awareness of belonging together, manifested in communion and in such corollaries as solidarity and friendship, and in common participation in common ideas. The correlative processes in the individual component of individual consciousness are not parallel but interrelated phenomena.

Sturzo says this interrelation is established by means of the mechanism of "projection," the activity of expressing ideas in certain concrete ways which render the ideas intelligible and communicable to the originator's fellows. This term is roughly equivalent to Sorokin's "objectification in vehicles" (the placement of ideas in symbols, signs, gestures, etc.), which, in turn, is the polar opposite of "internalization," which refers to the individual's incorporation of ideas reaching his mind by means of vehicles. Thus, to clarify the meaning of the term projection, it might be better to call it "externalization," since, for Sturzo as for Sorokin, it connotes the opposite of "internalization."

The projection of states of personal consciousnesses into the outside world is not only biophysical but also social and historical (5, 28). Sturzo returns frequently to this topic. Society, he says, is essentially the projection of human personality (299), or the projection of single activities in the interweaving of all activities (T. 288).

The projection of individual consciousnesses (more exactly, of their associative components) onto the social plane is multiple, simultaneous and continuous.[16] The projections emanate from the individuals belonging to a concrete society and are, by necessity, similar, because of the identity of human nature and the participation of members in the same circle of ideas, sentiments and so on. They are similar, but not necessarily identical and sometimes, for example in case of novel actions, may be quite at variance. But these deviating projections interact on the common background of the communion of the participants.

[16] This proposition has been derived from definitions of society scattered throughout Sturzo's work (see especially XVII and M. 31).

4. A unification of projections is achieved, though never completely, through the process of interaction, and in this way, collective consciousness is formed as a compound of the associative components of constituent individual consciousness. Therefore, collective consciousness does not exist as something other than concrete individual consciousness, since it is composed of them. This compound, the individual-social consciousness, possesses so-to-speak a dual nature. It is rooted in the individual consciousnesses, forming an inalienable part of them; and it is something which has inner unity which transcends the individual participants. On the one hand, this compound may be analytically resolved into individual consciousnesses and, on the other hand, it may tangibly influence individual consciousnesses and, through them, human actions. Such an analytical resolution is permissible because, according to Sturzo, collective consciousness adds nothing to the contributions of the individuals. The term connotes a reality, but it is the same reality as the individual contributions themselves, viewed collectively. These contributions, human thoughts and activities, although projected on the social plane, yet remain parts of the mental processes of the individuals so that they are real both individually and collectively. Hence, the term individual-collective consciousness.

Every society originates in this collective consciousness (32). And it is, at the same time, the force which holds together every society, even an artificial one like an army at war (177). Society may therefore be conceived as participation in ideas, sentiments, affections, values and interests (166) or it may be viewed as the "conjoined coexistence of several persons in their understanding, willing and expression" (301). Without individual-collective consciousness, society would be an unstable something, in perpetual motion and change. However this is not the case. Although society is dynamic, individual-social consciousness makes it coherent and stable while evolving through a process of immanent forces (24).

From Sturzo's emphasis on collective consciousness, one should not conclude that, in his view, the reality of society is identical with its being apprehended by reflection[17] (M. 90). The reality of a concrete society, according to Sturzo, is not tantamount to the *ideas* of the members that the society exists, but to the *fact* that the consciousness

[17] As one of his critics has done; cf. Chap. VIII, section 3.

of each member, actively or passively, necessarily involves the ideas and actions of others. This is a tangible reality. The fusion of the associative components of individual consciousnesses becomes part of the conditioning of each individual, as influential as his material and biological conditioning. Sturzo often asserts the existence and importance of conditioning and he rightly declares that there is no contradiction between the acceptance of this thesis and the postulate of free will (see Chap. IV).

On the other hand, Sturzo does not deny that, according to his theory, almost all social phenomena, like liberty, authority, law, and democracy, can be "translated" into phenomena of consciousness. "And why not?" asks Sturzo. Consciousness is the mechanism of the concretization of sociality, i.e. of the associative tendency of human nature, and therefore, "we shall find consciousness confronting us from the start in the collective processes" (M. 92).

As a final argument in favor of his thesis that collective consciousness plays the paramount role in social phenomena, Sturzo says: "When collective consciousness has not been formed, or is ill formed, the society does not exist, or does not function, or functions badly" (M. 91). In a rudimentary way, this reasoning follows the method of concomitant changes.

Summing up, one may say that according to Sturzo, a true society lives above all in the consciousnesses of those who belong to it; without that consciousness it cannot exist. On one occasion, contrary to his habit, Sturzo sublimates this basic proposition onto the philosophical level and says: "Society is a special form of cosmic solidarity" (T. 177). On the empiric level, a similar proposition reads as follows: "The individuals must reconcile [their personal rights] with a solidary coexistence [with] their fellow men" (N. 23).

4. The temporal dimension

Among the elements of the analytical definition of society, one finds the temporal dimension. The proposition that society has a temporal dimension is tantamount to saying that society is a process in time. "Society is predominantly a datum of *historical* consciousness," says Sturzo (3); it is noteworthy that this statement appears in the first chapter of *Inner Laws*.

What is time? Like St. Augustine, Sturzo does not offer a definition by reference to a genus and a specific difference, because there is no category under which time can be subsumed. Very ingeniously he says that time is the succession of limited presents, or more explicitly, that the consciousness of temporal being produces time as a succession of limited presents (S. P. 6). The term "limited present" is contrasted to infinity which is a present without limitations or succession (*ibid*).

By applying the time dimension, we arrive at the three tenses, present, past and future. The lead is given by Sturzo himself when he speaks of "society with the past" (the dead) and "society with the future" (the children) (311). These preliminary statements are developed as follows: Every moment of a process is real so far as it is present (XXV) which, for the sociologist, is the existence and the coexistence of men. When studying a process, we start from the present. . . . We seek in the past the laws of its formation and development; the activity preceding the present is conceived as causality, while the movement toward the future is understood as finality (XXV). On this conception of the human process, Sturzo bases all that he calls historicist sociology.

1. What is the present? Sturzo explains it in one of the most brilliant passages in all his writings. "It seems an instant. It is, and it is no more. And yet it is, for the instant of a little while ago . . . is the same that resolved itself into the instant of the present, and that continues to resolve itself into the continuous instants of the future" (S.P. 2).

Consequently, we may say that the relationship between the tenses is dialectical with the present being the synthesis of the past and future. Sturzo comes close to this idea in the following words: "The consciousness [of the process resolving the tenses into each other] is history. [Hence] one perceives in the present two elements in synthesis: the reality of the past in the present and, in the present, the actual memory of the past" (S.P. 4).

"All save the born pessimists, while they speak evil of the present . . . praise the past, and turn their hopes, whatever these may be, toward the future. Yet when this future becomes the present and the present the past, the roles are interchanged. The past with its bright memories . . . the future with its hopes . . . urge us to action to overcome the obstacles in the present, through labor and effort. . . .

And all this creates in us that personal continuity which is our present" (S.P. 1-2).

Sturzo develops these ideas in still another form: "The aim of action is practical thought, and as such is derived from theoretical thought. The two aspects, theoretical and practical, stand roughly for past and future. United, they form the present. Past and future are therefore in the present; they stand for reality and progress, knowledge and activity, history and philosophy" (S.P. 11). Insisting as always, on the supreme importance of consciousness, Sturzo adds: "The present is nothing but consciousness itself; without consciousness there could be no present and no history, only the materiality of crude facts" (S.P. 9).

Sociologically speaking, society is the coexistence of individuals in the present tense (299).[18] More explicitly, the material basis of every society is reducible to a group (plurality) of individuals who, united together, distinguish themselves from every other group. Of course, the element of distinction (between *this* society and another) is only a negative datum; it receives spirit [meaning] through the unifying principle, i.e. social consciousness (19). The meaning of these somewhat cryptic statements is probably this: if and when there are two societies, there are two different social consciousnesses. It is only by establishing differences between social consciousnesses that we differentiate societies and perceive their individualities.

In any case, every concrete society is specific and individualized (19-20). "From the day a concrete society has received form, it lives its own life . . . and fulfills its particular process" (21-2). Sturzo ascribes great importance to this individualization. In it, the individual feels the projection and enlargement of his personality, and in this way, the narrow and personal egoism of the individual is overcome as it develops toward group consciousness and spirit. But the concrete character of society confines the individual to *that* determined family, class, city, state, religion (20).

2. What is the sociological significance of the past? "It is customary," says Sturzo, "to discriminate between what survives and what does not; we think that the greater part is dead while only a fragment survives. . . . But it is difficult to take a true inventory, so closely is

---

[18] It is noteworthy that Sturzo declines the treatment of coexistence in terms of "formal cause" (M. 85).

all that forms the present knit with a long historical continuity. . . .
We forget much, so that much of [the past] is no longer actual in
memory. And yet the past is so [imperceptibly] transformed into our
present . . . that we cannot distinguish it from what we are today
(2-3).

Again, in his painstakingly consistent manner, Sturzo identifies the
past in consciousness: "If nothing [of the past] remained in [con-
sciousness], there would no longer be a process, for lack of continuity.
Actually, the present [is] always being enriched by the past. The
past may be said to exist after its fashion in the present" (S.P. 6).

But memory is a selective faculty so that we do not recall all of the
past that constitutes the present. It is sufficient that we are conscious
of our continuity and therefore at any moment we are able to reknit
our manner of understanding and feeling today with that of the past.
. . . This personal feeling of the continuity of life is bound up not so
much with the detailed memory of the events of the past as with the
continuous process in which the past resolves itself into the present
(S.P. 2-3).

Sociologically speaking, society in the past tense is tradition, that
is, the impact of the past on the present. Society, says Sturzo, is
fundamentally a datum of historical consciousness. "Society in the
concrete, i.e. a given society, . . . preserves its identity through the
consciousness formed among all its members that it is the same
[society] as [it was] in the beginning" (3); the word "all" is perhaps
a rhetorical exaggeration. The past is felt in the present as language,
customs, continuity of places and representative symbols. Among
such symbols one finds the succession of persons endowed with high
authority, the names of illustrious families, the recurring phases of
work, the return of popular festivals. This continuity is reenforced by
chronicles, myths, works of poetry (3-4), by such returning actions as
rites, formalities, legal institutions (32). The fusion of individual consciousnesses in the past is crystallized in laws, is incorporated in
towns, places, cities, monuments, works, churches, forms of costume,
of interaction, of living, and all that is expressed in works of thought
and art which develop in history (in its second meaning).[19] The
whole, to which Sturzo incidentally applies the term tradition, is born
of free initiative (T. 186), but develops into something which no

[19] Cf. the preceding chapter, section 3.

longer can be resolved into individual persons. We find elements which, under certain conditions, persist beyond personality itself. All this comes from persons . . . but, as an objective realization surpassing any person, is beyond the actions and reactions of single individuals (302). The permanent collective element can be identified only by means of abstraction (*ibid.*). Summarizing these ideas, Sturzo says: "The reality of social life—or [of] the present, which is the same thing—is a cluster of traditions, habits, ideas, sentiments which have found concrete expression in such public and private institutions as the family, or in the arts, and even in economic and material life" (S.P. 4).

Sturzo ascribes great importance to the existence of an irreducible residue of the past (which corresponds to what contemporary sociologists are wont to call culture). "Without the permanent element which cannot be resolved into single individuals, there could not be the very resolution into personality," and without that resolution "the whole effort of social activity would be in vain and incomprehensible" (303). Why the presence of permanent elements is necessary for the reduction, Sturzo does not explain. Probably, he has in mind the axiom that, if there is change, there must be something which changes, so that without a knowledge and understanding of the latter we would be unable to know and understand the former.

3. In the future tense, society is expressed in finality,[20] i.e. the pursuit, by associated men, of common ends. The finalistic element, says Sturzo, is inherent in every social formation (XVII). In other words, every social formation has a purpose (or purposes). "Society without future does not exist, or is a society which has existed, but now is ignored" (L. 8).

The finalistic element is not something superimposed on human nature (6). We are always moved by an inner finalism and give the "finalistic imprint to society" (310). Just as the individual consciousness, when projected, develops on the social plane, so are individual ends extended on the social level (7). Consequently, social purposes (ends) are tantamount to individual purposes (ends) carried out on the associative level (XVII).

[20] Speaking of finality, Sturzo again denies the desirability of applying to the sociological analysis of society the philosophical concept of "final cause" (M. 85).

The significance of a man's future depends on how well he feels the effective reality of this future in himself. . . . The future finds realization in the present as an effective beginning. . . . Thus the future resolves itself into the goal of human activity. Without an aim in action men are not men (S.P. 10-11).

These statements are in full accord with Sturzo's sociological synthetism: social ends are merely fusions of individual ends effected through the same mechanism of communion and projection which one finds behind individual-collective consciousness. However, "while the individual is the end of society, society is not the end of the individual" (7), a statement once again pointing to the inclination of Sturzo's synthetism toward personalism.

4. The discussion of society in its temporal dimension with reference to the three tenses allows us to draw these conclusions. The past is important insofar as it continues to influence the present; this influence is expressed in what we call culture. The present is manifested in the organization of human coexistence. The future influences the present by means of the representation of ends to be achieved, in other words, through social finality. The terms culture, organization, finality (social ends as ideas) form a triad in which the three elements of the triad correspond to the three tenses—past, present and future. Since the three tenses form a dialectical triad, the present being the synthesis of the past and the future, culture, social organization and finality also must form a dialectical triad: organization corresponding to the present which appears as the synthesis of culture from the past, and social finality, pointing to the future. The three elements of this sociological triad are innerly united, acting nowhere but in individuals and yet by far transcending the potency of any particular individuals since culture and social ideals are the emanations of collective (i.e. common) consciousness.

Sturzo never juxtaposed his statements in the manner just offered; but the present author believes that the reasoning above can be logically derived from his discussion of the temporal dimension of society and social dynamics. In addition, the writer has been encouraged to create a kind of superstructure upon Sturzo's statements on the subject of time by the fact that, in some of his works, Sturzo connotes the temporal dimension of society as its fourth dimension. Sturzo abandoned spatial terminology because he found no triad of dimensions in society analogous to the three dimensions of space. His view of time seems to have been inspired by Einstein's treatment of time as a fourth dimension, a formulation which achieved a fuller integration of our perception of outward phenomena. It can be conjectured that Sturzo felt that the temporal dimension of society could similarly provide the sociologist with an integral view of phenomena on a very high but still empirical level.

Therefore, the present author believes that Sturzo's ideas on the temporal dimension of society offer us one of the most penetrating and impressive sociological insights ever attempted into the total social phenomenon.

CHAPTER **IV** /

Sociological Laws

Sociological Laws

1. Are sociological laws possible?

STURZO'S SOCIOLOGICAL synthetism with its inclination toward personalism, poses before him this problem—are there, or are there not, sociological laws, taking "laws" to mean empirically testable propositions about regularities in social phenomena? A theorist embracing sociological collectivism easily answers the question in the affirmative: yes, there are sociological laws determining the behavior of the individuals in society almost to the last detail. There is probably no better example than the famous passage in Marx's *Critique of Political Economy* where he states that men enter into social relations of production *independently of their will,* and that the remaining portion of social phenomena form a superstructure which is determined by the configuration of its economic foundation.[1] On the contrary, for an intransigent sociological personalist, the answer must be: no, there are not and cannot be sociological laws because man is free. Historians of the type of Benedetto Croce belong here; but one may also imagine a derivation of a negative answer also from Watsonian behaviorism,[2] not because man is free, but because he is absolutely determined by conditioned reflexes acquired in the course of his life.

A sociological synthetist acknowledges both the reality of society and of the individual, but, conceiving of this reality as indivisible, he finds himself confronted by this difficulty: the existence of sociological laws seems to abolish individual freedom, yet the freedom of the individual seems to make sociological laws impossible. Sturzo is fully

[1] *Zur Kritik der politischen Oekonomie,* 1859, p. v.
[2] P. A. Sorokin, *CST,* p. 621.

aware of this antinomy and his resolution is in full accordance with his theory of the relationship between society and the individual. Let us begin by stating the two terms of this antinomy, as they appear in Sturzo's work.

1. *Man is free.* According to Sturzo, in his work "the freedom of the individual is a presupposition which is taken as proved" (162). This formula is not very felicitous because, logically, that which is proved is not a presupposition. What is more, the principle of free will can neither be proved nor refuted empirically. What Sturzo actually wants to say is that, in his thought system, the principle of free will is given the value of a postulate.

One finds in his work another formulation of the same idea which we shall retain: "Man is not determined, but a self-determining force" (XIX) (S.P. 9). This is an idea which receives more and more recognition in empiric science. A conspicuous instance may be found in a recent development in statistics, namely, in the theory of decision which, in contradistinction to the earlier denial of the freedom of decision or choice, is based on the assumption that man *does* decide; therefore, the founders of the new theory try to provide the eventual actors with adequate tools for making the right decisions.[3]

Man's freedom, however, is limited. Man's choices are more or less rational and therefore are conditioned by the environment which is physical, biological, historical and social. "The conditioning through the physical and historico-social environment is a necessity if man is to live and work" (90). Both the physical world and the social world condition [man's] birth, existence, development, activity. In his turn, every individual . . . conditions the existence of others. . . . Taken as a whole, his physical and social conditioning forms with the individual man a kind of existential solidarity" (162). These limitations merely curb, but do not abolish freedom. "Every determinism, whether external-environmental, or inner-instinctivist, makes out of society an agglomeration without self-determination, without creative activity, without intellectual and moral background" (M. 33). For Sturzo, such an agglomeration would not fit the term society.

2. On the other hand, *there are sociological laws.* Although particular laws are often mentioned and discussed in Sturzo's *Inner Laws* and *True Life*, their nature is touched upon only in passing in these

[3] Cf. A. Wald, *Statistical Decision Functions*, 1950.

works. An *ex professo* discussion of the topic can be found only in his treatise on *Sociological Method*, especially in Chapter II entitled "Sociological Laws." There, he tries to prove that the possibility of valid sociological laws is a necessary requisite for the very existence of the science of sociology (which, of course, is not tantamount to the proof that such laws actually exist); moreover, in this same section he discusses their nature and makes cautious statements about the degree of certainty our knowledge can attain of them.

But the existence of sociological laws had already been quite explicitly affirmed in *International Community* written twenty years earlier. There, we read: "Common sense admits two facts as indisputable: first, the cosmos (including humanity) has its laws; second, an ethico-social order is necessary" (I.C. 143).

a) "I have been asked," says Sturzo at the very beginning of the chapter on laws in *Method*, "whether there really exist sociological laws, and eventually what is their nature. That they exist cannot be doubted if one considers that the nature of society is organic" (M. 26). Here, the term organic is used approximately in the same meaning as in Cooley's work; in the terminology used in this investigation, the term synthetic should stand for it, connoting the two-sided reality of society and the individual.

"If human activity in society were not subject to laws," continues Sturzo, "if, in society, one could not discover constant norms . . . one should . . . acknowledge the defeat of sociology as a science which does not and cannot exist. There would only be laws external to men —laws of climate, soil, race and so on" (M. 31), but not "inner laws of society." The discovery of such laws is one of the major tasks of sociological study (T. 3). It is noteworthy that the term "inner laws" appears in the work entitled *True Life* and has also been chosen as the title of an English version of Sturzo's most important work on sociology.

In his methodological treatise, Sturzo adds: "If there were no possibility of schematizing [our knowledge of society] in terms of rules, norms, constants, and laws, we could not give ourselves an account of the associative phase of man's life and would be forced to remain on the level of [statements about] a series of loosely connected phenomena constituting an almost unintelligible complex" (M. 39).

b) What is the nature of a sociological law? As reported above, this is the second question which Sturzo was often asked to answer. Sturzo begins his answer by citing that some believe it is better to speak of sociological constants than of laws. He does not share this opinion. "The term 'law' has been transferred to science [from philosophy and jurisprudence]; in science, the original significance of command or norm issued by an authority has been lost, but the term has preserved the substantial significance of order and value. Transferred to moral science, history and sociology, the term 'law' received the character of a double analogy; one is related to physics and the other to ethical and juridical laws. In sociology we maintain the term 'law' instead of constant to connote both a human [social?] fact, individual and associative, and a normative fact, related to an intrinsically finalistic order" (M. 37). It must be noted that in his basic sociological treatises Sturzo often uses the term "constant" with approximately the same meaning as the term "law."

Sturzo is eager to emphasize that sociological laws are only analogous to, but not identical with, physical laws. "Sociological laws," he says in *Method*, "are not of the same nature as physical or mathematical laws, but are of the same kind as historical and moral laws. But even physical laws are mere approximations and are subject to gradual decay in time,[4] commonly after having been superseded by more general laws. [Some of them] are hypotheses helping science to advance, offering [to the investigator] a spring board and giving him the opportunity to arrive at a discovery illuminating a whole process which seemed confused and inexplicable" (M. 26).

Sturzo often repeats that his formulation of laws does not represent them as "deterministic" in the way physical laws are. One of Sturzo's most explicit statements on the subject reads as follows: "Deterministic laws are excluded: there never can be a state of necessity entailing war" (I.C. 114). Laws do not compel men to act in accordance with them; they "are based on the very nature of man, on his living and acting as an individual, single and associated, free and conditioned, orderly or tumultuous, intelligent or instinctive. It follows that the inner laws [Sturzo's term] of living and acting in society are complex and have so many aspects that it is difficult to find threads, bonds and coordinations" [between them] (M. 27).

---

[4] Of course, law is a statement about a regularity, not the regularity itself; hence the possibility of its "decay."

The main difference between physical and sociological laws is that the latter express only regularities, tendencies, and trends, not "necessary and invariant relations."[5]

How do such regularities obtain? First of all, as a result of the fact that man is not only free but also rational. "We are essentially reasonable, and the rational permeates all our actions. Rationality is not only the principle [in the meaning of cause, or moving spring] of our understanding of facts, but also the aim of our action" (310). This allows "the vision of laws derived from human nature, [especially] from its rationality" (258).

Second, the physical and social environment influences man's decisions and, being relatively stable, produces regularities in human behavior which may be expressed in the form of sociological laws. Of course, these laws "do not prevent each individual from freely affirming his personality, from taking his own course" (258). Nevertheless, in given circumstances most men would act in a similar way and thereby contribute to the emergence of sociological constants which are coterminous with sociological laws (M. 37).

c) How can sociological laws be discovered? "In every scientific analysis," says Sturzo, "one distinguishes between the active element [the cause] and the passive element [the effect] and tries to understand their interactions. The same must be done in the field of sociology. It is known[6] . . . that the active element of society is the individual man and that he is a living reality amidst other realities of different nature, that he is conditioned as to his existence, his individual and collective action" (M. 28).

Having read this passage one may be inclined to assume that Sturzo would begin his search for sociological laws by offering a theory of human nature and then deducing laws of human action in society from it. He does not, because his method is primarily inductive. "It is through being mirrored in others that we are able to perceive the laws which limit us in thought and action" (T. 178). But a much more important source of the derivation of sociological laws is historical experience. "History," he says, "enables us to learn the laws of our social nature" (T. 4). And, since he is an "historicist sociolo-

[5] At the present time, the rigid character of physical laws is subject to doubt.
[6] "It is known" stands for "it is postulated."

gist," he discovers the majority of the laws by contemplating history. On the other hand Sturzo declines as an invalid approach the use of statistics, though aware that it is commonly the main root of inspiration for contemporary sociologists[7] (M. 49).

"The search for sociological laws," says Sturzo, "is a delicate task for the accomplishment of which there is little scientific tradition and no rigorous method. It is therefore advisable not to attribute to these laws a definitive character, but rather to treat them as working hypotheses or lines of orientation until, on the basis of consensus among scholars, we can retain some of them as definitive laws" (M. 37, 63).

3. The resolution of the antinomy explored in this chapter follows of itself from Sturzo's treatment of human freedom and the nature of sociological laws. Absolute freedom (the complete independence of the individual will) and absolute determination (necessary and invariant relations between phenomena) are incompatible. But the antinomy can be resolved if limited freedom of man and the flexibility of sociological laws are both acknowledged. This is what Sturzo does when offering his often repeated formula: "a man is both free and conditioned." According to him, "it would be a mistake to think that there are no sociological laws because man is free, or that laws are deterministic because man is conditioned" (258).

Let us elaborate on the proposition that man is both free and conditioned. The term "conditioned" often recurs in Sturzo's work but is never defined (probably because of the assumption that the term is well known from philosophy). In Sturzo's sociological context, "conditioning" is tantamount to pressure exerted by the environment on the individual, inciting him to make specified choices; this environment is both physical and social. The kind of conditioning which originates in the social world is tantamount to the pressure exerted on individual A by the sum total of other individuals with whom A shares a collective consciousness. But A is not only a passive object of pressure; being social, he exerts a similar pressure on other individuals; more exactly, he shares in the pressure exerted on them by his participation in the concrete society to which they belong.

Consequently, an analyzing society must distinguish those influences on the lives of one's fellowmen which stem from free individual initia-

[7] See Chap. VII, section 2.

tive, and those which stem from the conditioning influence of the social environment and social structure, formed through the crystallization of human actions and patterns of action (T. 10). Both are real, and each has limited potency because of its limitation by the other. Most commonly, man adapts himself to conditioning, or else he tries to evade it. He can never act without at least partial conditioning; but he finds in himself, and in his initiative an impulsion to overcome a given situation (M. 15-16). He may overcome the concrete state in which he finds the physical and social world around him by displaying initiative, by exerting pressure on his fellows, or by trying to change the physical environment.

Consequently, when studying sociology, "one has to contemplate an impressive complex of phenomena from the point of view of psycho-social movements, which, on the one hand, are beyond individual free will and, on the other hand, are beyond the limitations of conditioning and, as a result, appear as constant configurations" (M. 38).

The complexity of social conditioning is well illustrated by Sturzo when he analyzes the nature of economic laws. "Economics . . . founded on physical elements and forces, is . . . subject to the laws of the material world. Yet the human factor, intelligence and will, plays the major part in economic causality. By his efforts man succeeds in regulating [the economic process], even in dominating it. The synthesis of the two factors, man and nature, gives us human economics, neither wholly free, nor wholly deterministic" (97).

Sturzo's solution of the antinomy makes him rather skeptical about the concept of social causation, especially since he is inclined to interpret causation in the obsolescent meaning of absolute determinism. Whenever he uses the term "social causation" he emphasizes that it does not imply necessary and invariant relations between phenomena. For example, if there were such relations, he says, we could not explain why a certain group of facts sometimes provokes war, but sometimes does not.[8] Moreover, when considering facts from the point of view of social causation, a single fact abstracted from com-

[8] At this place, Sturzo commits an often recurring mistake: a complex phenomenon like war is caused by a concurrence of definite conditions. Therefore, a fact corresponding to one of the conditions may have occurred, but remained without consequence because of the absence of the other conditions. Cf. my "War and Peace," *Thought,* Fall 1950.

plex reality lacks any significance whatever, since every socially relevant fact is a product of the long sequence of antecedents which have made it possible (M. 64).

2. Two basic sociological laws

It always seems that the meanings of definitions and abstract propositions become clearer when they are demonstrated in concrete cases. For this reason, a search through Sturzo's sociological work will help to formulate the laws which he believes that he found, to discover the sources and the foundations of corresponding statements, and to spell out the manner in which he discusses freedom and conditioning.

This search is facilitated by the fact that Sturzo offers a list of laws in *Method* which he had previously discussed in both *Inner Laws* and *True Life*. The treatment in *Method* is not a *verbatim* reproduction since each of the laws enumerated originally contained items relevant to the work in which it was first formulated. However an inspection of the indices to the Italian version of his basic treatises shows that not all of the laws appearing in his works are reproduced on the list in *Method*. In addition a reading of Sturzo's sociologically relevant works reveals many more propositions worthy of the term "laws." Consequently, the rest of this chapter is devoted to a confrontation of those propositions scattered throughout Sturzo's work which could be considered as sociological laws or their equivalents.

1. Sturzo gives a detailed explanation and makes frequent reference to two of the laws presented in his works, and for this reason they could be considered as fundamental to his edifice. The first is "the law of motion toward rationality" (216) which, for the sake of brevity, will be referred to as the law of rationality. This concept of rationality, the very key to Sturzo's social dynamics, will be studied in Chapter VI. At this juncture it suffices to say that, in Sturzo's thought system, rationality refers to the human faculty to discern good and evil, truth and fallacy, and also to a most important trait embodied in the structure of the social world, which combines the existence of order in phenomena and of immutable ethical principles. In this Chapter, we shall limit ourselves to the unfolding of the idea that *motion* toward rationality is a sociological constant, and that a set of

generalizing propositions about that motion could be called sociological laws.

In condensed form, the law of rationality may be formulated as follows. At any time and place, men, whether isolated or associated, display activities which aim at replacing what is around them by something better. The term "better" must be understood in a broad sense: "what is aimed at" may be considered to have a higher utilitarian value (for the actor or the group), or to be more just, or more beautiful, or to come closer to truth. The actions so inspired may fail: there may be no result at all, or the result may be worse than the situation at the beginning. But men may and often do succeed; then, for a while, they are satisfied. But just for a while; very soon, a new vision of something still better will appear and inspire further action.

It must be emphasized that Sturzo's "law of rationality" is not tantamount to the self-evident, almost tautological proposition that human action is always directed from less to more satisfaction or from more to less dissatisfaction; rationality would then be almost indistinguishable from finality. Consequently the law obviously defines rationality in another, more objective way, meaning a better adjustment to man's environment (physical and social) and a gradual closer approximation to absolute rationality, especially in its ethical sense. When speaking of the dependence of sociology on the existence of sociological laws or constants, Sturzo states: "If a partial but progressive victory of men over environment were not secured" (M. 31) sociology would have no *raison d'etre*. This is tantamount to the acceptance, in a mild form, of the doctrine of evolution toward progress. However the exploration of this idea is postponed until Chap. VI. It should be emphasized that, for Sturzo, the law of rationality expresses a tendency or trend (216, 241) which operates intermittently, being often interfered with by other tendencies conducive to semi-rationality or pseudo-rationality. But these interferences are also intermittent, having no common direction, while motion toward rationality has. At this place, we might supplement Sturzo's reasoning by introducing a general theorem on the outcome of the composition of forces (social as well as physical) according to which, in the final account, the constant factors win. In this case, rationality is the constant, always adapted to the circumstances of time and place. Here and now, something is more rational than something else was, and, according to Sturzo's optimistic view, what is rational here and now is, in the final account, more likely to materialize than its opposite.

It is obvious that Sturzo's law of rationality is not a law in the meaning of classical physics. It could not receive the form of a hypothetical proposition of the type "if conditions A, B, C are present, X follows." It could not, first, because there are no limiting conditions on which the operation of the law would depend (the "if-clause"), since the motion toward rationality is assumed to be omnipresent. Second, it never imposes itself on men with the necessity inherent in physical laws. Instead of being guided by objective rationality, men may indulge in activities of the semi-rational or pseudo-rational type. Summing up, we may say: motion toward rationality is merely a prepotent trend.

2. Another basic sociological law present in Sturzo's thought system is a law which might be called the law of a cyclic movement between polarization and unification; in Sturzo's catalogue, it appears in the form of two laws, one of polarization or duality, and another of unification. The term "polarization," as Sturzo acknowledges, has been taken from physics (127). The combined law may be summarized as follows: In society one sometimes observes a state of multiple nucleation tantamount to the dispersion of social forces among several centers, but this state is unstable. From it, society tends to develop toward the polarization of forces, or duality; if the polarized forces are crystallized around power or authority, duality becomes diarchy. Then, one of the components of a concrete duality or diarchy displays the tendency to absorb the other in itself, but success is never complete and unification is never definitive. After a while, centrifugal forces break out and society disintegrates into a multi-nuclear pluralism. This is the end of one cycle and the beginning of another.

The law under consideration is after all a law of a cyclic movement in three or four phases.[9] Let us pass them in review one by one.

a) Sturzo acknowledges that a society could be shaped according to the pattern of multinuclear pluralism, but denied any stability to

---

[9] The number of phases is reduced to three, if duality does not become diarchy and goes over into unity.

such a configuration.[10] His argumentation is not very convincing. "We do not accept pluralism as a symbol of a sociological system which could neither be coordinated nor function without passing through duality and crystallizing into diarchy" (258). This might prove that pluralism is undesirable, but not that it is impossible.

However a stronger argument might be presented in favor of his thesis. Opposing forces commonly are in conflict, and it is natural that conflicting forces be integrated in two, and only two camps. It is true that triangular conflicts are not unknown to history; for instance, this was the situation in the international arena shortly before the outbreak of the Second World War. But every triangular conflict is resolved by the formation of a coalition of two forces against the third, often followed after victory by a conflict between the two victorious allies.

b) Consequently, the trend is always from pluralism toward duality. For Sturzo, the appearance of duality within social configuration is a natural, not an artificial fact (M. 100). It can be derived from man's *liberum arbitrium,* which brings about the diversity of choices made by men in a given situation, and also from the recurring obfuscation of rationality by pseudo-rationality and irrationality (M. 101). Any social reality can be molded by the duality of the ideal and the practical, of the spiritual and the material, of the finalistic and the conditioned (24). But sociologically most important is the duality between reality in its static aspect and reality in becoming (246); more concretely, between the forces which insist on the conservation of the *status quo* and the opposing forces demanding change in the name of a social ideal. Sturzo calls these two forces the organizational and the mystical currents (297). In *Method,* he replaced these terms by another pair—the conservative and the progressive camps (M. 9). It must be conceded that, while both "organizational" and "conservative" are acceptable terms, both mystical and progressive are not, since they evoke misrepresentations: there is often nothing mystical in revolutionary ideologies, and, if they are like modern totalitarianism in all its modalities, they do not deserve being called progressive. The term "dynamic" might be suggested, since it seems to be less value-laden.

[10] Just as Spencer denied the stability of the homogeneous.

According to Sturzo, duality is often present despite the appearance of plurality, which seems to be there so long as we consider groups analytically and by means of abstraction. But when we consider them in action, we see that the forces coalesce in two's (255).

c) The duality of forces easily crystallizes into a diarchy; this happens within a group or even in a large society as a whole, through the emergence of two powers balancing each other (248, 252). The transition from unorganized duality to diarchy takes place when the mystical (progressive) current is so penetrated by rationality that it responds consciously to the necessity for power (254) finally, with power itself.

d) The transition from the stage of duality or diarchy to unity takes place when one of the opposite social currents becomes a mediator (256). The term mediator is rather unfortunate: one cannot be a mediator between oneself and something or somebody else. The examples Sturzo uses could be described better by such terms as dominance or absorption.

With respect to the stage of relative unification Sturzo poses the question whether unification is always carried out by the State, as many believe. He thinks that this is not the case and points to historical instances of unification through the Church (as in the Middle Ages) or even through the family; he could have (but did not) cite the Chinese family, prior to the penetration of Western influences.

e) But no unification is definitive. After a while, centrifugal forces break out and society disintegrates into multinuclear pluralism. To corroborate this proposition, Sturzo points to historical experience: no State, not even a totalitarian State, has ever achieved definitive unification; and the alleged unification of Western society into Christendom was not really complete (M. 101).

In *International Community* Sturzo studded his ideas about duality with concrete examples, such as the opposition between a monarch and parliament, or between a central power and a local government, or the State confronted with such real forces as the Church, the press, or the great industrial and commercial concerns (I.C. 52). One may conclude: first, that duality may appear within the framework of a definite group, or in relations between different groups; second, that in a large society there may be several simultaneous dualities. In the latter case, most sociologists would have spoken of pluralism.

Sturzo is eager to emphasize that his view on the impossibility of definitive unification is not an *a priori*, but an *a posteriori* conclusion, the result of painstaking sociological interpretation of complex historical facts which had to be classified, schematized and categorized (M. 99). He adds that he professed these views a half century before writing his *Method* (M. 104).

It is obvious that the complex law of polarization-unification, like the law of rationality, is not one which could be expressed in the terms of the formula "if A, B, C are present, X follows." The law points to the operation of a cluster of contradictory tendencies, some conducive to more and others to less integration in society; but the conditions under which one or another tendency prevails are not formulated (with the exception of the transition from unorganized duality to diarchy and from these to unification). In Sturzo's thought system, it cannot be otherwise: After all, the concrete man is the moving spring of the social progress. But while individual decisions are rather unpredictable, the accumulation of decisions in favor of more or less integration is predictable. Most predictable, according to Sturzo, is the coalescence of particularistic social forces into two camps which corresponds to the phase of polarization. Least predictable is the last phase, the disintegration after unity has been achieved. The time and the "precipitant" of the falling apart belong to the chance elements in human affairs. "Chance," says Sturzo, "is nothing else than one of the diverse elements in our physical conditioning and our boundedness" (XX). Perhaps this statement could be generalized to cover conjunctures in human social affairs, e.g., the almost unforeseeable intersection of tendencies[11] and trends creating that "impressive complex of phenomena" of which Sturzo speaks so eloquently when discussing the nature of sociological laws (M. 35).

A superficial interpretation of Sturzo's teaching about the law of polarization-unification can provoke the impression that Sturzo has himself indulged in what he calls "deterministic phenomenology." He is well aware of the possibility of such an interpretation and says: "Since all the diversity of life [tends] to polarization or duality, and the duality always tends to . . . unification, it might seem as though a cosmic force, a deterministic movement, drove [all the diversities] to

---

[11] Cf. my paper "Order, Causality, Conjuncture" in L. Gross (editor) *Symposium on Sociological Theory*, 1959, pp. 145-64.

duality and polarization. But the [driving] force itself is not dualistic. [The social world] is a world of beings of mind and will who freely move and act, though bound . . . within the circle of their . . . conditioning. Men do not *suffer* the law of duality, they act according to it [because it is their nature]. They are not brought deterministically to [unity], but they are one in their individuality and freely seek oneness in their final realization" (241). Every society that grows up out of human relationships is always "practically dualistic and tendentially unitary" (242). In its broad meaning, the law of polarization-unification is a general law which "no society, no institution, no human reality can escape" (246).

3. At this point, one should ponder the possibility of adding a third law to the two basic laws stated above, that of Individuality-Sociality" explicitly omitted in Sturzo's later treatises but stated in *International Community*. There, the following statements appear: "The fundamental law of every human society is: the more individuals increase in conscious personality, the fuller the development of their associative qualities and forces, the more the individuals develop and deepen the elements of their personality. . . . In order fully to understand this law, it is well to bear in mind certain fundamental notions: (1) The individual is social by his very nature and all his life is nothing else than a life of relations. (2) Every individual forms to himself the center of his own life, and acts and reacts among his fellows, who also form to themselves centers of their own lives, so that there seems to be a continual multiplication of each in others and others in each. (3) Hence, the more the individual develops, the fuller the development of elements relative to him. Thus by continual action and reaction society comes to be individualized in types, institutions, moral bodies, and the individual to be socialized in the institutions, circumscribing his life" (I.C. 45). On the next page, the law is explicitly called the law of Individuality–Sociality, and a few pages later, the assertion is made that "the law of individuality-sociality is always in force and functions according to the stage of development attained by the individual and social factors" (I.C. 50).

The omission of this law from later works does not mean that Sturzo would have repudiated the ideas just quoted, or would have come to the conclusion that his earlier statements had been faulty. More probably, after having written *The International Community*, in which he created his doctrine about individual-social consciousness, Sturzo came to the conclusion that what he had called the law of Individuality–Sociality was more than one law coordinated with other laws: the idea of individuality–sociality became central in his sociological thought. Therefore, the correlation between the individual and the social could no longer be treated as a "theorem" about society (which is the logical nature of any sociological law) but had to be conceived as one of the most basic postulates of his theory.

Under these circumstances, it is preferable not to succumb to the tempting idea of introducing one more item into Sturzo's own collection, namely, the "law" of Individuality–Sociality.

3. A few secondary sociological laws

In addition to the two basic sociological laws surveyed above, Sturzo rather briefly discusses several laws which may be called secondary.

1. "The social tendency," says Sturzo, "is toward the organization of every special associative social trend" (174). This organizational tendency is well expressed in the fact that no society exists without a form[12] (22). Some of the social forms are explicitly treated as sociological constants. Thus, one reads: "The family has always existed since there have been men on earth (30). . . . The perennial forces which have given it existence are the two basic instincts, the sexual and the parental" (32). "Wherever a social form exists . . . there is an intrinsic necessity of order and defense" (50) which gives rise to political society specializing in the performance of this function. Historical experience shows that there has been no society without religion, the tendency being toward the formation of specialized social forms devoted to the performance of the religious function[13] (66, 68, 76). Sturzo acknowledges however that out of the three fundamental social forms just mentioned only the family is a constant in the strict meaning of the word; as to political and religious associations, there is only a trend toward their separate organization, a trend however which is so strong that it may be classified among Sturzo's sociological laws.

[12] The individual forms (types of social groups) will be treated in detail in the chapter on Social Morphology.

[13] In his monumental work, A. Toynbee confirms Sturzo's position: "No individual human being and human community is ever without a religion of some kind" (A Study of History), vol. VIII (1954), p. 478.

2. Another secondary sociological law is that of autonomy–interference. The tendency to autonomy may be conceived as a derivation from the organizational tendency. The social forms, once organized, display a tendency to assert themselves, to achieve for themselves the organization they deem the most rational. Thus, for instance, a nation (a social form which Sturzo rightly distinguishes from the polity) tends to preserve its existence, personality and future with all its energies and at whatever cost (N. 16). Behind this tendency there stands a particular aspect of freedom which Sturzo calls organic.[14] The tendency to autonomy is inherent in human life itself. "Therefore, though interference may attenuate it, it is impossible for it to disappear completely. . . . An indispensable margin of freedom is necessary, and it is never absent from any social form" (118-9).

Autonomy, says Sturzo, does not mean separation from other social relations, but self-dependent existence, the independence of a specific and characteristic personality (I.C. 37). But, on the other hand, the individual forms are not complete realities,[15] though we habitually think of them that way by a habit of logical and legal abstraction. We speak of a family, but no one really asserts that the whole category of relationships of the members is exhausted within its circle. The same is true of the tribe, the village, the city, the State, or the Church (245).

Each social form tends toward autonomy, or independence. But autonomy can never be achieved in an absolute manner because, in addition to autonomy, there is interference, which means that influence is exerted by one group on another, so that, in the final account each form is bounded by others (117-8). That complete autonomy is never achieved can be demonstrated best in the example of the family. Among all peoples at all ages the family has been bound up with various political and social structures (38) as well as with religion (57). But once they have arisen, even interference cannot annihilate one of the fundamental forms of sociality so that the others can vie for dominance without it. Instead, a whole series of compounds of interference and autonomy take place, of which the following are typical instances (40).

a. Of the three fundamental forms, namely the family, the nation, and the Church, one of the three may overdevelop to the detriment

---

[14] See Chap. V, section 5.
[15] Probably in the meaning of groups absorbing their members *in toto*.

of the other two. This case obtains when the family form is in its patriarchal, tribal, nomadic stage, whether organized of itself or organized into military bands, (which takes place when there are permanent wars with neighboring tribes); another instance of this kind of interference is seen in the wars of migrant tribes for more or better land. A good specimen of this ideal type was seen in the Middle Ages when complete unification was attempted on the religious plane, and in modern times, a similar attempt at unification can be observed on the political level.

b. The second type of compound obtains when two social forms develop vigorously to the detriment of the third. This occurred when the dominant families combined with the priestly theocracy to the detriment of the political order. The same type of compound, but with different elements, was found in ancient Greece and Rome, where the religious form never achieved full autonomy but was forced to develop within the other two because the domestic form (*phratry* and *gens*) and the political form contested with each other for supremacy.

c. The third type of compound obtains when the three forms develop in approximate equality. In this case, relations between them commonly receive legal expression and the tendency toward unification on a higher level becomes operative (26-7). This situation is observed in modern democracies which adhere to the benevolent form of the doctrine of separation of Church and State, for example in the United States.

According to Sturzo, there is always a dynamic interplay between the tendencies of autonomy and interference, and periods of interference, struggle and temporary dominance constantly manifest the presence of social life. Autonomy and interference alternately prevail, so that it is even less possible to make predictions about them than it is to forecast the processes described in the law of polarization–unification.

3. A third secondary law concerns the transcendence of groups and the passage of consciousness from one group to another without loss of distinct personality, taken individually or collectively (20-1). At another place Sturzo defines transcendence as "the progressive passage of consciousness to another term that elicits it" (309). This is one of those cases where the meaning of a definition can best be clarified by a survey of a few instances. According to Sturzo, transcendence is

observable in the projection or extension of the individual onto the social plane which, as we know, is the very foundation of collective consciousness and therefore of social life; it is also observable in unification, and in efforts to overcome error and evil (308,310). The last instance probably covers cases when irrational developments which have occurred in a given social group are corrected by the interference of another group, e.g. the State or the religious association.

On the basis of these instances one may assume that the two "terms" between which the "processive passage" called transcendence takes place are, first of all, society and the individual. Although, in principle, transcendence is considered to be a two-sided process, passage from the individual to society appears to be much more important than passage in the opposite direction. "Society itself," says Sturzo, "indicates [man's] continuous aspiration to transcend the concrete experience of [his] actual life in wider participation" (310). This wider participation can be attained only through general ideas, such as the family, the fatherland, the Church. Nevertheless, transcendence is not at all passage from the realm of actuality to that of ideas. "The idea of fatherland is not merely an abstraction drawn from [observable] reality, but more than anything else is a social transcendence" (311). In the general context of Sturzo's work this means that, sociologically, fatherland is not the abstract idea connoted by the term but a concrete state of collective consciousness, the coalescence of citizens united by love of, and care for, the fatherland.

Sturzo himself is not very happy about the term "transcendence." He has chosen it because he could not find another word to render his meaning (309). Sometimes he uses the term transcendence in a more common (rather philosophical) meaning, as he does when formulating his philosophy of history (Cf. Chap. II).

However he expands the technical connotation of the term transcendence by referring the reader to earlier parts of his *Inner Laws* (preceding the chapter on transcendence) where he discussed several processes which fall under the concept before using the term, in order "not to introduce a new idea without elucidating it" (308), and there he tells us that he explicitly identifies with transcendence "the passage [of functions] from one group to another" (308). The most conspicuous example is the passage of functions to the State from the family, the religious group, and economic associations. This happens rather easily because almost every human activity displays some aspects of order and defense; but order and defense are the specific functions of the State; therefore, whenever any human activity is related to order or defense it may be easily transferred from the groups primarily involved to the State. But the State is not the only sinner. As an illustration, Sturzo presents the Hebrew theocracy at certain periods of its history when it carried out a multitude of functions not directly attributable to the religious form (52).

Sturzo calls the passage of functions "transposition," but, as he already explained, transposition is only one species of transcendence. It emerges that Sturzo's "transposition" is approximately the same phenomenon as the one studied by Sorokin in his *Social and Cultural Dynamics* under the heading "migration of functions."[16] Sorokin offers an impressive list of such migrations and makes an attempt to correlate them with the phases of the movement of cultures from one type to another, but alas, not very convincingly.

Like the laws previously surveyed, the law of transposition and transcendence[17] describes a mere tendency. It often happens that certain types of activities pass from the individual to society or *vice versa*, or from one group to another; but no definite conditions are offered in Sturzo's treatises.

4. Finally, Sturzo mentions a law of purification. There exists, he says, a typical law of purification in the family as a trend away from the dominance of animality (M. 82-3). The synthesis of the sexual and the parental instincts underlying the family, is at the root of this tendency. Animal egoism is overcome by conjugal affection, but of course retrogression toward animality is possible. The trend from polygamy to monogamy is also treated by Sturzo as an example of a general trend toward purification (42). In general, the process "between the primitive man who, for us, is on the border of animality, and ourselves . . . has been a continuous surmounting of the predominance of animal nature with its strong instincts so as to make possible life in common in kindred nuclei" (309).

In *True Life*, the process of law of purification is extended to become a kind of law of the success of "liberating currents," of which

---

[16] P. A. Sorokin, *SCD*, vol. III, pp. 181-216.
[17] Incidentally, the list of laws appearing in *Method* includes the law of transcendence, but not that of transposition.

there are three; first, the motion toward rationality, already studied; second, art, which is a vision of the good in symbols, sentiments and aspirations and may be conceived as "a cathartic purification of minds"; and third, religion, "which reveals truth and goodness" (T. 191).

One may add to this obviously incomplete list several statements made in other contexts. For instance, Sturzo mentions the "historical tendency toward democracy," though interrupted by retrogressions and long periods of collapse. True democracy, he adds, consists in the dynamic equilibrium of liberty and authority (G.M. 196). He finds, in history, the tendency of possession to become more and more "moralized," in other words, restricted through ethical conceptions curbing the power of men over men (P.M. 8). Here as elsewhere, purification and sublimation through "the liberating forces" is conceived as a prevalent tendency, not abolishing human freedom, since Sturzo is fully aware of the possibility of art vilifying human minds and of pseudo-religion.

5. The laws outlined above do not exhaust Sturzo's catalogue. But the present writer does not see any possibility similarly of formulating, on the basis of Sturzo's work, several of the other laws mentioned by him in the list offered in *Method,* as well as the indices of the Italian versions of *Inner Laws* and of *True Life.* Such are the laws of social consciousness, of resolution, of solidarity, and of conquest and achievement. Therefore, only a brief description of some of them is offered.

The law of social consciousness mentioned in the index to *True Life* is probably a reminiscence of the law of Individuality–Sociality discussed in *International Community;* but, in the text of *Inner Laws,* the term never appears; the references in the index point to numerous statements about individual-social consciousness explaining its nature and properties but not as a law in the meaning of Sturzo's doctrine.

The law of resolution stands in the index for the sum total of statements about the resolution of society into individuals, according to the synthetizing conceptions of society. Resolution is therefore an explanatory procedure rather than a statement about reality; scattered statements identifying resolution with full recognition of the value of individuals and mentioning that, if the egoistic interests of some prevail, this resolution does not take place,[18] do not change the picture, since these statements are irreducible to sociological laws.

[18] In the meaning that the individual is totally subjugated by the group.

As to the law of solidarity, it is surprising that, in *Inner Laws*, solidarity appears mainly in connection with economics. It is asserted that the formation of group economy, (i.e. of economy above the level of isolated men) is accompanied by "the emergence of solidarity and the imposition, on the members of the group, of an ethico-social tendency" (124). This is so because the economic structure creates communion and solidarity in the production and distribution of goods (150). Solidarity (identified with friendship) is also said to be necessary for the maintenance of durable relations between peoples (133) and the formation of nations (N. 4, 23). This again is not nearly enough to formulate a sociological law. Similarly the law of conquest and achievement (treated in *True Life*, pp 202-3), is merely a particular aspect of the law of motion toward rationality.

Furthermore, the following laws mentioned in the index to *Vera Vita* must be left without consideration: 1) the law of social coercion and the law of critical circles, because Sturzo himself calls them "alleged laws"; 2) the law of liberty and conditioning which is actually only an explanation of the relationship between the two; 3) the law "of life, knowledge and love" and the law "of the solidarity of evil" which deal with subjects beyond the scope of empiric science.

4. A few sociological constants

In addition to the fundamental and secondary sociological laws, Sturzo discusses several sociological constants which, after all, have the same meaning as his sociological laws. The most important among them are two pairs, authority-liberty, and morality-law, which he treats as "syntheses." The nature of the syntheses will be discussed in Chapter V. At this place the question arises, to what extent do these pairs belong to the number of sociological constants?

1. It is not possible, says Sturzo, to conceive of a society without a minimum of liberty. A society without liberty would lack any spontaneous force. A gang of slaves on the way to the slave market does not constitute a society. Human freedom is a necessary consequence of man's rational nature (163-4).

It must be noted that freedom or liberty is a social phenomenon appearing *within* social groups; the freedom predicated of a group, i.e. its independence from other groups, is covered by the concept of autonomy.

From these statements one may derive the following formula: a minimum of liberty is a sociological constant; where there is no freedom at all, there is no society, only a human aggregation of another nature. Sturzo is eager to emphasize that freedom does not impose itself on men, nor does it influence men deterministically, but leaves them the freedom of choice (174). This proposition seems to be tautological but is not. What Sturzo wants to convey is the fact that the constant called freedom is only a general tendency, which includes the possibility of deviations and exceptions, just as the other laws and constants do. In other words, man possesses the freedom to be or not to be free; he may reject freedom and create aggregations with no freedom at all; but, these would not be societies, and, as a corollary, the sociological laws would not apply to them.

2. Another constant is authority. "No society . . . can dispense with authority which is the principle of order" (161), while order is a necessary component of human coexistence. A society without authority would be a human aggregation lacking the means of achieving any social purpose; a fleeing army would serve as an example (164). Authority is consequently not something extraneous to the social body, or superimposed upon it, but is the necessary and constant projection of social will (64). There is a *law* or *natural necessity*[19] through which liberty and authority always coexist in every society (195). They limit each other, and their delimitation renders possible their coexistence (180).

3. A third sociological constant is morality, or the sum total of those common norms in force in a society which have become constant, i.e. customary.

4. Next comes the constant called law. The constancy of law is derived by Sturzo from the postulate that human activity requires: 1) association between men; 2) order in such an association; and 3) the guarantee of this order (60) which is the law. The constancy of law is not asserted with the same firmness as that of morality or liberty. But from such statements as "law is characteristic of every social form," or "law and legal authority commonly prevail over sheer force" (I.C. 50, 54), one may draw the conclusion that Sturzo assumes the existence of a sociological constant tantamount to the tendency toward the formation and maintenance of law. In other words, there is

---

[19] Italics mine (N.T.)

a law (a statement about regularity or uniformity in phenomena) according to which law (meaning an authoritative precept) tends to prevail in every society.

5. In addition to the constants appearing in the syntheses liberty-authority and morality-law, one can find in Sturzo's work a certain number of scattered statements about other constants. He says, for instance: "In nearly all epochs known to us, individual property and common property existed simultaneously, though in different measures" (106-7). Sturzo speaks even of an instinct for personal property which no State can destroy (119); what is instinctive is obviously constant. Another sociological constant is mentioned in the statement that friendship is the basis of community among men as among peoples upon which the whole social edifice is built.

5. Sociological laws in retrospect

In conclusion let us pose the question: what do the laws and sociological constants affirmed by Sturzo mean as a system.

Some of the statements passed in review seem to be elaborations of the obvious; but sociology deals to a large extent with phenomena which are obvious because they belong to the main stream of human life, and the obvious must be spelled out in order to give a systematic and consistent interpretation of the total network of tendencies and trends encompassing the life course of human beings. Of course, the laws and constants offered by Sturzo do not supply us with so complete an explanation of social life that by reference to one or some of them, we could understand everything going on around us in society. But such is not Sturzo's pretention. This can be summarized in the following way:

Despite the fact that man is a self-determining agent, one finds in all concrete societies certain situations and processes which are so common and recurrent that they can be considered as prepotent trends or tendencies or constants. They are not imposed on man from the outside, but are derived from the associative aspect of man's nature; this is why they can be called "the inner laws of society." These tendencies and trends are not deterministic; they do not compel men to act in a preestablished way; but with regard to the given and not chosen physical and social environment, the individual responds as a rational being, in a limited number of ways, according to those laws formulated by Sturzo and, of course, to many more not identified by him.

The laws and constants discussed by Sturzo are not asserted to form the totality of regularities and uniformities which obtain in society. He singles out those regularities which are sociological, i.e. pertinent to societies in the concrete, societies observed as wholes, not yet analyzed into economic, political, jural or other segments. Besides sociological laws, there are economic, political and other laws, but they remain, and rightly so, outside the scope of Sturzo's sociology.

One salient trait of Sturzo's doctrine about sociological laws and constants is its dialectical character. The vast majority of the trends discussed by him can be arranged in pairs of forces acting in opposite directions. There is motion toward rationality, but also motion toward pseudo-rationality and irrationality. There is the law of polarization, but also its opposite, the law of unification. There is autonomy and interference, there is liberty and authority. In concrete societies a continuous interplay of forces is going on. The outcome of their composition cannot be predicted in advance, because of man's original liberty. But, according to Sturzo, rationality is the dominant trait of human nature. Hence, his mildly optimistic statements about the final, at least temporary, victory of certain forces operating in society over their opposite numbers. We will return to this problem when discussing social dynamics.

While Sturzo's general theory of sociological law is drawn in firm lines, in full harmony with other parts of his doctrine, his presentation of particular sociological laws (except the two here called fundamental) is merely a preliminary sketch.

CHAPTER V

Social Morphology

Social Morphology

1. What is social morphology?

"WE MUST and should study the morphology of society" (T. 7). "If sociology is to contribute something to knowledge about men in society, [it can do so] through the study [either] of morphological formations [or] of the historical process" (M. 138). These explicit quotations from Sturzo leave no doubt that, for him, morphology is a legitimate part of sociology, despite his horror of "abstractionism" and his inclination to identify [social] types with abstractions and therefore to interpret the forms of sociality, the basic unit of analysis in his morphology, as "methodological schemes" (B. 4).

Sturzo acknowledges the legitimacy of social morphology which, by its nature, is a static approach, despite his insistence on the historicist or dynamic nature of society. This superficial inconsistency may be resolved in the following way. Sturzo denies the validity of a static conception of society and of any conception which would ascribe to society the kind of stability we ascribe to buildings or geographical configurations. For him, society is always in motion. This is in accordance with the view predominant among contemporary sociologists who teach that society is immediately given to us in interaction, i.e. in the behaviors and motions of individuals.

This idea is often exaggerated. For instance, Gurvitch becomes impatient whenever he finds a statement ascribing *some* stability to society; for him, society is an eternal formation, deformation and reconstruction of social equilibria.[1] Sorokin, who sees in interaction the basic unit of analysis, and who ignores the distinction between

[1] G. Gurvitch, "Le concept de la structure sociale," *Cahiers Internationaux de Sociologie,* Vol. 19 (1955), pp. 6 ff.

motion within a given society and motion transforming it,[2] nevertheless fully admits the logical necessity to conceive of society not only as containing change, but also as that which itself changes.[3] On the other hand, many sociologists, especially those who belong to the functional school, after paying lip service to the proposition that society is a network of interactions, proceed to devote almost all of their attention to social statics, which places them far from Sturzo in this regard.

Sturzo not only asserts that society is predominantly dynamic, but he actually unfolds a predominantly dynamic sociology. Nevertheless he offers a well developed although not all-embracing morphology, mainly in *Inner Laws*. Valuable additions can be found in his other works. In any case, he completes a static study of dynamic phenomena.

There is no incompatibility between the two lines of thought. We must distinguish between a static *conception* of society and a static *study* of dynamic phenomena. To collect data for social statics, the observer so-to-speak makes snapshots of particular societies at specified moments, establishing who are the actors, what are their aims, their relations, and so on. A detailed reproduction of such findings in words or on charts would not be sociologically relevant, since it would remain in the purely descriptive level. But the procedure may be repeated at different moments relative to the same society and the results of the several observations may be compared. This comparison may reveal sheer chaos, in which case the observations have been sociologically fruitless. But they may reveal some constancy, some order, or somewhat definite tendencies. The same actors may be found to behave in recurrent ways, to aim at the same goals, to maintain the same relations among themselves. Such a result is sociologically relevant. In a continuously moving society, we perceive "structures or scaffolds," to use Sturzo's own words (T. 4).[4] These man-made structures, he continues, are necessary for further individual actions, and, let us add, their perception is necessary for an intelligible treatment of dynamics: they serve as anchors and as supports to which dynamic propositions may be attached.

In point of fact, one does find at least relatively stable elements in

[2] Sorokin, *SCD*, vol. IV (1941), pp. 587 ff.
[3] Sorokin, *ibid.*, vol. I (1937), pp. 154 ff.
[4] What is found is the structure, the movement which is directly observed.

society. One of them is culture, to which Sturzo refers many times although only in passing and generally without using the term. Another element of stability is the individual, the self-determining agent who acts according to his particular nature. Keeping in mind that what is called a personality in psychology and sociology must be distinguished from a philosophical concept of human nature in general, personality may be identified with the cluster of the individual's attitudes, i.e. of acquired (learned) tendencies to act in specific ways under specified conditions. This is probably what Sturzo has in mind when he writes: "Man . . . acquires habits of mind and body which may be called stable or transient forms through which he manifests his will" (23).

These particular attitudes are acquired by the individual in interaction with other individuals, but the acquisition is both selective and creative because the individual freely chooses to internalize one of the many alternatives to which he is exposed. The most drastic case is observed when the child or adolescent, exposed to detrimental influences, selects those attitudes which may correspond either to the mores of society at large, or to those offered for imitation and internalization by the "bad boys" in delinquent or subversive groups etc. When selecting and incorporating attitudes into his personality, the individual often performs a creative act (in the same way as an invention may be creative); the internalized attitudes are then modified and adapted to those which already form part of the personality.

Once selected and adapted, the attitudes remain relatively stable. But society (meaning here a social group) consists of definite individuals (this is convincingly demonstrated by the "snapshots" mentioned above). *Ergo*, the actions of the individuals in society must be relatively stable. Since this is so, the comparison of snapshots yields knowledge about reality. Consequently, social morphology is scientifically warranted despite the dynamic character of society.

Although this line of thought cannot be directly imputed to Sturzo, it seems to underlie his sociological theory of morphology.

2. *What is a social form?*

Let us now go a step farther. An individual social structure discovered by the mental superimposition of snapshots is sociologically relevant if the result can serve as a model for the understanding of society.

To serve as a model, a concrete social structure must be recognized as a specimen of a type, constructed by empirical induction, or by comparison of many concrete structures. This is what Sturzo is actually doing, as he acknowledges in the following statement: "We look after common elements among social nuclei" (B. 7). Where the term nucleus seems to connote men in a durable grouping, Sturzo calls these relatively stable and recurrent nuclei "forms of sociality" or "social forms," often treated as synonyms and sometimes replaced by the terms societies and social groups.

The starting point of Sturzo's treatment of social forms is "sociality." As explained in Chapter III, sociality is an abstract term designating the associative aspect or component of individual consciousness; it becomes concrete and therefore real when this potentiality is actualized in the consciousness of one or another individual. "The inner principle in which we find the source of the concretization of sociality, [that] which beyond all other phenomena and material structures proves to be the specific, definitive and original element of sociality embracing all social forms . . . is provided by the rational capacity of individuals to acquire consciousness of their associative nature" (8, 13). At this point, let us not go any deeper into the nature of rationality, since we will do so in the chapter on social dynamics (VII).

Concrete sociality is observable in the mental processes and actions of men. But, because the very nature of human consciousness is both individual and social, concrete sociality is projected onto the outside world as family, class or caste, nation or State, or church (5). The projection (externalization) occurs because "individuals . . . seek to achieve something through their own activities" (12-13); the term "own" must be understood as connoting joint or associative activities, as in the following statement: "The social forms involve manifold activities of individuals in which cooperation passes from being potential . . . to becoming actual and efficacious" (25). Actual and, let us add, durable or recurrent cooperation, gives rise to "collective realities" and these, to be realities, call for a form (25). In other Sturzian words, "every individualized society is such through a form; there can be no society in the concrete without form" (22).

The social form is then declared to be the mode or specific reason for the concretization of society (22-3). At this place, Sturzo speaks of the concretizing of *society*, whereas in the statements cited above he spoke of the concretizing of *sociality*. The referent is the same, since the concretization of sociality connotes the individual aspect of the phenomenon, and the concretization of society connotes its collective aspect. Whenever sociality is concretized (in cooperative actions of individuals), there is a concrete society, and whenever there is a concrete society, there must be a cluster of concretizations of sociality.

What does it mean that a social form is the mode or specific reason of the concretization of society or sociality? For Sturzo, the reason for the concretization of society, or the reason for the appearance of one or another social form, is the existence of human needs which seem to be best achievable through durable association. The "mode of the concretization of sociality" points to the particular type of relations to be established between the members of a social form, depending on whether this is a family, a city, a State, a Church. The connection between particular types of relations and particular forms has been lucidly explained by Sturzo in *International Community* where social relations occupied the center of his attention. "Sociality," he says there, "cannot remain a matter of purely individual relations, but tends to some form . . . of organization, i.e. to the establishment of a hierarchy of forces" (I.C. 48). "Human society seeks to give form to the constant or semi-constant elements in human relations. That is, it tends to create and develop social types justifying their demands, molding their customs and enforcing their laws so that by a kind of gradual crystallization institutions emerge able to withstand the flux of events and the anarchical forces of destruction" (I.C. 36).

On the foundation of the above statements, one could draw up a tentative definition of social forms congenial to Sturzo's general sociological theory. First one has to consider the analytical definition of society. Out of the four traits composing it, the last, the temporal dimension, must be omitted because social form is a type, an abstraction, and as such has no logical relationship with time. Of course, this does not prevent the individual societies corresponding to one or another form from having a temporal dimension. However, another trait, that of specificity must be added. Every society must have a form, says Sturzo. But there is no general form of society; there are numerous forms of which one, just one, is observable in any concrete society being studied. The specific form differentiates a given society from the majority of societies, but not from all societies because there may be and there probably are many concrete societies having the same form. Therefore, we could never say that an object under observation is a social form without pointing it out as one of many types.[5] Summing up, a social form may be defined as a plurality of individuals possessing collective consciousness of the necessity to act jointly and associatively for the attainment of specified ends in a specified type of organization.

This statement seems incompatible with Sturzo's own words: "I preclude the typicity of social forms" (B.S.). These words seem somewhat enigmatic when compared with the extensive study of the types of social forms in *Inner Laws* and elsewhere. The negative statement just reported and the positive fact of the study of definite social forms can be reconciled in the following way: Sturzo has found a number of types of social groups which constantly recur and therefore can be studied in social morphology, but he denies that the number of social forms appearing here and there are classifiable in a fixed number of types: he does not preclude the possibility that additional, so-to-speak, sporadic or erratic social forms may eventually emerge.

3. The fundamental forms

1. The main contention of Sturzo's morphology is that there are three and only three fundamental social forms, namely the family, the polity (the State) and religion (in the meaning of pluralities of human beings associated through the community of religion). These forms, he says, are given to us in the historical, i.e. experimental (observable) reality and are constant in all civilizations and ages (25). They are omnipresent because they answer the requirements of human nature in its three permanent and basic aspects. The family secures affection and continuity (of the race); the polity guarantees "order and defense" without which no social life is possible; religion provides men with ethical and finalistic principles (25, 51n.).

Hypothetically, the satisfaction of these three basic needs should be

---

[5] This situation is analogous to the one characteristic of criminal law: we cannot assert that an action is criminal without having found that it possesses the traits of one of the types of crime (murder, rape, theft and so on). The Germans denote this trait of crime by the untranslatable term *Tatbestandmässigkeit*.

achieved through the respective forms. But we have to distinguish form from content, meaning "the whole practical activity in which men engage within the various forms" (B. 51). Observation shows that the scope and the range of these contents are not always in full accordance. First, in primitive society, political and religious associations exist early in an embryonic state, from which they tend gradually to evolve. Second, it sometimes happens in the course of history that one or even two of the fundamental forms are absorbed by the other. Third, the phenomenon of the "passage" of functions from one group to another, mentioned in the preceding chapter, cannot be excluded.

2. One may ask the question: Is it certain that there are three and only three fundamental forms? The question may be raised especially with respect to the economic phase of social life, since Sturzo maintains that economy is only a secondary form of sociality. In this regard as in many others, his view coincides with that of Sorokin, who also denies that economics has a place among the top-level cultural systems which together form the "sociocultural supersystem." But, unlike Sturzo, Sorokin also denies the fundamental character of the political phase of sociocultural life.[6]

What are the reasons for Sturzo's negative stand on this question? First of all, he asserts that a pure economic form of sociality, i.e. one which is neither domestic, nor political, nor religious, does not exist. The economic form, according to him, enters all of the fundamental forms and conditions the manner in which they develop and attain their ends (26). This is not very convincing since, as Sturzo himself has shown, there is the phenomenon of interference, i.e. reciprocal influence takes place between the forms. Relative to each of the fundamental forms one could assert that it sets conditions under which the other ones function and develop.

Second, he asserts that "an economy is not autonomous and has no finalism of its own, but shares in the finalism of the fundamental forms" (97). Since physical determinism is present in economy, the objects manipulated by men in economic activities are subject to the mechanical determinism characteristic of the physical world; therefore, economy never succeeds in becoming a fundamental and autonomous form of sociality. It rests on the fundamental forms and simultaneously

[6] Sorokin, *SCD*, vol. IV (1941), pp. 122-4.

becomes an almost necessary ingredient in their structures; this is true even of religion and religious associations (98).

The meaning of the statements just reported is probably this: material things are often of great importance in the fixation of human relations and in the creation of "scaffolds and structures." This is true, but one still wonders whether one should not add to the list of man's basic needs (which engender the fundamental forms) the need for material things for the very survival of the individuals who compose societies. It is rather awkward to describe say, General Motors or Bell Telephone Co., only in terms of the conditioning of domestic, political and religious life. It seems that dependency on mechanically determined physical objects precludes, for Sturzo, the very possibility of autonomy in a social form; a form depending on something else is not a self-determining body. But in the final account, human reason and human will, according to Sturzo, mold the economic forms into what they are. The crucial question is—whether they do, or do not, pursue their ends independently of domestic, political or religious ends. Of course, they do—and therefore a realistic sociology of Sturzian inspiration should not deny to economy a place among the fundamental forms of sociality. Sturzo's admirers should not be shocked by these doubts since he was the last man to assert that his sociological theory was final.

3. Let us return to Sturzo's fundamental forms. The family is the first natural nucleus (31; T. 204). The perennial forces behind it are the two basic instincts, the sexual and the parental. On this background something develops which could be called "family consciousness" (32); in contradistinction to polity and religion, the family consciousness is always particularistic, exclusive, distinct from the totality (10). Despite all the oscillations of social factors, the family is always present as one of the fundamental and constant elements of social life (49).

Although the family is a response to one of the basic exigencies of human nature, it needs guarantees. These guarantees are trifold: inner, political, and religious (32-3). The inner guarantee is based on the very process of the domestic form of sociality, on the natural growth of cohesion among the coexisting family members, the habit of being together and, commonly, the presence of affection, which helps the family to resist outside forces directed toward its breakdown.

The political guarantee is tantamount to the recognition by the state that the family transcends the mere fact of association, which gives the family the character of an "institution" (39). By the way, Sturzo does not succeed in offering a clear and consistent definition of this term[7]—it seems that no one, at least no one in sociology, has ever succeeded. On the basis of Sturzo's work, the best approximation to a definition would probably read as follows: an institution is a recurring set of durable and important inter-personal relations guaranteed by the State and the law.[8] However in the present context, a definition of institution is not of great importance; what matters is the fact that the family is usually protected by the State, which is not tantamount to saying that State law entirely molds the family. On the contrary, the family creates its own laws and actualizes them in the kind of autonomous movement which characterizes each of the fundamental forms of sociality (40). Finally, the religious guarantee is never absolutely absent, although among nonbelievers it is replaced by various forms of pseudo-mysticism (53).

4. The polity (the State) functions to maintain order in the relations between individuals and subaltern groups, and to defend the collectivity against extraneous forces (50). There is some difficulty in delimiting the political form from the other fundamental social forms, because "every social content may be envisaged as [belonging to] the category of order" (57), and because the function of order and defense may be fulfilled by the two other fundamental forms or hierarchies of organizations (50), which was the case in feudal society. But a polity exists when a social nucleus specializes in the fulfillment of the fundamental exigencies of order and defense. For Sturzo, the State is an organization by intrinsic nature because the State is specifically organized to satisfy the needs of order and defense, and these ends cannot be achieved except through organization (I.C. 49).

Although the State recognizes a social order, it is important to note that the State is not its sole or even main source: men elaborate and express a social order because they are rational beings. Disagreeing

---

[7] The statement cited in section 2 is *not* a definition.

[8] Sturzo's view is at variance with the now prevailing view that institutions are complexes of patterns of behavior. Cf. however B. Malinowski, *A Scientific Theory of Culture* (1942) who identifies institutions with social groups.

with the ideas of many social philosophers, Sturzo says that the State is not a "perfect" society (I.C. 47; M. 102-3). The State represents the political form of society, but is not society itself. It controls public power, but is not the whole of social power; it deals with economic interests, but not with the whole of economic life; it promulgates laws, but does not create them.[9] The State is the political and legal organization of society, but must never be confused with society itself (N. 134).

Like the family, the polity is a manifestation of the individual-social consciousness of order and defense at the very root of the political form of sociality (64-5). Political consciousness is (predominantly) the consciousness of an elite, of a ruling class, in contradistinction to national consciousness, which is the consciousness of a people in contact with other peoples (70).

In polities the existence of authority in combination with liberty is of strategic importance; but since order and defense are spread throughout the social texture, authority is not limited to the State.

In his treatment of nationalism vs. internationalism, Sturzo devotes particular attention to the Empire, one species of the State. An Empire consists of a ruling people and ruled peoples and must possess a military potential superior to that of all countries on which its beam of influence is shed; the idea of Empire is tied with that of hegemony (N. 231).

The inner urge to expand is the motive force in the formation of an Empire. It may derive its tensile strength from the geographic position of a prominent people; or from prevailing economic facts; or from the centralization of business which extends over a wide territory (such was the case of Venice, Holland, England). Population pressure is never a prevailing factor. Expansion is an inherent law of Empire. Imperialistic expansion may occur even when the wish of the people is hostile to it, and even when the leaders want to stop such adventures (N. 233-4). The urge to expand may be called imperialism, as distinguished from nationalism (see below section 4).

5. Religion, the third of the fundamental forms, is founded on the feeling of limitation relative to the mystery of life and death and the

[9] Probably in the meaning that a simple *fiat* of the State authorities is not sufficient to introduce new patterns into the behavior system of the citizens, and that additional conditions must be present. Unfortunately, the legislators often overlook this *de facto* limitation of the power to legislate.

need to explain cosmic causality and ethical law (66). Sociologically speaking, religion is not so much a personal sentiment as a group bond, a moral and social union (67). One should distinguish the spirit in the religious form from the technical and juridical organization of the religious society (72).

The existence of religious associations belongs to the number of sociological constants since there has never existed nor does there now exist a civilization not based upon a philosophical, moral and religious complexus, which serves as the unifying principle of its social nuclei and helps to idealize the facts of ordinary life. The lay, a-religious complex of modern civilization is negative and has no positive plan for the reconstruction of philosophy and morals (58). One could add, of course, that Marxism makes just such an attempt and has become a kind of secular religion[10]; but in countries where Marxism has gained political and social supremacy, it has been unable to provide men with a genuine motive to live and to work, a fact proven by the necessity experienced by the governments of these countries to reinstall the so-called capitalistic incentives for work.

4. *The secondary social forms*

Let us now turn to what Sturzo calls the secondary forms. They are either 1) intermediary groups between the elementary nuclei of a society, or comprise the margin of social formations, or 2) men in grouped geographical categories which, as social forms, have achieved a certain autonomy (153).

As already stated, Sturzo does not believe in the possibility of an exhaustive classification of the secondary forms. He does not offer a definitive catalogue, but mentions, 1) villages, towns, provinces; 2) racial, national, religious minorities (the latter are distinguished from religious associations as fundamental forms); 3) universities, especially the medieval ones endowed with wide autonomy; 4) colonizing companies, such as those of India and the Americas; 5) modern literary and scientific associations; 6) political parties and religious sects on the respective margins of the State and the Church; 7) class organizations which assume an autonomous character; 8) companies of merchant adventurers; and 9) monastic orders (154-6).

[10] Marxism as a secular religion is well discussed by W. Gurian, *Bolshevism*, 1952, pp. 5-23.

1. Sturzo submits three of the secondary forms to detailed study; namely, the economic association, the international community (both in *Inner Laws*) and the nation (in *Nationalism and Internationalism*). Relative to the former, his main effort is directed to proving that economy cannot be classified as a fundamental form; this aspect of Sturzo's teaching has already been reported. The peculiarity of economy is that it is not only a special social form, but is also a particular manner of conditioning social life, which refers to its function of providing means of subsistence (95). Crude material facts are transformed into social values by human solidarity, expressed in actions of the altruistic type, and by the tendency to form a common economy. Then, the material conditions of life become a moral (behavioral) factor of living in common. But as already mentioned, Sturzo says that economy never becomes autonomous and has no finalism of its own; it shares in the nature and the finalism of the fundamental forms of sociality. Specifically economic forms serve as instruments for the fundamental social forms and provide a liaison between the various types of societies (124).

Sturzo attaches great importance to those economic groups which express the pre-established interests of the possessing and nonpossessing classes. They are in almost continuous conflict because of the impermeability of their structures (M. 11), in other words, because of the slowness and difficulty of vertical mobility.

2. The international community is secondary because it can be resolved into another form of sociality, namely polities or States. The international community may be considered as their amplification or synthesis (129). International communities can be formed in many ways; Sturzo mentions the affinity of language and civilization; colonial expansion; armed conflict resulting in the formation of a central organization; expansion of a unifying religion as in the cases of Christianity, Islam and Hinduism; political alliance and the gravitation of peoples toward a hegemonic center; or general understandings conducive to the formation of organizations like the League of Nations (130) and the United Nations.[11]

None of these facts is self-sufficient; the formation of an international community requires consciousness of moral affinity and communion (in the sense explained in Chapter III) (130). The results may be

[11] The reference to the United Nations has been added in the Italian version of *Inner Laws* (*Società*).

connoted by the term "friendship," once again an optimistic exaggeration on the part of the author. Friendly relations, he continues, are reenforced by legal forms, religious rites and public festivals. Among peoples (polities) having reached this stage of communion, the maxim *pacta sunt servanda* is in force (131). It is true that history presents us with many cases of pacts which did not presuppose any tie of friendship (132). But every pact transcends its political meaning of practical utility and reaches the ethical plane. Relationships between peoples, even if initially utilitarian, either create solidarity and friendship, or else they dry up and cease to exist (133). According to Sturzo, the normal course of development from initial contact, discovery of moral affinity, friendship consolidated in pacts, may sometimes be reversed, so that development may proceed from pacts to friendship to discovery of moral affinity. According to Sturzo's general view of the nature of tendencies observable in social life, both lines of development cannot be treated as instances of mechanical determination; human reason and human will stand behind each step and may arrest the development at any particular stage and turn it around—from more to less friendship or *vice versa*.

3. The nation is not explicitly classified by Sturzo among the secondary forms, probably because he treats it in a special monograph where the problems of classification did not arise. But Sturzo's view on the subject is evident: "Among the communities based on solidarity," he says, "the nation holds a place midway between the family and the State, sharing with the family the feeling of natural affinity and tending along with the State to the goal of civil increment of order and defense" (N. 23). The nature of the nation is treated along the general lines of Sturzo's sociological synthetism with some inclination toward personalism: he does not ascribe to the nation a "spirit" or reality beyond the single individuals who compose it, but sees in it the simultaneous reflection of the consciousnesses of its members; the nation cannot be conceived outside of the framework of society or community or family groups (N. 17, 23).

The general properties of the nation and the ideas and sentiments engendered by this social formation are treated by the author as follows: "Nation is a community based upon solidarity, organized on the foundation of tradition, history, language and culture" (N. 4, 23). The nation is not the political organization of society, nor its religious organization, nor a voluntary society freely formed and dissolved. It is rather "the binding sense . . . of a people which, becoming aware of itself, seeks to distinguish itself from any other and to arrange its existence in the best possible manner according to historical circumstances" (N. 16). In general, Sturzo's nation corresponds to what is now commonly called an ethnic group which has reached a certain level of self-consciousness. "Nation means the individuality of a people; this cannot come about without stable geographical continuity, an historical and cultural tradition, economic interest, awakened consciousness of the past of the people. The individuality of a people means just a *de facto* differentiation between one ethnic group and another" (N. 13).

Like many authors, Sturzo oversteps the bounds of his own definition of a nation when he numbers Switzerland and Belgium among the social formations called "nations" because of an identity of language and culture. This is the result of a semantic confusion, found predominantly in the Romance languages and adopted also in English, wherein the terms nation and state are not sharply distinguished. The Germanic and Slavic languages do not follow suit, so that authors writing in these languages would never apply the term "nation" to Belgium or Switzerland. Semantic quarrels are fruitless since there is no authority to impose one or another connotation on the users of a term. For this reason the term "nation" has almost disappeared in contemporary sociological literature. However it could be preserved to connote the fusion of State and ethnic group achieved in England, France, Italy, Spain, and so on, and forming the content of the social ideal denoted as self-determination of nations.

Sturzo, however, does not believe in self-determination as an absolute principle. "The rights and duties that spring from the maturation of a nation," he says, "are only historical and relative" (N. 24).

Sturzo offers precise distinctions between the terms national consciousness, national sentiment, national ideal, and nationalism. National consciousness is the feeling that comes to the surface with the reawakening[12] of a people. National sentiment is akin to patriotic

---

[12] Probably Sturzo means not only the reawakening of people after a long period when the national sentiment was dormant (*e.g.*, the Czechs during the 17th and 18th centuries), but also the initial awakening of national (ethnic) consciousness in a social group possessing the other requisites of a nation.

exaltation. National ideal is a longing to obtain what is lacking to bring about the realization of the completion of a nation (N. 24). Nationalism is both a theoretical conception and a practical activity which tends to overvalue the nation and to make it a dominant, or perhaps an absolute principle (N. 25).

Finally, Sturzo makes a distinction between nationalism and imperialism, the latter connoting the tendency to build or expand empires. The former has almost always a popular basis and is diffused among the whole people while the latter is limited to the ruling class or the ruling people (N. 239-40).

5. *Syntheses*

1. Members of social groups, i.e. of concrete, individualized social forms, hold together, act together, and share many values differentiating them from members of other social groups. They are tied together by specific social bonds. According to Sturzo, they are united primarily by collective consciousness, the foundation of the whole system of social bonds.

Collective consciousness is a mighty, but informal and inarticulate bond. What is more, it is necessary to maintain the stability and cohesion of social groups. In the inner structure of social groups (as well as in their interrelations) one may distinguish particular forces of cohesion which, in Sturzo's work, are called "syntheses." He names three pairs of such syntheses: liberty–authority, law–morality, duality–diarchy, but unfortunately, he does not offer an explicit definition of the term synthesis. One may even wonder whether *each* of the elements of the three pairs is a synthesis, or whether synthesis means *conjunction*, on the top level, of the elements of each pair. On the basis of his work, the latter interpretation could refer to liberty–authority, which are declared to coalesce in social order. It is not clear whether the same could be asserted of morality and law which are said to tend toward equilibration under the banner of equality, but no tangible reality is shown to embody this equilibration. And it is almost impossible to ascribe a synthetizing capacity to the pair duality–diarchy, each of which (but not the two together) could be conceived as a synthesis (equilibration) of forces eventually forming the duality or its species, the diarchy.

Therefore, the first interpretation imposes itself, ascribing the value of a synthesis to each term of each of the three pairs. This interpretation is corroborated by the statements from *Inner Laws* where Sturzo summarizes the syntheses as follows: authority is the active, unifying and responsible consciousness; liberty is the consciousness of individual personality and its autonomy; morality is a rational consciousness applied to human actions; law is consciousness of equality in justice; duality is consciousness of social organization, either organizational or mystical; and diarchy is consciousness of social power (301).

To make things still more difficult, the term synthesis is sometimes used to connote the coalescence of smaller groups into larger ones (see below, section 7). Therefore, it is preferable to use the term "synthesis" as little as possible and to discuss the first two pairs as "forces of cohesion." One could hardly object to designating authority, law and morality in this way, but one may raise doubts whether liberty (which, in Sturzo's work, appears in four modalities) can be similarily designated, since liberty, as shown by experience, is often disruptive. But, in Sturzo's view, liberty, together with authority, is an indispensable component of order, which is not so much one of the forces of cohesion as the tangible result of their operation.

In addition to the four terms appearing in the first and second pairs of Sturzo's syntheses, one must consider the terms "force" and "power" as related to authority and the term "justice" standing behind the law. In Sturzian sociology, these terms are interrelated in a rather complicated manner and connote not items in a sterile classification of concepts, but real and important social phenomena.

2. To understand this complicated system of concepts, one has first to define the terms which comprise it. Force is treated by Sturzo as a kind of independent variable, more exactly, as something which is known or given and to which the other objects under study are related directly or indirectly.

Power, says Sturzo, is force which has achieved superiority over [primacy among] other forces (G.M. 188); for example, social force is conspicuously present in the State, but by no means only there. Authority is power which is legitimate (recognized; *ibid*). The meaning of this definition of power is demonstrated by the cases of Ireland and Poland. If no collective consciousness emerges after a people has been conquered, as happened in both of these countries, there will be a duality between the conqueror and the conquered people, so that the conqueror's force will be powerful but not authoritative (G.M. 186).

The fact of recognition (meaning, of course, inner recognition, not obedience based on the obvious impossibility to resist) makes power legal. This is probably what Sturzo means when saying: "we can conceive of the use of force as either rational (lawful, by legal authority) or irrational, i.e. dissociated from legal authority or unlawfully exerted by legal authority" (I.C. 54). Consequently, law and authority are rational elements, while force and power are irrational. But law and authority are not synonyms; authority is a modality of power and, more remotely, of force; it is first of all the ability to issue commands and to enforce them, while law is a social force generated by the popular recognition that those in authority are entitled to issue and enforce commands.

a) Law is a necessary attribute of authority; on the other hand, without authority, law cannot exist. Consequently one is entitled to say that law materializes in the power to act and to require others to act; hence the duty to act and to allow others to act (I.C. 146). The relationship between right and duty is treated by Sturzo in a manner at variance with the one prevailing in modern jurisprudence. Every right, says Sturzo, imposes an obligation on the part of the person concerned; in exchange, the correlated person has a concomittant obligation [and, obviously, a right corresponding to the obligation of the former]. The double chain of subjective and reciprocal rights and duties constitutes in itself an organic social structure (213). The modern jurist would agree that every right calls for a corresponding duty, but always the duty of *another person*: to the right of the creditor the duty of the debtor, to the right of an officer to issue commands the duty of the subordinates to obey. Right and duty are the two sides of a juridical relationship, in the image of the convex and the concave sides of a sphere.[13] The relationship between rights and duties mentioned by Sturzo, namely a combination of reciprocal rights and duties between two persons (e.g. in the sales or labor contract), is only a common, but not a necessary aspect of legal phenomena.

Behind the law, there stands the fundamental principle of justice. About the latter, one finds in Sturzo's *International Community* this rather unexpected but realistic remark: "the painful efforts of all the theorists to find a measure for justice shows that such a quest lacks practical value" (I.C. 193). This certainly does not mean that justice

---

[13] This idea is vigorously developed by Leo Petrazhitski, *Law and Morality* (1904-7, in Russian; English translation, 1955).

is only a conventional or external fact. It is an act of consciousness expressed in the formation of rights and duties and tending toward the achievement of equality or equivalence in individual-social relations (238). The lack of an objective and immutable measure for justice means only that law in the concrete cannot be derived from pre-established postulates; it always reflects the interpretation of justice at a definite time and place. "Laws, whether customary and moral, or written and codified, contain at once constant and fundamental principles, and voluntary, conventional, traditional, or political elements. The greater or lesser conformity of such laws to the requirements of human nature depends on a complex of facts" (I.C. 144).[14]

b) The counterpart to authority is liberty, which appears in four modalities: original liberty is the autonomy of human personality, to be realized in a social order; expressed in the latter, original liberty appears as organic liberty, final liberty, and formal liberty.

Organic liberty, the free initiative in the creation of social groups and the freedom to create, modify, develop and multiply their organs, is permanent in social life; it can be hampered but not suppressed (174-5). This statement from *Inner Laws* is hardly compatible with the one appearing in *Guerres Modernes*, where one reads: "There are always social organs; but organic liberty does not always exist" (G.M. 210). This is of course a more realistic statement: organs may be imposed on a society by power which is not authority and consequently is not related to liberty.

Final liberty is the freedom to choose the immediate end [of action] (177). "Triumph of liberty [probably, in the formal meaning] may become a goal of action; this is an act of finalistic liberty" (G.M. 211).

Formal liberty is connected with the juridical crystallization of society. The particular liberties covered by the term "formal liberty," have always existed in varying degrees, although in the past they were not envisaged as liberties for all (179-80).

c) The counterpart to law is morality. Sturzo's definition of morality has already been reproduced (cf. Chap. IV, sect. 4): morality is the sum total of common norms which are in force in a society and which

---

[14] This treatment of justice is in full accord with Sturzo's original treatment of rationality distinguishing between what is rational here and now and what is absolutely rational (cf. Chap. VI).

have become constant in it. They become constant or customary through the repetition of acts, more exactly, in the spirit by which the acts are animated. But only "good customs," righteous norms, expressing practical rationality, belong to morality (204). This limitation is essential for "there is no period in history in which we do not find traditions, usages, institutions conflicting with the principle of natural solidarity and with the fundamental laws of morality" (188).[15]

d) Now we can turn to the consideration of some specific relationships between each of the forces of cohesion (syntheses).

Authority is so closely linked to law that their definitions could not have been given without reciprocal reference. But authority is also linked with morality and religion. The nature of this link is explained by Sturzo in the following way. To be authority, "power needs more limitations than the one presented by the law. Organic [legal] limitations do not suffice; they must be supplemented by limitations accepted by all" (P.M. 13-4). Two factors give the ethical limitation real efficacy: first, general conviction dominating the collective consciousness, and second, supporting religious conviction (P.M. 14). A peculiar situation obtains when ethical norms formed in the past are now subject to doubt; since a conflict of ideas often becomes a conflict of forces, political power, for a certain time, liberates itself from normal limitations (P.M. 15-6) and becomes naked force.

Finally, authority is linked with liberty. Let us begin with one of Sturzo's most startling statements. Liberty and authority are not diverse or opposed elements of society, but correspond to the same exigency of the social personality of men (171). Authority is the will of the people; liberty belongs to the personalities (G.M. 191). Organized liberty is authority; organized authority is liberty (G.M. 213). Each delimits the faculties of the other whenever they come into contact (185).

Liberty summons authority by rebound, and the social resultant of their synthesis is order or the tendency toward order. If this is not the case, the formal delimitation of authority and liberty has resulted in an excess of one side or another (180). In general, their delimitation is not a sociological *a priori*; in other words, it is not determined by some inner necessity; it is an outcome of social life (185).

[15] Cf. the statements of R. Redfield reported and commented on in the next chapter.

In a few instances, Sturzo ingeniously demonstrates the interplay of the two elements of the diad liberty–authority. Election is an act of authority based on liberty; this is the first and most elementary synthesis of the two (G.M. 193). A parliament is free to pass a law; but in so doing it performs an act of authority. The government is free to offer and to sign an agreement (G.M. 216); but this again is an act of authority.

The relationship between liberty and authority is once more epitomized by Sturzo in the following manner. Authority may be considered as *reductio ad unum* of the wills of the members when, according to Sturzo, all participate freely in authority (177). This is one of Sturzo's rather frequent statements in which one can perceive a kind of social optimism transcending the boundaries of empiric science. Of course, Sturzo does not overlook the possibility of conflict in the framework of polities. However what appears as a conflict between authority and liberty (e.g., a revolutionary movement aiming at the overthrow of existing authority) is actually a conflict between two sections of a diarchy both led by an authority of their own, each section being formed around a specified principle (183-4).

6. Social organization and functions

In addition to his detailed analyses of social forms and of the forces of social cohesion, Sturzo's morphology contains relatively short statements about the organization of social groups, their functions, relations and integration. Let us summarize what he has to say about these problems.

1. The coexistence of men in society is always organized (an idea sometimes unfortunately expressed by Sturzo in terms of the organismic analogy). The individuals are organs of society, meaning that each contributes to the achievement of social ends. Not all contribute in the same way; the specification of functions by individuals is what makes organization. But apart from individuals, there are no organs of society (7).

A social formation receives its individuality and its specific character from its organization taken together with its ends. This allows Sturzo to say that society is "organico-finalistic" (6). When acting as organs of society, the individuals express their consciousness of being in communion with one another and acting as a whole (62). This statement is one of the clearest expressions of Sturzo's sociological synthetism.

The organization of men in concrete societies does not deprive them of freedom. It may seem that only individual activity is free. This is incorrect, says Sturzo. In common activity freedom is complete, though there is consciousness of mutual conditioning (T. 199).

The individualization of every particular society, manifest in its organization, is treated by Sturzo in the perspective of his sociological synthetism with its inclination toward personalism. It is derived from the need inherent in each individual not to lose his own individuality in an association with others (20). This does not mean that man is unable to overstep the limits of small groups. To do so, he must be conscious of a higher social unit that would comprehend them (ibid). In this way, the idea of the hierarchy of social groups (to be discussed somewhat later) makes its appearance.

Two major methods or plans for moulding group life must be added to complete Sturzo's sketch of social organization. In his earlier works, Sturzo called them the methods of authority and liberty, warning that we should not confuse these *methods* with the terms used to connote the *syntheses* which follow from them. In *Method*, he suggests that the methods of authority and liberty could be called the methods of coercion and persuasion, respectively. Thus, the method of liberty (persuasion) describes the process of organization based on conviction, self-control, self-discipline, and respected and cherished tradition, while the method of authority (coercion) describes the process of organization based on fear and imposed control and discipline (196, 198).

2. As already stated, Sturzo describes society as "organico-finalistic." In addition to organization, social groups possess finality. This means that the social forms do not appear as aimless motions of human activities. They are permeated by finalism since they help men attain their ends. The social forms, says Sturzo, "are the projection [of natural ends of human activities] into concrete reality" (25). In this projection, individual finalism becomes social finalism. As already explained (cf. above Section 3), the particular types of social forms correspond to the main types of human ends to be achieved; according to Sturzo, this correspondence is the *raison d'etre* of any social form, although, in practice, there may be discrepancies.

In accordance with his basic theoretical standpoint, Sturzo does not assume that the special forms arise by an inner necessity only in the forms themselves.[16] The human forms do not emerge independently of human will. Men create them while more or less aware of the utility of the forms in attaining human ends. Therefore, Sturzo says that the social forms originally appear as ends of human activities (*finis operantis*), but once arisen, "the social forms are consolidated in ever closer correspondence to human needs, organized as more or less permanent means for the attainment of further ends, and transformed if they are no longer adapted to changing conditions of human activities" (25); Sturzo says that man's incessant urge to act can outdate the utility of a given form but this lack of adaptation of a formerly well adapted form can be transformed only if the conditions of human activity (among them, human vision of new possibilities) have changed. The instrumental role of a social form is of paramount importance since "the coordination of various human activities . . . is a typical function of a human group" (XVIII). Thus, starting with finality in the meaning of *finis operantis* (the goals pursued by the actors), Sturzo penetrates deeper into the functional performances of social groups in the meaning of *finis operis* (the objective contributions of specific groups to the survival and well being of society). Here are a few instances:

"The fundamental requirements of human nature are the preservation and development of the individual and the species. This postulates social life . . . as necessary and coexisting [with individual life] from the time of the first appearance of human life on earth" (I.C. 143).

"From the strictly sociological standpoint, whenever a social form exists . . . there is of intrinsic necessity a function of order and defense" (30). This means that order is one of the necessary conditions of the existence of a social organization.

At another place Sturzo says: "Liberty and authority are necessary and *therefore* original elements of sociality" (177). He calls their co-presence "a law of necessity" (195) making possible the projection of sociality.

"Human experience leads us to believe that men, in order to remain organized, need as much the rational element which forces them to

---

[16] The opposite position could be held only by a sociological collectivist.

accept the limitations of society as the coercive element which prevents us from evading them" (N. 256).

The quotations above make it clear that Sturzo is not satisfied with stating the fact of the coalescence of individual ends and social ends, but asserts the intrinsic necessity of the former experience for the latter. Such statements bring Sturzo quite close to the doctrine of the contemporary functionalists. We will return to this idea in Chap. IX (section 5).

7. Intergroup relations

The particular social groups (forms) of various types do not remain strangers to each other. They enter into relations, communion, inter-action, and the network thus formed may be conceived as an immense crystallization of humanity (B. 4). The simultaneous existence and the intertwining of the activities of innumerable groups appears before our eyes and makes evident the complexity of the social process (XX).

1. Sturzo treats the integration of smaller social groups into larger bodies by using the category of synthesis, but in a meaning quite at variance with that of the forces of cohesion. Sturzo explicitly uses the term synthesis in discussing the international community to denote "an amplification of polities or states." It is evident that similar syntheses are observable throughout the social texture. A federal State i.e. composed of member States, may grant ample autonomy to the villages, towns, provinces, and may then be conceived as a syn-thesis of these smaller units. A family may be complex, i.e. consist of several generations out of the members of which several "nuclear families" (composed of parents with their children) are formed. A religious group may be articulated into many subgroups on various levels. Large industrial associations may be conceived as syntheses of individual plants, shops and auxiliary organizations.

2. Above these syntheses, Sturzo contemplates two more. One is what he calls "a society," "a concrete society," in so far as it is super-imposed on the social forms already studied. This line of thought appears quite clearly only once, namely, when he states that some of the secondary forms of sociality are intermediary types between "the totality of a society" and the elementary nuclei (153). The totality of a society appears then to be a synthesis of the elementary nuclei

corresponding to the fundamental form taken with some of the secondary forms. It appears therefore that the term society is used by Sturzo to designate two different objects of observation: on the one hand, any social group, simple or complex; on the other hand, only a social group of a higher rank embracing many social groups of lower ranks and belonging to various types. In the passage referred to, society is called "the totality of a society" and roughly corresponds to an ethnic group, but in some cases to the multi-national state; it seems to be identical with what Parsons calls society in contradistinction to a partial social system.[17] Many of Sturzo's statements about society in the concrete reported in Chapter III are obviously applicable only to these totalities; only in their framework does one find a particular culture based on history and tradition, and a well developed social consciousness which is rudimentary or almost absent in many small functional groups.

3. Above these "totalities of society" corresponding to peoples or ethnic groups one finds civilizations. "The sphere of human personality," says Sturzo, "may . . . widen out into immense circles[18] or civilizations transcending single peoples" (T. 208). The central point is the religious orientation to which science and philosophy converge. Religion is at once philosophy, ethics and history. . . . The foundation of this [super] group consciousness receives value and stability from a religious idea" (T. 209). Every civilization is so deeply rooted in social groups and the spirit of the peoples composing it that it is impossible to confuse one with another, contemporary or preceding. Differences, ideal and practical, rooted in the sentiments, habits and convictions of people living in the same circle of civilization [and others belonging to other civilizations] are of real importance whereas racial and similar differences are not (M. 54-55). It is relative to these syntheses that differential sociologies are postulated by Sturzo, as reported in Chap. II.

4. In this volume, the framework of Sturzo's sociology is consistently reduced to the level of empiric science, but an accurate report cannot ignore the fact that Sturzo describes an "ultimate synthesis" which this writer feels is beyond the scope of empiric science. This

[17] T. Parsons, *The Social System*, 1950, p. 19.
[18] The term circle is preferable to the term cycle used in the English version of *True Life*.

ultimate synthesis unites natural (empiric) society with the "supernatural," which Sturzo says is the quintessence of the history of man on earth (T. 4, 229). On this level, the social bond is love (T. 11). However, Sturzo emphatically denies the existence of a society corresponding to humanity, because humanity as such is not unified by a specific collective consciousness.

5. If and when systematized, Sturzo's social morphology provides us with an impressive theoretical synthesis. The foundation consists of innumerable groups of the functional character—domestic, political, religious, economic and others. Already on that level, multiple and diversified syntheses are observable. But, in their turn, these syntheses are integrated into what Sturzo calls "the totality of a society," peoples or ethnic groups. The ascending movement does not stop here, but reaches to the level of "civilization" (distinct from functional groups called "international communities") of which there are only a limited number. And these, in Sturzo's philosophical and theological, but not strictly sociological vision, are subject to the ultimate synetheis—the synthesis of the human with the divine. It is remarkable that Sturzo consistently denies the possibility of a synthesis corresponding to the term humanity. Men are united with God in the framework of particular civilizations, units in which the religious spirit forms the strongest bond. So long as there is no all-human religion (which, for Sturzo, could not be anything but Christianity), there can be no synthesis connoted by the term "humanity."

CHAPTER VI /

Social Dynamics

Social Dynamics

1. What is social dynamics?

WHILE STURZO's thought requires a preliminary exploration to determine how morphology (i.e., social statics) is possible in his thought system, no such deliberation is needed with respect to social dynamics. Sturzo's sociology is "historicist" and consequently essentially dynamic. "History," he says, is "an inner process of society. Society always presents historical novelty, an aspect of revelation, an inward dynamism" (T. 5). "A concrete society is never stable or definitive; it is processive and dynamic" (13). "Every [concrete] society lives its own life and fulfills its particular process" (22). Nevertheless, he finds it possible to draw a generalizing image of the social process, to formulate abstract propositions about social dynamics, despite his negation of "abstractionism" (which is not tantamount to the denial of the validity of abstractions (cf. Chap II). Abstract knowledge of society, he says, may be obtained [first] through the study of morphological formations, but [second and still more] through the study of the historical process (M. 39). "If the temporal [dimension] is omitted, [the investigator] is deprived of the means of studying the social rhythm" (T. 7), which is absolutely essential for the understanding of society. Such are the most explicit statements of the Italian master on the subject.

What is social dynamics? There is no doubt that, for Sturzo's historicist sociology, social dynamics is identical with the historical process. "The whole of human activity on earth," he says, "is a continuous process which we call history" (T. 198). "History is a process without discontinuity; the past resolves itself into the present bearing with it the good and the evil realized by events" (C. & S. 128).

139

"History begun in time has never been arrested, never turned back, never repeated itself, but has gone forward" (T. 198).

At this place an important problem arises: does Sturzo really identify social dynamics with the sum total of *all* human actions on the associative plane? This is a problem which divides contemporary sociologists; they have to decide whether social dynamics is tantamount to change or motion of society, or is only one of its species, characterized by sub-total change in social structures or systems. The former position is held by Sorokin[1] for whom the broad conception of dynamics is vital since only on its basis can he assert that change belongs to the nature of social and cultural systems and therefore postulate that sociocultural change is immanent. The latter position was that of F. Giddings who used the very appropriate term of social kinetics to connote motions going on within the framework of structures without changing them; it is now that of Parsons and, more or less explicitly, of the functionalists.[2]

There is no doubt that, in principle, Sturzo does not distinguish between kinetics and dynamics—otherwise he could not have identified the historical process with the sum total of human activities. Most events taking place among men immediately become "the past," history in the meaning of "the course of events" (cf. Chap. II); they are trivial events in which the human drive "to achieve and fulfill" (see next section) is actualized within the framework of existing structures. This line of thought has been chosen by Sturzo despite his predilection for the interpretation of history as the sum total of events "over and above the domestic and economic contingencies," events which remain in man's memory and become part of the historical tradition of a group.[3] This interpretation would almost necessarily confine social dynamics to actions and movements which affect the existing structures or at least tend to affect them. To demonstrate his sociological theorems he naturally chooses events covered by the second interpretation of history much more frequently than trivial

---

[1] In his definition of dynamic sociology, Sorokin covers both social kinetics (operation of social systems) and dynamics (change in them); saying that dynamic sociology is the study of repeated social processes and changes, repeated cultural processes and changes (*SCP*, p. 367).

[2] Cf. my *ST.*, p. 83 and my "Basic Concepts of Sociology," *AJS* 58 (1952), p. 185.

[3] Cf. Chapter II, section 3.

activities covered only by the first interpretation, so that actually his theorems in the realm of social dynamics concern themselves mainly with facts transcending the routine operations of men in existing social structures.

2.   Finality and rationality

Sturzo's dynamics is based on the triad—human liberty, finality and rationality. "The source of [social] movement is human liberty" (T. 198). "This free action is not blind; it has finality" (Inf. 110). Furthermore, an individual end is nothing but the conscious rationality of the practical actions of individuals (7), while social ends are derived from the individual's consciousness of being in communion and acting accordingly (8).

What comes next is rather startling: finality is identified by Sturzo with striving for *some good.* "Even when men start from wrong assumptions and are moved by passion, what they aim for and what they achieve is *for them* a good" (Inf. 110).

Saying that human action, the basic unit of dynamic analysis, has finality does not however open any promising line for further investigation, at least on the sociological level. But behind finality there is rationality, a principle which, in Sturzo's thought, plays the part of the moving spring of the historical process, i.e. of the immediately given aspect of social dynamics. "We are reasonable essentially and the rational permeates all our actions," says Sturzo (310).

What is rationality? Sturzo states explicitly that he uses this abstract term because an analytic procedure makes it necessary to present human factors in their abstractedness (310). But the term is used to designate a concrete factor in the individual. Like sociality, rationality is a "human faculty," a concrete factor in the individual (11) which is not imposed on him, but is part of his nature; as such, it is common to all men. That rationality also has other meanings in Sturzo's system will be shown later, but they too are logically related with the one now under scrutiny.

What are the specific traits of this "human faculty?" In his picturesque language Sturzo declares it to be "a light shining in the individual and making him what he truly is, man" (11). Let us emphasize the preposition "in": this is an inner light, perhaps the innermost trait of man.

In empiric science, a picturesque sentence must be translated into more prosaic language. On the basis of statements scattered throughout Sturzo's work, one comes to the conclusion that rationality must be analyzed in two dimensions.

1. First, rationality is a merger of truth and good; whose contrasts are error and evil (310). Both aspects appear in Sturzo's work, sometimes with emphasis on the former, sometimes on the latter. As good, "rationality is the should be, the deontological which presses upon us in the guise of a laudable, desirable and attainable ideal" (15).

As truth, rationality is connected with the postulate that "the world in which we live is a rational world which we rationally interpret in knowing it and living by it" (279). As human faculty, this aspect of rationality appears in man's ability to know reality, at least to strive for knowledge of it, and to adapt one's actions to the knowledge so acquired.

Rationality is not just an abstract name for an individual characteristic. It describes those concrete intellectual and ethical factors found in the urge to act to fulfill oneself in a continuous succession of voluntary acts (11). Since rationality is a merger of truth and goodness, this urge to act determines the finality of action in the concrete by giving an orientation toward the true and the good.

Now let us consider one more rather enigmatic statement which Sturzo makes about rationality as a human faculty. In discussing the influence of ethical conceptions on facts he states: "Historical facts and moral rules have a common principle in human nature— conscience,[4] directed instinctively or reflectively, by reason" (Inf. 110). But how can reason direct conscience and ultimately, the ensuing action instinctively? Is not instinct another faculty than reason? The difficulty might be overcome if one takes into consideration that, in Sturzo's terminology, the term "instinct" often connotes habitual or learned behavior which is based on the acceptance, with the participation of reason, of certain patterns or norms of behavior. In this meaning, instinct means something like a share of reason. From such an interpretation, it follows that Sturzo's theorems about the rule of rationality in human behavior concern themselves with almost all human actions, except those based solely on innate reflexes.

[4] Should it not be consciousness? One translation of the article from the Italian has the same word connote both conscience and consciousness.

2. Let us now contemplate the second dimension of rationality, its stratification into three levels. This dimension of rationality is implicitly present in Sturzo's work where one finds statements about concrete or "inner rationality," and sometimes "true or pure rationality," as well as statements about manifestations of rationality on a level intermediary between the two. Let us call the three levels subjective, (or personal) objective, (transpersonal or historical) and pure (or abstract) rationality. The distinction is necessary to integrate some Sturzian propositions which, at face value, seem incompatible.

As already stated, one of the startling points of Sturzo's doctrine of rationality is the assertion that what man aims for and achieves is, for him, *always* a good; and what is good is rational, according to Sturzo's definition of rationality. On the other hand, Sturzo often speaks of semi-rationality, pseudo-rationality (what is believed to be rational but actually is not), semi-rationality or irrationality (the vision of right obscured by emotion, passion, prejudice and so on). *Ergo*, not every human action is actually rational. This apparent contradiction can be eliminated only, if and when we distribute the particular propositions among the three levels of rationality which, of course, are meaningfully interrelated.

a) On the subjective or personal level, rationality means that human action is directed to truth and good as conceived by the actor. "There is always," says Sturzo, "an effort to overcome error and evil," which, as we know, are contrasts to rationality. "This movement is given not only in the present tense, in the passing moment, but may be perceived in the past and the future as a necessary projection of the ego" (31). As stated in Chapter IV, these propositions are tantamount to the postulate that man always acts to move from less to more satisfaction or from more to less dissatisfaction, in other words, from the level of reality to that of aspirations and values.

The finalism of the individual man, in other words, rationality expressed in action, is naturally reflected in society which is nothing else than associated men. "We are always moved by an inner finalism and give this finalistic imprint to society," says Sturzo (310). Just as the individual consciousness, when projected, develops on the social plane, so individual ends are extended on the social plane (7). Consequently, social purposes (ends) are tantamount to individual purposes carried out on the associative level (XVII); they are derived from the consciousnesses of the individuals of being in communion and of acting accordingly (8). On that background, one may assert that "society cannot lack finality animating it and holding the individuals associated. . . . Social crystallization is multiple and is expressed in a plurality of coexisting societies [i.e. social groups] with actually divergent interests" (M. 17).

b) Above the level of personal rationality, there is the level of historical rationality. On this level, rationality is no longer identical with a human capacity. It is transpersonal and connotes what is objectively rational here and now but was not then and there and may no longer be under changing circumstances. Men living in a certain age may judge the institutions and behaviors of a previous age, or of another civilization, as being irrational or semi-rational. But, pondering the social situation in its totality, they may understand and concede that, then and there, no better approximation to rationality was possible. Such approximations are commonly embodied in the mores and prevailing ideologies of a given time and place. Then, most individuals thought and acted along the lines of these approximations. Then, those "laudable, desirable and attainable ideals" which, according to Sturzo, press upon us because we are rational beings, coincide with culturally accepted patterns of behavior.

c) This is, however, not the highest level of rationality. There is, above the level just surveyed, the level of "the rational world in which and by which we live" (279). The rationality of the world in which we live may be conceived as an absolute idea; but it takes concrete and particular shape in each of us and thus becomes concrete (17).

In this way, a logical relationship between personal rationality and pure rationality is established. Of course, on the highest level, the deontological aspect of rationality must appear in the form of absolutely valid norms and ideals.[5] Empirically, this is unknowable. But an approximation to it may be achieved by the comparative study of culturally approved and imposed systems of ethics. Sorokin (in cooperation with the present writer) has found, in five major European nations, during approximately one and one half thousand years, "A kernel group of actions which . . . tend to be considered criminal in almost all societies and at all periods."[6]

[5] On absolute morality cf. Chap. V, section 5.
[6] P. A. Sorokin, *SCD*, vol. II (1937), p. 577.

In a posthumous paper by the prominent anthropologist R. Redfield we read: "It is clear that there must be some restrictions on violence within the small group or little community; it could not persist if custom allowed any man or woman to attack and destroy any other. It follows that within every group it must be thought wrong to kill anyone you choose, wilfully. And it follows that a sense of oughtness or rightness will, in every group, attach to these restrictions on violence . . . The universality of the nuclear family is another commonplace. . . . In nuclear families, however different from one another, are generated many of the qualities that never depart utterly from the central human tendency: personal interdependence, warmth of sentiment for another; associations that support, as significant and important, what is intimately learned in life from one's cherishing elder or one's older siblings."[7] These lines are obviously written in the functional style, whereas the absolute morality implicit in Sturzo's sociological doctrine is philosophically derived. The explanations differ, but the facts are identical: there is a central core of morality which is independent of the caprices of human will.

In Fichter's *Sociology*, one finds these statements: "the concept of ultimate value may refer . . . to the *minimum consensus* found in all societies concerning certain principles of behavior. All societies everywhere put prohibitive sanctions on incest, murder, blasphemy, lying (?) and stealing. All societies place a high value on fidelity, friendship, love and justice. . . . The psychic unity of mankind is exhibited not only in basically similar human intellects and wills, but also in a minimum social conscience.[8]

As to the ontological aspect of rationality on the top level, one may wonder whether it is not identical with that postulate of order according to which there are invariant relations between phenomena; of course, to be acceptable to Sturzo, the postulate must be given a narrow interpretation and be reduced to the assertion that there is *limited* order, in other words, that there are necessary relations between *some* phenomena, but not between their totality.[9]

[7] R. Redfield, "Anthropological Understanding of Man," *Anthropological Quarterly*, vol. 32 (1959), pp. 12-3.

[8] J. Fichter, *Sociology*, 1957, p. 304.

[9] Cf. N. S. Timasheff, "Order, Causality, Conjuncture" in L. Gross (ed.) *Symposium on Sociological Theory* (1959), pp. 146-7.

3. The relationship between the three levels of rationality is treated by Sturzo as follows:

The finality of a particular action is determined by rationality in the subjective, or personal meaning. It might actually be pseudorationality or irrationality, but each subjective finality is interwoven with the finality-rationality of the actions of other group members, and in that compound, rationality in the historical or social meaning prevails. For instance, authority is always combined with constraint and penalty: individuals may dislike it, but "when constraint and penalty are lawful and just (and these are data of reason felt in the collective consciousness), then their inner rationality overcomes the repugnance to . . . the exercise of force" (10).

Why does objective rationality prevail? At this place, Sturzo could have used one of his excellent, but little developed insights, namely the idea that, in collective consciousness, there are elements which cannot be resolved into individual consciousness. These elements, (corresponding to what we call culture) commonly succeed in bringing deviating choices of individuals back to the course expected by society and, in the majority of cases, closer to objective rationality than the pseudorationality of the deviant actions.

Why does historical rationality strive for absolute rationality? "Between ethical conceptions and social realizations [in particular cultures] there will always be enough distance to justify men in revising their norms and in dreaming of ideals that can be at least partly realized" (I.C. 112). "There is always need to revise the prevailing ethical conceptions to bring them in conformity with human reason" (Inf. 111). "In each realization of rationality there will be deficiencies, therefore, reforms will always be neccessary, and there will always be a struggle to eliminate these deficiences" (N. 72).

In their attempts to eliminate these deficiencies, and to conform with historical rationality, men are guided by their often blurred and sometimes faulty vision of absolute rationality. In consequence, we may say: Sturzo's ideas about mutations in transpersonal or historical rationality, somewhat reminiscent of Stammler's ideas about natural law with variable content,[10] should not be interpreted as relativistic.

4. The lengthy discussion of rationality has been necessary to present

[10] R. V. Stammler, *Die Lehre vom richtigen Rechte,* 2nd edition, 1926.

clearly Sturzo's ideas about rationality as the moving spring of social dynamism. These ideas may be summarized as follows:

The present state of a society is always the result of human activity, directed by finality and concrete rationality. Looking at any historical process at any moment of its unfolding, one may distinguish two dialectical elements, one negative and the other positive, which point to the continuous passing from the potential to the actual, from the past to the future. Negatively, rationality shows men that what was achieved in the past under the banner of rationality now presents itself as wanting, incomplete, even bad. Positively, rationality is the source of ideas which, if realized, will constitute a corrective supplement (14). In other words, "the good things achieved . . . call for others to be achieved in their turn. . . . Here is the thread of history—the activity of the group directed to its own welfare, stretches into the future" (203). In still other words: "Man, as he gains in self-consciousness . . . takes his own inward progress as a measure for a better estimation of . . . the past and present. He thus rejects as repugnant and inadequate to human nature many practices, beliefs, rules and criteria that at another age or in another environment were judged to correspond to the greatest individual and social good and hence to the intimate laws of nature" (I.C. 144).

The portion of Sturzo's theory concerning itself with rationality seems to stand quite outside the general stream of contemporary sociology. However one may perceive in it an anticipation, in unusual terms, of those quite recent developments in sociology which stress more and more the value concept. To this idea we shall return in Chapter IX.

3. Is there evolution and progress?

Some of the statements above, taken out of context, provoke the impression that Sturzo's theory of social dynamics is evolutionary and assumes as many earlier sociologists did that evolution is oriented to progress. But it will be shown that there are statements against a necessary evolution and progress in his works. Once again, we meet a thesis and antithesis in Sturzo's work and we will try to resolve the antinomy by finding a synthesis in his own work. Let us first quote a few statements clearly expressing the thesis and the antithesis.

1. Almost in the very beginning of one of his sociological treatises, Sturzo speaks of "the formation of society from its most rudimentary beginnings down to the most advanced stages of present reality" (T. 3). "The first natural nucleus has been the family (204). The domestic form contains within itself, though in germ only, all the other forms of sociality. The need for order and defense, as the families multiply, [has imposed] a patriarchal structure, the prelude to a political construction [and] has increasingly limited the influence of the root family. The religious form, from a pure family religion, has tended to develop into a wider complexus such as a tribe of several tribes held together by an extra-domestic religious bond" (27-8).[11] "The first beliefs only gradually took concrete form in positive cults. . . . The prevailing type of the family [has] influenced the religious organizations. For instance, the matriarchal type conceives of the deity as feminine; the earth or the moon is her symbol. In the type of family found in the period of big hunting, the totemistic religious conception prevails. . . . In the great patriarchal family of the nomadic shepherds it is the worship of the sun and the stars" (66-7). As to the family itself, "the historical process, as a movement toward rationality [has been directed] toward monogamy" (188). Statements like these obviously follow the line of classical evolutionism, with definite stages following each other and with so-to-speak natural correlations between the stages observable in particular segments of social reality.

Other statements point to a mild progressivism. "As little by little the conquests of human thought and life penetrate into human consciousness, the laws of nature and its needs are more intimately felt and have their rationality better realized (I.C. 145).

Even when rationality [has been attained] on the highest level possible then and there, the process cannot stop and must find further realization in an unceasing becoming (16). Thus, an advanced society can aspire to reach equilibrium expressing a still better order (180). In other words, the attainment of a state considered satisfactory or even good does not preclude the aspiration for something still better and higher. Thus interpreted, the motion toward rationality may be visualized in the image of eternal ascension, or unlimited progress.

b) In contrast with these statements however, one finds explicit denials of evolution and progress; "History is neither evolution nor progress, [but process] a continuous activity. In this [process] . . .

---

[11] The translation has been substantially amended by the present writer.

progressions are never more than partial [and] relative (T. 198). At another place Sturzo says: "There exists a perennial striving to cast off the irrational from the rational; but [there is] no constant progressive motion. We find only particular and relative progress, shot with regression and involution (16). "Historical experience is not a straight line, nor progressive, nor assured against deviation" (36). Historical experience is full of indisputable facts of decadence, of data about harmful consequences sometimes caused [by actions aiming] at just ends; such as has been the breakdown of family economy, and later on, guild economy (T. 182-3).

Sometimes Sturzo explicitly rejects more specific or partial evolutionary doctrines, for instance, the hypothesis of evolution from primitive communism to individual property. Such a hypothesis, he says, is not supported by sure data (105). In any case, "history does not present us with an evolution from a type of common property to that of individual property, but with varied and simultaneous developments of the two types of property" (108).

c) As Sturzo acknowledges, "between the idea of a constant rational becoming and that of process not intrinsically progressive, there might seem to be an irremediable conflict" (17). He resolves that antinomy in two ways. First, he states that the purely rational and the purely irrational do not exist in concrete reality; consequently, the movement falls within "relativistic lines" in which both the rational, the pseudorational [and semi-rational] are represented.

Second, Sturzo denies not evolution as such, but a particular kind, or interpretation, of evolution. He says: "the idea of deterministic evolution is denied by history and human experience" (16, 31). "While we cannot admit a deterministic human progress, we must grasp the fact that humanity makes progress in its experience" (72).

The conditioning of the historical process by the anticipated future is never deterministic (90). This means that *this* particular past does not determine what the *particular* future will be. What is determined, is that men will demolish or at least remold what they have achieved in the past whenever they have a vision of a better future; and such a vision is likely to appear sooner or later.

Historical experience points to a flexible and partial evolution under the impact of rationality, which, after many setbacks, still brings about a gradual improvement of human society.

The two trends discussed above—the tendency of personal rationality toward achieving the demands of historical or transpersonal rationality, and of the latter to evolve toward absolute rationality, form, for Sturzo, the very backbone of the historical process as a whole. Restating in a somewhat different manner the two formulas above, we can say:

In the short range, the historical process tends to achieve transpersonal rationality, or a state of things rationally optimal under given circumstances; but, in the long range the historically given stages of transpersonal or historical rationality move toward absolute rationality. It must be emphasized that both movements, the short range and the long range, are only trends, so that their progressive character may be interrupted by movements from more to less absolute rationality, from more to less historical rationality.

Let us now choose from Sturzo's work instances of historical movements illustrating the above propositions. The family has evolved from polygamy to monogamy, from the less to the more rational (on the absolute level). But, in its time, the polygamic family adapted to its environment was more rational than would have been the monogamic family transplanted into an unsuitable environment (18).

Similar conclusions can be drawn from the history of war, vendetta and slavery. In war, the irrational element of armed force is introduced (136). But collective consciousness has tended to transform it into a legitimate means. Hence, the concept of rational and just war has emerged (138). Sturzo's argument might be expanded as follows:

From the point of view of absolute rationality war is irrational. But there were times when war served rational purposes, such as unifying into large polities fractionary states which had no *raison d'etre* but endured through dynastic inertia; or, on the contrary, providing liberty to formerly subjugated nations (this was the case of the Dutch war of independence against Spain) or to newly born nations (such was the case of the American war of independence).[12] Other more rational ways could and should have been chosen to achieve the ends; but they were not, because of the obstinacy of those in whose favor the principle *beati possidentes* played. Therefore, in these cases war was rational. But, as forcefully emphasized by Sturzo, absolute rationality demands that war be entirely abolished (Inf. 108).

"Vendetta, an historical instance of a criminal system [of conduct]

[12] The illustrating cases have been provided by the present author.

was still to a certain extent justified in primitive society not yet endowed with political organization." It was a primitive system, based on the premise "an eye for an eye" and the notion of the solidarity of a group in the guilt of any of its members. It was due to a state of social structure at a time when there was no police force to guarantee order and safety. . . . The solidarity of the family groups and the collective responsibility for the crime of any of the members provided a certain [measure of] social security, but often led to the punishment of the innocent, to group hatred which continued for generations, and to terrible chains of violence (Inf. 100). A time came when it could and really was "broken by some higher ecclesiastical or political power." Now "the vendetta belongs, like slavery, feudal serfdom and polygamy, to a period of civilization that is past" (Inf. 101). In the terminology used in this work one can say that vendetta ceased to conform with historical rationality, since its functions could be achieved on a higher level, coming closer to absolute rationality.

Concerning slavery, Sturzo reasons as follows: Slavery is a social institution opposed to the fundamental rights of the human person; *ergo*, it is intrinsically irrational (let us add, in the absolute meaning). But historically, slavery arose from a complex of economic, psychological and social situations which made it not only possible . . . but even general and normal; it was thought to be rational even by the great thinkers of the ancient world (217). Moreover, slavery survived and even revived in Christianity despite its flagrant contradiction to the spirit of the Gospel—an obvious case of pseudorationality (Inf. 97), or of adjustment to economic and social situations and their rationalization or vindication by arguments of dubious value. Similar statements are made about the passing away of bloody sacrifice to Deity, ordeals, and duels (I.C. 147).

Sturzo is so sure of the final victory of rationality that he makes parenthetic predictions. In modern society, two institutions are, in his opinion, utterly irrational, war and the ugly wage system;[13] so he predicts that both will pass away (I.C. 14, 207).

But in the past and present the rational and the pseudorational are sometimes so intimately interwoven that they can be separated only analytically. As an example Sturzo discusses the temporal order of

---

[13] Sturzo prefers a "middle way" on the basis of the "deproletarization of the proletariat."

the Middle Ages under which both the feudal and the ecclesiastical systems suffered from disunity, instability and weakness. The absolute monarchies subordinated everything to their power, even the Church, at least in certain aspects. This was an historical necessity, hence, a movement toward [transpersonal] rationality. But the means used were often neither rational nor legitimate. The *raison d'etat* was the pseudo-rational element which accompanied a movement which, in turn, was fundamentally rational (285, 292).

In conclusion, one may say that rationality is the moving spring of social dynamics; rationality, as a human faculty, urges man to strive for something better than he has; rationality on the historical level is a set of directions addressed to men forming a social group, especially "total societies," in their efforts to achieve those improvements which are possible here and now; and absolute rationality is the ultimate point of orientation, never reached, but always shining as a light or a guiding star.

4. *Mechanism, determinants, rhythm*

1. While the theory of the moving spring and of the direction of social change are presented by Sturzo in grand style rarely attained elsewhere in sociology, his works contain only scattered propositions about other elements of social dynamics, especially about the mechanism of social change. Relative to this problem, now we possess in sociology a commonly accepted scheme emphasizing innovation through invention, acceptance and diffusion, perhaps supplemented by Toynbee's scheme of challenge-response.[14] Sturzo's discussion of the problem is somewhat different. It is grounded in the time dimension of society, the unification, in the present, of the past and the future plus the continuous emergence in individuals of the urge to exert their rational faculty, to correct the errors of the past, to improve and extend the achievements available. He is obviously interested only in so-called social inventions, i.e. purposive innovations in social structure and, without enumerating them, discusses three mechanims—leadership, struggle, and the growth of social consciousness.

a) In their striving for a better future, says Sturzo, men rarely act alone. Men of vision "give birth to a collective finalism which is the

[14] The pattern of challenge-response forms one of the major themes in his *Study of History* (1936), vol. I.

welfare of the group and of its members. . . . Those who have the adequate properties and qualifications will guide the others; [commonly] there will be dispute, discussion and even conflict over what should be done; affirmations and negations will succeed each other as partial visions of welfare" to be achieved (201-02). In this way, Sturzo introduces the second partial mechanism of advance, i.e., struggle, at least between ideas.

b) Without contrasting finalism [of individuals and groups] there would have been no struggle and without struggle society never could . . . overcome the pluralistic stage which is static and non-progressive (M. 17). Here Sturzo obviously goes back to one of his basic sociological formulations, the law of duality–unification, and asserts that the more sociological diarchy is real, effective, and dynamic, the more dynamism in the lives of the people, the more advanced their civilization will be. . . . The reason is obvious: the dynamic element is (or appears to be) the attainment of an ideal, the affirmation of a faith, the promotion of a good, the conquest of rationality, the achievement of a better future, in the face of a reality whose spiritual well-springs seem to have run dry (251).

In accordance with the law of duality–unification, the struggle pushing ahead the motion toward rationality is conducted in the framework of two camps, the conservative and the progressive. The conservative camp may become reactionary, and the progressive, revolutionary (M. 9). Both among conservative organizers and progressive reformers there are some who are moved by selfish interests or false concepts; but a fundamental drive toward common good is also present. There are periods when ethical conceptions and social facts are in conflict; then the progressive camp receives vigor and collective life takes on the rhythm of progress. But it is not less necessary that society be saved from the perpetual perturbance of pseudomystics and the revolt of discontented mobs. In this sense, even the reactionaries may fulfill the [salutary] function of serving as a bridle (Inf. 115-18).

The two camps represent the opposition, latent or open, between reality statically considered and the ideal visualized as the potential result of social dynamism. A stable social organization represents a certain amount of security and is affirmed as definitive (*qua* optimal) by the conservatives. For the dissenters, i.e. those who belong to the progressive camp, the potential future is conceived in terms of ideal justice, wider prosperity, overcoming of an evil, sometimes as a liberating cataclysm (246).

The conflict may be decided in favor of one or another force. But in history we find neither the pure suppression of one of the antagonists, nor an irenic immobility in cooperation. One of the camps seems to have gained final victory; but then the victor undergoes a dichotomy, or the vanquished regains strength, or a third current supervenes when the diarchy has collapsed (257). After all, "struggle is . . . a stage of transition in the movement toward a particular end to be achieved by the victorious force" (M. 18).

Sturzo's emphasis on struggle is reducible partly to the dialectical scheme to which he is inclined despite his basic disagreement with Hegel, and partly to the influence exerted on him by a mild form of social Darwinism (such as that of Ratzenhofer which was strongly represented in European sociology in the days of Sturzo's youth)[15] but mostly to his life experience which was a continuous struggle for the victory of a definite social ideal.

c) Sturzo mentions only briefly a third mechanism of social dynamics, namely the growth of collective consciousness. "A collective consciousness can grow only in two ways—by the expansion of an initially small group which, in assorting ideas and materializing them in fact, obtains large assent; or by a new social organization which appeals to others for support" (N. 265). Moreover, the integration of smaller groups into larger may obtain. For instance, there are many historical cases of the rise of one family to predominance over others which is tantamount to unification into extra-familial complexes, such as fratries, gentes, tribes, clans (40).

In conclusion one may say that Sturzo's doctrine on the mechanism of social change does not contradict the prevailing doctrine on the subject. The latter treats the phenomenon on the surface; inventions are made and are accepted if specified conditions are present. Sturzo digs deeper and points to the very roots of man's inventiveness and tendency to accept innovations.

2. Sturzo does not proceed to any survey of the possible determinants or factors of social and cultural change. Among the many discussed in sociological theory, he naturally pays most attention to

[15] Cf. my *ST*. pp. 63-4.

the problem of the influence of ideas. He denies the thesis of the idealists according to which ideas develop immanently and then influence social facts. For him, ideas develop concomitantly with changes in facts and are no more than new alternatives for human choices; men remain free to accept or reject them and to act accordingly. He demonstrates his position best with respect to the ideas about slavery and their alleged impact on the social fact of emancipation.

Before the emancipation of the slaves "became a *fait accompli,* it was assumed by theorists that [emancipation] was impossible, or at any rate was bound to produce serious and unbearable consequences for society as a whole. After the abolition [of slavery] ethical theorists began to say that one could prove the timeliness, the reasonableness, even the moral obligation of the measures taken. Then, but only then, were the ethical theories of the pioneers and the men of vision, of the humanitarians and genuine Christians seen in a new light (Inf. 99). The earlier arguments of the philosophers, jurists and economists in support of slavery and against the possibility of abolition show us two things: first, that their reasoning was bound up with a determined historical situation; and second, that it does not hold good for another social situation. They projected onto a static plane; they took what was relative and mutable for conclusive and immutable. Unfortunately, it is a very common optical illusion, to see the relative world *sub specie aeternitatis* (I.C. 234-5). It is startling how close Sturzo's position comes here to the views of the modern sociologists of knowledge.

3. About the rhythm of social dynamics (i.e. its differential velocity) Sturzo has little to say. On many occasions, Sturzo emphasizes that, although society is predominantly dynamic, movement is generally slow and requires the concurrence of many conditions. The main reason for this is that the backbone of the specific personality of the group, its collective consciousness, tends to be stable. "To change the collective consciousness, there must be change in social, economic or political conditioning" (N. 267). He emphasizes the slowness of the formation of the ruling elite, wherefrom more often than not leadership comes forth. This formation is by no means an automatic process. Large political elites, he says, cannot acquire the necessary experience only through participation in the central government. Additional gate-

ways to that experience are activities in municipal and local bodies, journalism, universities and so on (G.M. 203, 205-9).

This naturally takes some time. At another place, speaking more specifically of "moral achievement" which is obviously one of the aspects of social dynamism of the progressive type, Sturzo says, "For every particular moral achievement, history teaches us that four conditions are necessary: 1) an educational formation; 2) a political order; 3) social maturation; and 4) a continuous process of acquisition and readaptation. For that reason, ethical achievements are difficult and slow" (n. 212). These statements are so short as to be cryptic. It is however clear that to each of the conditions, especially the third one, a process in time, sometimes a lengthy process, must correspond.

On the other hand, "the [social] rhythm can be artificially accelerated, especially through legislation. A new law often presents itself as a [purely] external bond, binding only by sanctions. . . . Then, a temporary separation between the ethical and the juridical obtains, until an inner assent [to the law] is induced; this brings out the ethical side of the law" (223). Or else the law sooner or later passes into oblivion.

Sturzo is aware that the rhythm of the historical process may be still more accelerated by revolutions. But revolution is almost never mentioned in his work. Although he acknowledges the right of revolt against a political power waging an unjust war, he certainly is fully aware of the great danger of any revolution—the impredictability of its outcome. Therefore, he never saw in revolution an adequate means of progress.

5. *Dynamism vs. stasis*

In the final account, nothing in the historical or social process is final. The law of polarization–unification plays its part and together with the law of the motion toward rationality brings about continuous change. But although nothing is final, during a certain time the results of efforts aiming at the embodiment of rationality, personal and transpersonal, are considered as achievements. The tendency to achieve, we know, is embedded in man's rationality. The tendency to achieve brings about greater welfare, molds the course of history on small and large scale. Achievement gives vitality and collective personality to the social group; renunciation of achievement [which occurs in exceptional cases] petrifies and eventually dissolves the group personality. Achievement is considered as conquest. In sociology, the notion of conquest must be extended to cover gain in all possible realms—moral, intellectual, religious, political, economic, social welfare in the internal life of the social group and its relations with other groups. Every form of welfare already achieved must be guaranteed, defined, and lived again and again; therefore, conquest is always a becoming, in the continuity of action (T. 203).

Sometimes, when a condition of incompleteness and deficiency prevails, people may have little or no awareness of it A society in this situation decays into a period of stasis or immobility which is commonly accompanied by the abasement of personality (15-6). But stasis is more often a condition of delusion. Men are often inclined to think that they have built institutions to last forever; in actuality, the reality of institutions is only a moment in the process (244); in other words, the process itself is mentally arrested. We are inclined to overemphasize the stability of the historically achieved forms of sociality, especially of the fundamental forms. But their stability often conflicts with the instability of their social environment, a result of the inherent dynamism of the social process. This dynamism often tends to void or at least to remold the institutions. If change is not achieved, tensions between the form [expressed in the institution] and content [as provided by the flow of the social process] obtains; such tensions are conducive to the great crises of history, e.g. revolutions.

It may seem that, in the dynamic conception of society as a continuous process of realization, society is reduced to something intrinsically unstable, in perpetual motion and change (24). It is actually unstable in that it is always changing. But change is a process in time. The historical process is gradual; the individual steps conducive to absolute rationality cannot be made here and now *ad libitum*; the conditioning environment, physical and social, plays the part of a brake, and attempts to jump over insuperable barriers are irrational. Therefore, relative to social change, time is often measured not in hours and minutes, but in decades, sometimes in centuries. Social crystallizations, especially institutions, last without negating social dynamism only so long as they continue to offer men the opportunity to go ahead under the full protection of the established forms.

After all, the "axis of dynamism is social consciousness" (34). Of course, the concrete content of social consciousness steadily changes, but the social consciousness of a group endures in the feeling of the individuals composing it that they belong together not only with their contemporaries, but also with those who passed away and those who are to come. This makes society "coherent and stable and makes it evolve in a process realized by immanent forces" (39) embedded in each particular and unique society.

Dynamism dominates Sturzo's sociology. But, as shown in the preceding chapter and also in this section, it does not deny its static aspect. "Between the dynamic and the static," says Sturzo, "there is the interplay of the motor and the brake" (222).

CHAPTER VII

Don Sturzo's Critique
of Sociological Theories

Don Sturzo's Critique
of Sociological Theories

UNTIL THE last decades of the nineteenth century, a sociologist inclined to theoretizing, in other words, to theory construction, often proceeded as if he were acting *in vacuo*; he added his interpretation of society to those already existing without giving them too much attention.

Then, the situation changed. The sociologists of various schools and trends became aware of each other and began a kind of *bellum omnium contra omnes*. The demolition of theories indicated by others was often allocated more mental energy than the creation of new approaches.

Gradually, the situation changed again. It became clear that the demolition of theories offered by other thinkers did not prove that the wrecker was right in his own constructions. It would have been otherwise if the number of possible theories were limited; then, the elimination of all but one would be tantamount to the proof of the correctness of the latter. Several French sociologists (e.g. Gobineau and Durkheim) used "the geometrical genius" of their nation in attempts of this kind; but their efforts were not crowned by success precisely because it is impossible to construct an exhaustive list of theoretical possibilities.

In consequence, when constructing a sociological theory of his own, the contemporary sociologist looks around and locates his version in a fairly well occupied field. He explains how his views differ from those already expressed and tries to demonstrate why his theory is superior to those of his predecessors; but the demolition of the latter is no longer in the forefront of his preoccupations.

This was the situation in the 30's and 40's of this century when

Sturzo was writing his major sociological works. He was never interested in systematic surveys of theories he found around himself, but did not evade polemics with those which, he believed, dominated the field of sociology. Unfortunately, like most European sociologists of that time, he had an incomplete knowledge of American sociology. It is a particular pity that he did not come across Cooley's work, which he probably would have found congenial to his thought. Naturally, his major works could not take into consideration the great advance made by American sociology in the 40's and 50's.

Despite these handicaps, it is essential for a complete understanding of Sturzo's sociology to know his statements about the theories which came into his field of vision. As already mentioned, he never made a systematic survey of these theories (such as made by Lester Ward, M. Kovalevsky and Pitirim Sorokin). But what appears in the form of scattered statements can be systematized; such a systematization is the purpose of this chapter.

To achieve this purpose, the theories to be surveyed will be distributed among the following classes: 1) positivism; 2) neo-positivism; 3) Marxian sociology; 4) organicism; 5) psychological sociology; 6) philosophical sociology; and 7) neo-systematic sociology.

1. Positivism

Positivism is the sociological theory most frequently discussed and combatted by Sturzo. Unfortunately, he rarely mentions names so that sometimes the targets of his attacks cannot be identified beyond reasonable doubt.

Comte is cited three times: first, to reproduce his definition of sociology as "the positive science of society," which, says Sturzo, is still the current definition (M. 110 n.); second, to oppose what Sturzo calls "pan-sociology." or a total science of society, absorbing history, jurisprudence, [social] philosophy and [parts of] theology (M. 110);[1] and third, to mention Comte's "cult of humanity" which is confronted with the contemporary cults of nation, race or class (M. 58).

For Sturzo, the main exponent of positivism is Durkheim whose

[1] The inanity of such a pretention on the part of sociology is discussed in Chap. II.

"sociologism"[2] is considered especially hateful—by the way, the term "sociologism" is explicitly used by Sturzo (M. 78).

For the positivist, says Sturzo, society is a *tertium quid* (M. 31), something existing above and independently of the two or more individuals composing it. Durkheim's treatment of collective consciousness as a mysterious entity standing above men and exerting irresistible constraint on them is abhorrent to Sturzo. Sturzo was probably not familiar with L. Gumplowicz whose views were still more extreme than those of Durkheim and could therefore have served as a still better repellent: for Gumplowicz, man is wrong when he believes that *he* thinks; in actuality, the *social group* does it.

But let us return to Sturzo's explicit criticism. For the positivist, he says, the social [organization] is the true and deterministic cause of all human achievements, such as language, religion, morals, art, law, politics, economy. The social [organization] would then be an irreducible phenomenon incapable of resolution into others (XIII). Of course, this is incompatible with Sturzo's sociological synthetism, especially since the latter is inclined toward personalism. The sociologistic conception, believes Sturzo, goes beyond positive experimentation[3] and becomes the main thesis of a social philosophy. What he wants to say, is this: the sociologistic interpretation cannot be logically inferred from observation and therefore contradicts the epistemological premises of positivism as stated by Comte, for whom "the facts must speak for themselves." Positivism, more explicitly sociologism, cannot, according to Sturzo, satisfy a logical mind which finds no reason why it should stop at social structure as an ultimate and irresolvable phenomenon; on the contrary, it finds reasons for proceeding further and, behind the social facts, discovers a primordial fact (XIII) which, for Sturzo, is the "individual-social consciousness" unifying society and the individual, making of them two faces of the same reality. Emphasizing the collective aspect of that complex phenomenon and neglecting the individual one, ascribing to society a self-sufficient entity and value, positivism, more particularly sociologism, falls into the error of abstractionism (XIV) which, for Sturzo, is tantamount to a scientifically impermissible *pars pro toto*.

[2] Sociologism is a term introduced by Sorokin in his *CST*, pp. 433 ff., to designate sociological theories falling under the definition of sociological collectivism as treated in Chap. III.

[3] In the meaning of observation.

At various places, Sturzo takes to task the "positivists," probably still identified with the sociologistic school of Durkheim, for more specific errors. They insist on the conditioning of men by environment, which is a fact; but they err when seeing in that conditioning something extra-human, existing *per se* and determining man's behavior (15). Human initiative is treated by them as pure appearance without reality; according to them, man does not possess either liberty or spirit; he is merely a highly evolved animal. They treat social phenomena from the materialistic point of view, assuming that this point of view is a firmly acquired part of modern culture (29).

This materialism is apparent in the positivists' treatment of the problem of justice. For them justice is merely the subordination of the individual to society, which is always represented by the dominant class. This subordination is expressed in laws and rules which make life in common possible. Consequently, justice appears to be an expedient but conventional mechanism corresponding to the stage of social evolution and the correlative stage of development of collective needs. In other words, justice is relative so that what is just here and now is or was not just then and there (237).

Summarizing his views on positivism of the Durkheimian type, Sturzo mentions that sociology has been sired by positivism and concedes that the positivists have carried out quite interesting studies. "But all the material [collected by them] lacks a soul . . . it cannot produce a scientifically valid synthesis" (T. 6; cf. M. 115).

2. Neo-positivism

Let us now shift our attention to Sturzo's treatment of modern forms of positivism, in the first place, of neo-positivism. Sturzo never uses this term; but when he subjects to critical examination the scientific validity of propositions based on statistics, he has in mind one of the major characterisitcs of neo-positivist studies, their quantitativism, i.e. the assumption (rarely stated explicitly) that only what is measurable is scientifically knowable.

Statistics, says Sturzo, is a delicate instrument, the abuse of which easily leads to illogical and erroneous conclusions. The statistical study of social phenomena is based on the criteria of the constancy, recurrence, and variability of certain facts under given circumstances and in definite time and space limits. It contributes to the acquisition of knowledge about facts, according to types and preëstablished categories. But types and categories simplify the concrete facts and present them in abstract terms; thereby, qualitative and realistic knowledge is impoverished and even altered. Statistics help little in the identification of facts and in the ascertainment of their coincidence and connection (M. 42). Such criticisms are familiar to the American sociologists who have passed through the period of acute feud with the adepts of the case study method and the statistical method.

Sturzo clarifies the reason for his scepticism of statistics by citing the instance of the declining birth rate observable in many societies. Statistics show that industrialization contributes to this phenomenon. But, on a similar statistical foundation, it can be shown that the agricultural population of western and southern France has reached an exceedingly low fertility, so that depopulation has been prevented only by foreign, predominantly Italian, immigration (M. 42-3). *Ergo*, a firm correlation between industrialization and low natality does not exist.[4]

In general, says Sturzo, to each statistical finding another can be opposed; therefore, quantitative data are not conducive to the establishment of social causation. These data, which are always on the level of abstraction, must be reevaluated by transferring them to the concrete level. This can be done only by trying various hypotheses, from the simplest to the most complex, until they yield a result having qualitative value (M. 43). He seems to be unaware of the fact that many "statisticians," i.e. neo-positivists, do this.

In his "sixteen theses" (cf. Chap. I, section 5) Sturzo is even more severe in his condemnation of statistics. As already reported, thesis No. 12 reads as follows: "Statistics applied to social facts does not prove anything, since it puts under one denominator facts which are apparently similar, but are qualitatively diverse. [The statistical method can be used] only for the purpose of provisional ascertainment which may be indicative [symptomatic?] and classificatory; but one must avoid drawing any scientific conclusion on the basis of assumed similarity and alleged frequency" (M. 64).

[4] In developing multi-factor analysis, modern statistics has overcome Sturzo's objection.

It is natural to continue by discussing Sturzo's evaluation of social ecology which, after all, is merely a modality of neo-positivism.[5] Sturzo does not deny the value of ecological studies and human geography (which he does not sufficiently distinguish). But, he says, there is no reason to think that, sociologically, the facts discovered by the two approaches could occupy a central position in the edifice of social science (M. 29). Overemphasis on the two factors in question is conducive to error. For instance, the ecologically minded sociologists (Sturzo should rather have mentioned a representative of human geography) would say that temperate climate is propitious to the advance of culture, and points, for corroboration, to ancient Greece, the Greek colonies and Rome. But he could not explain why the same climatic factors which produced the great civilization of the fifth and fourth centuries B.C. did not do the same in the Middle Ages; or why England, Holland and the Scandinavian countries, which are certainly not favored by a moderate climate, have contributed so much to scientific, religious and artistic culture. Of course, he continues, one should not deny that climate is one of the conditioning factors of human development and that the coldest zones of our planet are thinly populated. But who denies that man is an animal whose body is conditioned by the climate (M. 30)? What Sturzo rightly reproaches in the ecologists and geographical determinists is the assumption that ecological and geographical factors completely determine the course of the historical process, which they by no means do.

At the present time, geographical determinism is dead, and most contemporary ecologists perform valuable studies in one or another of the aspects of human life in society without pretending to possess a key to the door behind which we could find a complete explanation of social life. In other words, contemporary ecology is hardly a competitor in the race for the best possible formulation of "sociological theory of the highest range" to the number of which the Sturzian theory belongs.

3. Marxian sociology

The Marxian theory which, although not primarily sociological, contains a number of sociologically relevant propositions, is often discussed in Sturzo's work. This is only natural since a large part of his activity

[5] Cf. N. S. Timasheff, *ST*, pp. 212-5.

consisted in opposition, in actual social life as well as in theory, to the Marxian forces operating in the Italy of his time. From that opposition Sturzo got a vivid and correct understanding of what Marxism really means as well as of the attraction exerted by it.

Between Sturzo's emphasis on liberty, conducive to a sociology based on the proposition that man is a self-determining agent, and the materialistic and absolutely deterministic theory of Marx, there can be no bridge.[6] Since "the economic structure presses upon the social type," it is natural for human minds to be misled and to make of economics the sole law (= determinant) of history (101). The historical materialism thus engendered had a following for half a century, says Sturzo. This is an understatement; not only does historical materialism today dominate at least the official thought of one third of mankind, but even outside the area where it is imposed *ratione auctoritatis* it continues to influence, sometimes in subtle forms, the development of social science and political thought.

Where is the error of Marxism? For Sturzo, it is obvious: historical materialism is as wrong as every "analytical" theory; in other words, as every theory singling out one specified factor and making it the "unique fundamental principle." If only one factor is relevant, then its unfolding determines the development in its totality; this and not another development becomes an absolute necessity. Sturzo cautiously adds: "We do not deny the influence of economics on society. We deny that it forms the whole sociological and historical causality" (101). In actuality it is one, just one, of the many conditioning factors of human activity in society.

But Sturzo is not satisfied with this general objection and points to some of the more specific errors of the Marxian doctrine. "The error of Marx and the belated Marxists is that of blaming capital for the faults of capitalism and of dreaming of a society without capital" (125). However, this reproach is valid only relative to a vulgarizing modality of Marxism, but not to Marxism on the higher level which does not deny the necessity of capital, that is "of savings employed in production" (125). But Sturzo is rightly sceptical concerning the

---

[6] John Oesterle (cf. Chap. VIII, section 4) is quite wrong when ascribing to Sturzo the use of a terminology which suggests Marxian notions of being and becoming. Sturzo often and emphatically states that Marxism is a dangerous fallacy (M. 83 and 95).

possibility of a perfect [social] structure in which inequalities would be smoothed away by a regime working automatically and happily complete (126). At this place he invokes his law of duality according to which the schism of society into two camps, the conservative and the reformist, is inevitable. Moreover, class struggle, whose sublimation onto the theoretical level has formidably fostered European socialism (M. 53), is not a unique phenomenon. Because of "egoistic regression," struggle develops in all the forms of sociality, even the loftiest, including the religious ones. "What wonder," concludes Sturzo, that the "world of economics founded on material interests . . . should be perturbed by perpetual and fundamental conflicts" (127).

4. Organismic sociology

Although Sturzo often speaks of "social organism," he is well aware of the fallacy of the organic sociology and vigorously denounces the organicists, i.e. the sociologists who try to build up their science on the foundation of the postulate that society is an organism, so that propositions true for the latter could be automatically transferred onto the former. Sturzo is aware that organicism in sociology is a thing of the past. But he correctly points to the non-scientific survivals of organicism which one meets in the doctrines ascribing ultimate reality and value to social class (Marxism), the State (Fascism) or the race (National Socialism).

He submits organicism to sharp criticism. "The idea that society is an organism which develops from simple to complex forms," says he, "is as old as human speculation" (M. 53) about man and society: "The starting point of organicism is that society is a real organism with its own structure and life. Hence the endeavor to create a social biology. The play of analogy however cannot create a science. To speak of social biology [means simply] to transfer biological data into the social field on the ground of analogical or imaginary resemblances" (XII). One of the major errors of organicism is to consider society as something morphologically fixed once and forever, and not to observe it historically as it goes through phases of progress and stagnation (M. 33).

The main reason for Sturzo's opposition to organicism is the same as his reason for opposing sociologism: like the latter, organicism sees in society an entity existing outside and independently of individuals and determining their conduct (M. 34), a position incompatible with Sturzo's sociological synthetism.

5. *Psychologistic sociology*

The rejection, by Sturzo, of positivism in all its forms, of Marxism, and of organicism, can be expected by one familiar with his strong belief in the spiritual nature of man. One could perhaps expect that Sturzo would experience some affinity with sociological theories explaining society in terms of mental processes. But no: he vigorously rejects that "psychologistic sociology" which was in vogue during his formative years and is still influential in our day.[7] This position is determined by the fact that psychologistic sociology, like positivism, is "abstractist," in other words, it singles out one factor to explain the totality of social phenomena. He chooses for thorough demolition the instinctivist and psychoanalytical trends in psychology, and expresses in shorter form his rejection of behaviorism and of social psychology, insofar as they pretend to offer a complete explanation of the world of social phenomena.

The instinctivist approach to society is formulated by him as follows: Society is considered to be "a product of nature" based upon man's instincts more or less identical with those of the animals. The adepts of instinctivism believe that the law underlying the concretization of society (here Sturzo introjects into the theory under examination a concept of his own) is that of the associative (= gregarious) instinct; they accentuate the imitation aspect of human action (obviously a reference to G. Tarde) and overemphasize instinct and similar psychological facts related to verbal communication and to the formation of local traditions.

In so doing, he continues, the instinctivists treat problems on a superficial level. Valuable intuitions remain unexplored. Sociological theory is impaired by the influence of related sciences; analogies (between social and psychological facts) are treated as true similarities and sometimes given the value of causal explanations. This, he says, is not the right way to find laws of human action in society, one of the major tasks of sociology (M. 27).

[7] Cf. my *ST*, pp. 141 ff.; the term "psychologistic" is used by the present writer by analogy with "sociologistic."

Still more emphatic is the rejection of psychoanalysis, again as an "analytical theory" singling out one of the factors of human life and giving it the value of an all-embracing synthesis. The moving spring of human, social activity is identified as *libido*, an undifferentiated and potential energy arising in the unconscious depths of the human mind. This energy is actually narrowed down to the sexual instinct, which is supposed to begin influencing human action in early infancy, in forms which men cannot but experience as abnormal. "The Greek myth," says Sturzo, "is borrowed to represent what it does not, the psychopathy of an instinct [which] from the start [is] essentially perverse" (37).

Psychoanalysis is, then, wrong not only because it explains the totality by a part; the choice of the part selected to play the role of the moving spring is most unfortunate. It is based on "the confusion of the normal being with the abnormal, or the assimilation of the child to a diseased subject suffering from sexual neurosis." This results in the presentation of consciousness as of a mere reflection of *libido* which appears as "the center and source of all thoughts, all human activities, even the loftiest, like art and religion" (37-8). It is true that the psychoanalysts speak of catharsis which could be identified with Sturzo's purification.[8] But Freud's catharsis is no purification at all. It consists in the growing of the consciousness of the libidinous tendency, in the passing from the pre-conscious to the conscious, from the indeterminate to the determinate, while, in Sturzo's view, the process of purification consists in the overcoming of animal instincts.

Sturzo summarizes his evaluation of psychoanalysis as follows: "Making use of various elements of psychology and sexual pathology [it] seeks to construct a sociology that would be the negation of all true characteristics of society" (38). This criticism remains applicable in our day. There exists no definite psychoanalytical school in sociology. But the impact of psychoanalysis is felt in the work of several contemporary sociologists (especially T. Parsons) while the vogue of "the interdisciplinary approach" makes a further invasion of psychoanalysis onto sociology easy and dangerous.

Without ever naming it, Sturzo rejects behaviorism as a valid approach to sociology. "Sociology has been made too materialistic. [It has become] a science of outward relations or psychological reactions

[8] Cf. Chap. IV, section 3, No. 4.

(an obvious reference to the stimulus-response scheme) without including the thoughts and affections of individual men" (T. 17). Sturzo rightly assumes that, in society, there are more than outward relations and chains of stimuli-responses, and naturally fills the gap by pointing to his predilected idea of motion toward rationality (*ibid.*).

On the other hand, "the deterministic sociology which seeks to resolve the forming and deforming of societies into . . . the elementary needs of sense life does not give a true society, but merely a determined way of living like that of other categories of animals." But "animals have no society in the same meaning of the word as related to human society, nor would men if they would be subject to the pure determinism of their material needs" (11).

Neither has Sturzo any use for social psychology. What is called social psychology, he says, can give nothing more than a continuous resolution into individual psychology (XII): in other words, facts considered sociopsychological are in actuality phenomena of individual psychology erroneously interpreted. "True psychology," says Sturzo, "leads unfailingly to the rejection of every foundation of the concept of a [sociopsychological organization] distinct from the individuals composing it" (*ibid.*).

There is however a kind of psychologistic sociology which is neither instinctivist, nor psychoanalytical, nor behaviorist. To be sure, one has only to name V. Pareto, W. I. Thomas and Max Weber. Out of these "big three" of the first quarter of the twentieth century, Sturzo only mentions Pareto whose work (as well as that of Weber) seems to him to be full of data, but depressing with respect to theory (M. 9). Like most European sociologists of the time when Sturzo composed his major sociological works, he was not familiar with W. I. Thomas.

The only one of the group whose work is explicitly though briefly discussed, is Max Weber. Sturzo acknowledges that his own work contains elements borrowed from the great German scholar, namely the idea of social typology. But, he adds, Weber's ideas on the subject are quite at variance with his own ideas on social forms. Weber's ideal types confine sociology to the subjective constatation of facts, types and symbols, leaving to philosophy the task of the objective verification of the referents. In this way, sociology is impoverished while, on the other hand, the intrusion into sociology of various "speculative sciences" is fostered (M. 111).

Sturzo is hardly right when he asserts that Weber evades the task of the objectification of subjective experiences. On the contrary, Weber insists on the interpretation of social facts on the two levels of causality and meaning and shows, by examples, how the latter task should be achieved. But Sturzo's phrase about the limitation of social inquiry to subjective meanings which actions have for the actors points to one of the essential weaknesses in Weber's thought system. This weakness is mitigated by the fact that, in applying his theoretical conceptions to the discussion of concrete cases, Weber often takes into account the average or typical meaning of human actions in society. Between such interpretations and Sturzo's ideas on human actions originating in individual-social consciousness a bridge could easily be constructed.

6. *Philosophical sociology*

Sturzo is obviously not only a sociologist, but also a social philosopher, though he is inclined to deny this and on the verbal level is right, since he incorporates his social philosophy into sociology (cf. Chap. II). In any case, he has high respect for philosophy *tout court* (to use one of his phrases). Nevertheless, he rejects sociological doctrines of philosophical inspiration, namely idealism, institutionalism and voluntarism. Let us survey his ideas on the subject.

Sturzo often mentions "metaphysical" or "idealistic" sociology. He has in view theories which could best be labelled "ideal-realistic." These are theories which ascribe prime or ultimate reality to ideas and see in social groups their emanations or concretizations.[9] Of course, his target is primarily those students of society who are still under the influence of Hegel. They are now rare birds, except in Italy where, until recently, sociology proper was repressed because of the dominance of Benedetto Croce whom, in his sociological treatises, Sturzo mentions only once to say that he borrowed from that philosopher and historian the term "process" but not the "Crocian" theory (M. 14).

In the metaphysical conception, says Sturgo, society is conceived as a principle, will, force, idea, spirit which actuates itself of itself and realizes itself in various forms of human life. According to this con-

[9] Represented also in B. Malinowski's *A Scientific Theory of Culture,* 1942.

ception, history is the sole expression of the becoming of society, which leaves no place for anything like "social dynamics," or a sociological treatment of becoming. History is then paramount and only historical explanations of human destinies are possible. Sturzo concludes his description of the characteristics of "metaphysical sociology" by a brilliant comparison with positivism. Historicism (in the meaning of the idealistic conception of society) and positivism, he says, correspond respectively to romanticism and naturalism in the arts and letters (XIII).

Then comes the criticism: although the idealistic conception of society helped to deepen the study of social facts and to widen the scope of inquiry in the fields of religion, art and sex, it contains a fallacy, since, like positivism, it attributes to society a self-subsistent entity and value and thereby falls into the error of abstractionism. Consequently, it must be rejected as incompatible with the concrete or total approach to society (XIII–XIV) which, for Sturzo, is the only gateway to true sociology (cf. Chap. II).

Despite his rejection of Hegelian metaphysics and sociology, Sturzo often uses the dialectical method of reasoning and the terms involved. He even acknowledges his indebtedness to some (unnamed) Hegelians who have elaborated the dialectic of human thought and action (M. 15). Nevertheless, it would be quite wrong to look at Sturzo's thought as crypto-hegelian. Sturzo rejects with indignation a mild attempt made by John Oesterle to find, in his work, such an inspiration. "I have sometimes used the Hegelian (as well as Marxian) terminology," he says, "to facilitate the understanding of my criticism of theories [which] I have combatted in all my writings" (M. 95-6).

It is startling, but quite logical, that Sturzo returns to Durkheim in this context, this time not as a positivist, but as an idealist who sublimated social consciousness onto the level of an extra-temporal entity, something like Hegel's Absolute Spirit or Idea (M. 111), though without his dialectical ornamentation. Sturgo obviously has in mind Durkheim's *Jugements de valeur et jugements de realité* (1911), but explicitly rejects any interpretation of his own work as an imitation of Durkheim's "general sociology" (M. 110)—a term appearing in the work just referred to and forming there the highest level of sociological analysis.

Another philosophical approach to sociology mentioned and rejected by Sturzo is the "institutional theory," today much in fashion among French jurists. "They seem to consider the institution as if it were an entity brought into existence by an external superior being, setting it up as a logical *a priori*, [above] the individuals . . . For such jurists, the reality of institutions lies entirely in their being unitary units" (243). Sturzo rejects this approach just bceause it emphasizes unity, while in his thought duality permeates the whole texture of social life.

To evaluate Sturzo's criticism we must keep in mind that, from among the French institutionalists, Sturzo mentions only Hauriou (M. 75 and 97 n., both times misspelled Hanrion) whose views are of Platonic inspiration while the later institutionalists have shifted to Thomism. Second, in Hauriou's writings, a distinction is made between *institution–personne* (a social group), and *institution–chose* (a stable complex of rules of conduct). His followers have dropped the second connotation of the term (prevalent in American sociology) and retained the first.

It is obvious that Sturzo's criticism is pointed to the institutional conception of a social group. Here as elsewhere, Sturzo's negative position is determined by the fact that the theorists under examination conceive the institution as standing on its own feet, independent of the will of the men constituting it (M. 33-4 and 75).

While Hauriou believed that " the directive idea of an institution" (but not the institution itself) was independent of human will, the later institutionalists do not differ so radically from Sturzo as he believes. True, they ascribe reality to the social group (institution); but this is, for them, not an independent reality; it is a reality derived from the individuals and their wills and obtaining because of their converging adherence to a "directive idea," the idea of a task to be performed by the group.[10]. It is a pity that there never was an exchange of views between Sturzo and the institutionalists. It is probable that such an exchange would have fructified both theories and brought them closer together.

Finally, among the sociological theories of philosophical inspiration rejected by Sturzo, one finds "voluntarism"; as is usual in his work, no names are cited but it is obvious that he has in mind belated followers of J. J. Rousseau, more frequent in political philosophy than in sociology. For the exponents of voluntarism, says Sturzo, every

[10] Cf. my *ST*. pp. 263-5.

society, e.g. the family or the polity, is voluntary. There are no necessary societies; their formation is the result of a contract, tacit or explicit, by which the individuals surrender one to the other a part of their liberty for the advantage of life in society. Such theories . . . tend to deny the imposition of an absolute authority and of coercive law as [incompatible with the rights] of human personality. For Sturzo who insists on the intrinsic necessity of authority (though not absolute) and of coercive law, such ideas seem to be incoherent (12)—which they really are. Since voluntaristic sociology is more a myth than a reality, let us conclude our discussion of it at this point and turn to the last item on the list we offered in the beginning of this chapter.

7. Neo-systematic sociology

The same regret which has been just formulated relative to a lack of an encounter between Sturzo's ideas and those of the institutionalists can be expressed with respect to the ideas of neo-systematic sociologists.[11] Out of their writings, Sturzo quotes just one sentence from Robert McIver's Society: "society is a system of social relationships in and through which we live."[12] Commenting upon it, Sturzo says: "Such a definition is acceptable to a phenomenologist[13]; it is however merely a constatation of a fact without any explanation which could be philosophical, and therefore should be avoided"; or it could be accepted by a positivist for whom the idea of a "system" and especially of "a system in which we live" could give the opportunity

[11] This term is introduced in place of "analytical sociology" used in my Sociological Theory, pp. 234 ff. The term "analytical" may provoke the impression that the work of other schools, e.g. of the neo-positivist one, is not analytical. Cf. G. Lundberg "Some Convergence in Sociological Theory," AJS 62 (1956), pp. 31 ff. The term "neo-systematic" points to the focal position of system in the conceptual scheme of the authors earlier treated as analytical sociologists and emphasizes their difference from the older systematic sociology in Germany (best represented by L. von Wiese).

[12] Society, Its Structure and Changes, 1939, p. 9.

[13] Here and elsewhere, Sturzo uses the terms phenomenology and phenomenologist in a meaning quite at variance with the one ascribed to them by the members of one more sociological school of philosophical inspiration, best represented by A. Vierkandt and G. Gurvitch, in his earlier works. For Sturzo, phenomenology is a manner of looking at facts (phenomena) as they appear in immediate perception; while for the members of the school just mentioned, the term connotes perception of phenomena through a sophisticated procedure called by some of them "ideational abstraction." Cf. my ST, p. 267.

to construct a *tertium quid* outside the individuals as such (M. 32). Such an interpretation would be in the style of sociological collectivism and would therefore be unacceptable for Sturzo.

But, he continues, McIver is neither a phenomenologist nor a positivist; his definition is merely descriptive, ascribing to the term "system" the meaning of a complex of relations.

8. *Conclusion*

In concluding this survey, one cannot but express admiration for the breadth of Sturzo's perspective: with several exceptions (mentioned above) he has found the opportunity to establish and substantiate a definite view on the major sociological theories current at the time of his writing. Taken together, these particular appreciations and criticism offer an excellent opportunity to penetrate into the very depth of Sturzo's own thought.

Two *motifs* dominate the master's thought on the critical level. First, he rejects *ab ovo* all theories guilty of abstractionism, which in his language is tantamount to the substitution of one or another part of social reality for the whole. The sociological interpretation of society must be "concrete"; the term "total" would perhaps have better conveyed Sturzo's idea. Hence his implacable denunciation of all kinds of monistic determinisms. Today, this is almost commonplace, though more in principle than in practice. Survivals of older monistic interpretations continue to exist surreptitiously, and Sturzo's vigorous criticism is therefore by no means antiquated.

Second, out of several "total" explanations of society, those which explain society by making it the ultimate reality (sociologism) as well as those which explain it in terms of the embodiment of ideas are particularly unacceptable to Sturzo. There remain two explanations, one individualistic or personalistic, seeing in society a mere juxtaposition of individuals, and another synthetistic, making the reality of society and the individual indivisible. It is noteworthy that Sturzo has not allocated much space and mental energy to the refutation of the former; as to the latter, he has not fully recognized that the institutionalists and neo-systematists are brethren in arms, and has treated them either as sociological collectivists, or as "phenomenologists," in the meaning of authors satisfied with statements on a superficial level.

In general, like Sorokin, Sturzo commonly discusses theories in their extreme form, and does not take into consideration that in mitigated form they may contain partial but still valuable truths. But in his polemics with the sociological collectivists, he has many times forcefully expressed his own views—quite a few of his polemical statements, deprived of the spearheads directed against adversaries, have been used in the preceding Chapters (II-VI).

One must regret not finding in Sturzo's work discussions of several authors whose ideas are rather congenial to his own, for example, Sorokin and Gurvitch. But one should not forget that Sorokin's *Social and Cultural Dynamics* was published in 1937–41 and Gurvitch's *Essais de sociologie* in 1938, that is *after* the publication of Sturzo's *Essai*. The same is true of many works in the functional style to which some Sturzian propositions come very close. We shall have the opportunity to confront Sturzo's work with those just mentioned, but, alas, are unable to guess what would have been Sturzo's attitude with respect to them had he the opportunity to read them.

CHAPTER VIII

Don Sturzo's Critics and Interpreters

Don Sturzo's Critics and Interpreters

1. Sturzo's impact on sociologists

STURZO'S SOCIOLOGICAL theory is both original and profound. It is original when it looks at social phenomena from a novel point of view and it is profound when it digs below the superficial level that satisfies so many sociologists. Nevertheless, the fact that Sturzo's sociology has not attracted very much attention cannot be doubted. American surveys of Italian sociology frequently omit Sturzo's name. It is not mentioned in G. Gurvitch and W. Moore, *20th Century Sociology* (1946), or in H. E. Barnes, *Introduction to the History of Sociology* (1948). In a short survey of Italian sociology published in ASR in 1957, one finds these statements: "Don Luigi Sturzo . . . is often identified as the man responsible for the rise of modern sociology in Italy. That he was in the vanguard . . . cannot be denied."[1] That is correct but not very instructive.

More astonishing is the fact that one finds very little about Sturzo even in books of Catholic inspiration. In the index to M. Williams' *Catholic Social Thought,* one finds fourteen references; but in the corresponding pages of the text, one finds only that Sturzo said something about something, but the content of his statements is not summarized. Although Sturzo is undoubtedly the greatest among contemporary Catholic sociologists, E. Kilzer and E. Ross in their *Western Social Thought* (1954) mention Sturzo only in two footnotes, in these words: "Sturzo is another important Italian sociologist" (together with Pareto, p. 346, n. 28), and: "Reacting against the monistic neo-Hegelian philosophy of the Italian universities, Sturzo

[1] V. Rappaport, S. Cappanari and L. Moss, "Sociology in Italy," *ASR,* vol. 22 (1957), p. 443.

developed a social philosophy inspired by Catholicism. He saw human history as part of a process of becoming, in which society and the individuals who compose it together develop according to a divine plan, toward a supernatural destiny. Taking theological truths as basic, he conceived of sociology as an empiric science of all human activity within the historical process" (p. 309, n. 14). This summary is not only superficial, but in some regards misleading.

Why has Sturzo's sociology received such scant attention? One may surmise that Sturzo is passed by because, despite his denials, his sociology belongs to the class of philosophical sociologies, in other words, sociologies grafted on one or another philosophical system. But G. Gurvitch, whose sociology is conspicuously philosophical (he was originally a phenomenologist, but now calls himself a "hyper-empiric dialectician"), is commonly considered to be one of the most prominent contemporary European sociologists; and K. Mannheim, an isolate among philosophical sociologists, is widely read and approvingly quoted in this country.

There are two other plausible reasons. One is Sturzo's insistence on introducing into sociology the problems connected with the impact of the supernatural on human society (cf. Chap. II). The other reason is the manner in which the author formulates his ideas. His critics (cf. the further sections of this chapter) often complain about his difficult language full of neologisms, elliptic and sometimes cryptic propositions. This cannot be decisive because many sociologists do the same and still have a wide audience; for example, T. Parsons.[2] What makes Sturzo's works really difficult is the extreme brevity of many of his statements, making them subject to misunderstanding; his predilection for a dialectical confrontation of incompatible propositions; and his tendency to formulate multiple propositions on the same subject, of the type "A is nothing but X"; then, "A is nothing but Y"; and then, "A is nothing but Z", requiring great mental effort to resolve the antinomies thus posed. (The present writer experienced these difficulties when writing his *Sociological Theory*. He first planned to devote to Sturzo a section in the chapter on "Philosophical Sociology," but had to abandon the plan since composing Sturzo's ideas into a few pages of reasonably understandable text proved to be almost imposs-

[2] Cf. Ellsworth Faris' review of Parsons' *Social System* in *ASR*, vol. 18 (1953), pp. 103-106.

ible. It might be different now, after two years of work on the present volume.)

The difficulty of Sturzo's language is aggravated by the fact that his works have not appeared in their original Italian, but in French or English (in one case, German) translations, which try to reproduce the master's statements almost word for word, with no regard for the enormous differences in the ways of expressing ideas in these languages. This secondary obstacle is not insurmountable. Later on, at least some of Sturzo's works also appeared in Italian. Better translations could be made if there were more interest in his work. The meaning of elliptic and cryptic statements can be deciphered, and apparent inconsistencies can be resolved into coherent systems.

In any case, Sturzo's sociological work has remained almost terra incognita. The publication of *Inner Laws* and *True Life* in English moved Paul Furfey, of the Catholic University of America, and Robert Pollock of Fordham University, to deliver lectures on these works and to write long essays, which unfortunately did not appear in English (cf. below section 5). In addition, there have been four reviews of *Inner Laws* in the United States, three short ones and one long one (by John Oesterle) plus two articles by R. Caponigri.[3]

In 1953, Robert Pollock prepared a remarkable anthology of excerpts from Sturzo's work.[4] The anthology is excellent, but it is, by its very nature, only a preparatory step toward the detailed cognition of a complicated scientific work.

Several articles and reviews in Italian have been devoted to the interpretation and critique of Sturzo's treatises, and an article in German has been published. In 1953, a three volume symposium in honor of Sturzo's eightieth birthday (which occurred in 1951) was published.[5] Among the numerous papers, five are devoted to Sturzo's sociological doctrine; in addition to this, a paper by P. Sorokin contains several references to Sturzo. But no real discourse between Sturzo and his fellow sociologists has ever taken place. A few articles in Italian appeared after Sturzo's death.

[3] A. Robert Caponigri, "The Ethical and Social Bases of Italian Politics: Sturzo and Croce," *Ethics*, vol. 59 (1948-9), pp. 35-48; and "Don Luigi Sturzo," *Review of Politics*, vol. 14 (1952), pp. 147-65.

[4] *Thought*, Summer 1953, pp. 165-202.

[5] *Scritti di Sociologia e Politica in Onore di Don Luigi Sturzo*, 3 vols., Bologna, 1953.

To the best of the author's knowledge, this is the extent of scientific literature about Sturzo's sociology. This literature, with eventual rejoinders by Sturzo, forms the subject matter of this Chapter.

2. *Two short American papers*

A short and entirely adverse critique of Sturzo's *Inner Laws* appeared in *Orate Fratres*.[6] The author, Father E. Kilzer, says: "Sturzo's language is frequently abstract to the point of obscurity and contains strange words seemingly coined to the occasion. . . . The book cannot be classed among Don Sturzo's more important writings."

Sturzo replied to Kilzer in a few lines in a footnote in *Method*. "Father Kilzer believes that such abstract terms as physicity and the like have been invented by me; he is wrong; they have been current in European sociology for perhaps a century" (M. 77n). Sturzo's rejoinder is correct relative to continental European sociology until the time of the first publication of his *Inner Laws* (in French in 1935); but abstract terms were never in vogue in English and American sociology and today they are rapidly declining in continental Europe too. The future belongs probably to those works written according to the canon of "moderate operationism."[7]

Another review of *Inner Laws*, by Paul Honigsheim, is a model of brevity.[8] The reviewer first summarizes Sturzo's theory with emphasis on its personalistic aspect ("society is the sum total of individuals") and on the eternity of ethical rules—Sturzo's fine doctrine on the gradual approximation of human societies to absolute rationality seems to have escaped attention.

Honigsheim's summary is followed by an attempt to trace the dependence of Sturzo on forerunners, a task justly declared to be not easy, for no references are given by Sturzo. Nevertheless, the reviewer believes that the following is obvious: "Large parts of the system correspond to the leading Catholic neo-Thomistic social philosophy of the Dominicans and Jesuits. Eliminated are the traditional theory of social contract and evolution of state authority out of paternal power; maintained is the right of the individual within the same

[6] Vol. 19, No. 4, February 1945, pp. 191-2.
[7] Cf. N. S. Timasheff, *ST*, pp. 310 and Hornell Hart, "Operationism in sociology and psychology," (unpublished MS).
[8] *AJS*, vol. 57 (1945), pp. 160-1.

limits as in almost every Catholic school. Emphasis is given to the role of love in social life and in acquiring knowledge, an originally Platonic —Augustinian element, now appearing again in Neo-Thomism. The examples used denote the influence of the culture-historical-anthropological school of Father Schmidt, itself based on a Catholic Platonism."

The review continues as follows: "Even the non-partisans of the author's philosophy can adhere to his theories that general rules can be conceived only as based on history, and that the history of primitives and history strictly speaking must both be incorporated into the one historical science." However, the area of agreement between Sturzo and his critic is not correctly drawn. Sturzo derives from history not "general rules" (of conduct) but sociological laws, which are not rules; and nowhere does Sturzo explicitly advise historians to incorporate pre-history (which, by the way, is more and more frequently being done), into their histories.

The review concludes with a discussion of the future of Catholicism so far as it is based on Sturzo's social philosophy, as Honigsheim calls it, despite Sturzo's claim that a social philosophy is an undesirable hybrid (cf. Chap. II). This part of the review is obviously outside the scope of this volume.

It is astonishing that Sturzo almost did not react to Honigsheim's discussion of his work. In a footnote in *Method* (109-110), he reproduces the two passages quoted above without confirming or denying Honigsheim's guesses about his spiritual genealogy, which would have been very helpful for the correct location of his sociology in the total history of social thought. In a few lines, Sturzo expresses disappointment that his work is understood as an instrument for increasing the influence of Catholicism, and states his hope that even those who do not share his ideas and reject his methodology would evaluate his work objectively, according to its inner value.

3. The controversy with F. Mueller

Franz Mueller's review of *Inner Laws* in the ACSR[9] resulted in a four-phased polemic with Sturzo, the only case of its kind known to this writer. The reason is probably that Mueller's review begins with

[9] *ACSR*, vol. 6 (1954), pp. 109-11.

a statement which must have hurt Sturzo badly: according to the reviewer, the sub-title of Sturzo's work in its English version—new sociology—is a misnomer, since, for the most part, the book does not deal with sociology, but with social philosophy, philosophy of history and political sociology and is rather a study of society in the abstract. The Introduction to the book is said to unfold ideas akin to Alfred Weber's *Kultursoziologie*. This is hardly correct: Alfred Weber studies concrete historical configurations (continuing in the direction set by Danilevsky and Spengler) while Sturzo, despite his insistence that society exists only in the concrete, is eager to discover, *by abstraction*, traits common to various (if not necessarily all) societies.

After some mordant remarks about Sturzo's manner of presenting ideas, Mueller regrets the ambiguity of many of Sturzo's statements, especially those describing society and consciousness. In Mueller's opinion, though Sturzo explicitly rejects the individualistic conception of society, quite a few of his statements seem to have a nominalistic slant. Mueller then assembles a long list of apparently contradictory statements about the nature of society, which he concludes as follows: "Though all these statements can be given a sound and satisfactory interpretation, it would not be surprising if some readers" were misled.[10]

Finally, Mueller reproaches Sturzo for the excessive use of the notion of consciousness and offers a selection of statements taken out of context: society resolves itself into consciousness; justice is an act of consciousness; authority is responsible, unifying, and active consciousness; the specific element of every international community it the consciousness of moral affinity; autonomy is consciousness.

It must be conceded that the statements are somewhat puzzling, to use Mueller's expression. However they become intelligible and plausible if one considers that, for Sturzo, "individual-collective consciousness" is identical with social reality. Then, the identification of society, justice, authority, international community and so on with consciousness points to a common denominator of all these phenomena *qua* social phenomena. Nevertheless, it must be conceded that the brief and apodictic statements reproduced above require too much

---

[10] A summary of the majority of statements cited by F. Mueller has been offered in Chapter III, section 1.

mental effort on the part of a reader who does not intend to become a specialist in Sturzian sociology.

Mueller's criticism provoked Sturzo to write a letter to the editor of the ACSR[11] which appeared in the October, 1945, issue. In this letter Sturzo emphasized the central position of consciousness in his sociological system and offered new and sometimes clearer formulations of some of his predilected ideas. "When rationality [which is part of human nature] becomes conscious of itself (and it takes place only in individual beings), society can develop, organize itself and answer to the deepest exigencies of personal and community life." This is the very meaning of one of the statements which had puzzled Mueller—society resolves itself into consciousness. What Sturzo wanted to say, can be rephrased as follows: "Society is impossible without consciousness," a statement explicitly endorsed by Mueller.

Furthermore, in his letter Sturzo rejected any interpretation which would make his a theory of society "in the abstract," a curious travesty of Sturzo's sociology, which he developed as the science of society "in the concrete."

Finally, Sturzo has explained his "phraseology" so vigorously attacked by Mueller. This phraseology, says Sturzo, "is not altogether new and is taken from the modern usage of lay philosophy" which no longer comprehends and appreciates the scholastic terminology and technique.

The next phase of the polemic was a rejoinder by Mueller which appeared in the same issue of the ACSR as Sturzo's letter.[12] Mueller begins by saying that he has no objection to Sturzo's preference for the diction and phraseology of modern lay philosophy if and insofar as this would encourage non-Catholic sociologists and philosophers to discuss Catholic social thought. Yet, he continues, he is afraid that even those used to a non-scholastic approach will find it difficult to read the *Inner Laws* and to grasp its fundamental theses—which, in the present writer's opinion, is true.

Mueller continues by acknowledging that consciousness is a necessary condition of specifically human association; but, he says it can hardly be conceived as its formal cause. But Sturzo nowhere asserted that it was and could not do so because he was writing a book on

---

[11] *ACSR,* vol. 6 (1945), pp. 182-3.
[12] *Ibid.,* pp. 183-4.

sociology, not on social philosophy, and therefore consistently avoided a purely philosophical terminology.

There follows, in Mueller's rejoinder, a rather surprising statement: "If society, justice, authority and so on are all defined in terms of consciousness, then the criterion of their differences seems to be missing." As stated above, consciousness may be considered as forming the common denominator of the phenomena mentioned above, which still could and should be differentiated depending on the various *contents* of consciousness.

After having insinuated that overstressing consciousness may lead the reader to identify Sturzo's philosophy with that of Berkeley, Mueller inflicts the final blow: "Sturzo does not contribute to our understanding of the true nature of society by saying that it is neither objective, nor concrete, but abstract.[13] The social philosopher must give an answer to the question 'what is meant when we say that a society acts or is acted upon.' If we say that in reality only individuals act and are acted upon, then scoiety does appear as mere nomen."

Sturzo's final counter-attack has been conducted in Part Two of his treatise on *Method*, together with the refutation of Oesterle's critical article (see next section). In that joint answer to his critics, far more attention is paid to Oesterle than to Mueller, partly because the former's article is much longer and more specific than that of the latter, partly because Sturzo had already refuted some of Mueller's statements in-the letter summarized above. For the same reason, our survey must be brief.

Against Mueller's insinuation that, after all, Sturzo is a nominalist (and not a universalist) Sturzo has this to say: If the [philosophical] question of universalism is posed, there is nothing wrong in recognizing that society is "universal" [in the meaning that all societies possess the "essence" of sociality]. But where does one find that essence? Only in associated individuals. Just as humanity is actuated in every single man, sociality is found only in concrete societies. Society [in the abstract] has no other existence [to be distinguished from essence] but in our minds (M. 75-6).

Against Mueller's fear that the reader would be led to Berkeley's

---

[13] It is hard to understand how F. Mueller could have read such a statement into a book explicitly and recurringly insisting on the contrary.

thesis, *esse est percipi*, Sturzo points to several passages in *Inner Laws* which, if properly understood, would show that Mueller's charge was unfounded.

As to the alleged overemphasis on consciousness, Sturzo asserts that between Mueller's formula (consciousness is a necessary condition of human association) and his own formula (consciousness is the principle of the concretization of sociality), there is no real difference. Mueller, says Sturzo, has not paid attention to the term concretization which could have been replaced by that of the individualization of a particular society. Sturzo is sure that his formula is better and tries to demonstrate it in a few examples, which, it must be conceded, are not as telling as the author believes them to be (M. 92-3).

4. Oesterle's criticism

John Oesterle's article on Sturzo's *Inner Laws* (which appeared in the form of a book review)[14] is the only paper available in English which discusses Sturzo's sociology point by point. Oesterle has high appreciation for the book. "It has . . . a profundity of observation and a wealth of material notably lacking in the books usually written on sociology. . . . Now in the field of sociology we have someone like Don Sturzo who . . . possesses the qualifications and the intellectual discipline necessary to approach the subject matter comprehensively" (pp. 520, 533).

This high appreciation of the book as a whole does not prevent the reviewer from raising many objections (some of which coincide with those we met in Mueller's review—the two papers appeared almost simultaneously). We shall extract the most important critical remarks and summarize Sturzo's rejoinders which form a large portion of the second part of his *Method*.

1. "The historical [approach] as used by Sturzo is in reality philosophical rather than historical, if we keep the terms in their literal distinction. History, as Sturzo wishes to use it, involves philosophical and theological judgments which, instead of being properly within the sphere of history, exhibit . . . its relation to philosophy and theology" (p. 533). In general, Sturzo's "understanding of historicism as the systematic conception of history as human process . . . concerns

[14] *The Thomist*, vol. 8 (1945), pp. 520-33.

rather the philosophy of history which is not the same thing as history conceived as philosophy" (p. 521).

In *Method,* Sturzo leaves that criticism unanswered, probably because he had substantially clarified his position in the article "Philosophy and History" published in 1946 and amply quoted in Chap. II of this volume.

2. "Throughout the book," writes Oesterle, "Sturzo gives the impression that the abstract is to be associated with the unreal or the misleading, or that the abstract is a form of reasoning in the mind apart from a foundation in reality. Hence he tends to gravitate between some form of the wholly abstract and the concrete individuality. However there are, apart from the wholly abstract, three degrees of abstraction which approach a greater universality without ever departing from their grounding in reality. Thus we can and should, in scientific procedure, consider society other than either merely a concrete entity or . . . some form of pure abstraction. We must understand the nature of society as drawn formally from its concrete existence which gives us a real entity distinct from and of course related to the individuals forming this society. This is not the abstract to be confused with the ideal nor the abuse of the abstract that would mislead us but rather that abstraction which, in conformity with scientific procedure, would inform us. . . . The study of a subject such as sociology terminates in the concrete order of the particular societies, but our arrival at that stage of investigation presupposes a sound understanding of the nature and characteristics of society and the social order itself" (529).

Replying to Oesterle, Sturzo negates the supposition that he identifies the abstract and the unreal; it lacks any foundation in his work. "If I had understood the abstract as something unreal or misleading, I would have done one of these two things; either I would have denied the concretization of society (while it is stressed in my sociology), or I would have denied the possibility of abstraction from reality, which cannot be derived from any of my statements provided they are not taken out of context" (M. 73-4). Sturzo adds that, contrary to Oesterle's conjectures, he (Sturzo) uses the abstract term "sociality" to designate society in the abstract and reserves the term "society" to connote society in the concrete, while Oesterle prefers to use the term society both on the abstract and concrete levels. This is common usage, but it is misleading (M. 77).

3. Like many others, Oesterle disapproves of the role Sturzo assigned to consciousness. "Consciousness," says Oesterle, is "a somewhat unique abstraction in itself. . . . In its ordinary significance, to be conscious is to be aware of one's acts or to act knowingly. This does not add a special quality to man. It is true that Sturzo emphasizes group consciousness. But what does it really imply other than that one member of the group is aware of another member of the group? If it means more than that, better terms could certainly express it. . . . As Sturzo appears to use it, it is a means to establish the identity or unity of society. . . . If consciousness is the unifying element of a society, we are not apt to see in society anything more than a series of associated consciousnesses of individuals. But this is hardly how we understand society and in fact act in the social order" (529-30). Furthermore, from Sturzo's doctrine on consciousness, Oesterle derives the proposition that Sturzo subordinates common good (welfare) to individual good.

Out of Oesterle's arguments, Sturzo chooses to refute first of all the corollary and shows that his critic's imputation is wrong: for Sturzo there can be no individual good which would not also be a common good, and *vice versa*; what is supposed to be individual good only, is no good at all (M. 86-7).

As to Oesterle's main argument, Sturzo asserts that his term "consciousness" is better than any one which could be suggested. The importance of collective consciousness may be proven, believes Sturzo, by establishing, on the basis of historical evidence, a kind of correlation between well developed collective consciousness and an adequate functioning of society (M. 91).

4. Oesterle believes that Sturzo has wrongly extended the importance of duality in social life. It seems to him that, doing so, Sturzo simply has transferred the notion of man's mode of action—it can be called a basic contrariety in man—into the social order. Reason and sense, he continues, form a natural contrariety and hence a duality. We could thus expect a similar situation in men acting together. Further, change in the physical order proceeds through contraries. By an extensive elaboration Sturzo has transferred the principles of

man's mode of action and that of change in general to social movement as a means of rendering the social process intelligible (523).

Sturzo's rejoinder runs as follows: he has not imposed the principle of duality on reality for some *a priori* reason, but has inferred it from painstaking study of historical reality. "My critics," says Sturzo, "are opposed to my thesis of an incessant cyclical movement; they prefer to represent society as stabilized through order and progress from less to more perfect states" (M. 100). But, concludes Sturzo, their thesis is not supported by history.

5. Closely related to the criticism just examined is another one: Sturzo, it seems, overemphasizes motion and change at the expense of stability; "Sturzo's development of process and change in terms of duality and diarchy often gives the impression of universal mobilism, for, even though the duality tends to unification, still any real unification . . . never appears to occur." Furthermore, "he describes the sociological duality as a conflict, latent or open, between reality statically conceived and its becoming . . . While the structure of the physical universe, including man, is such that there is always change, yet there are successive terms to all changes and it is in virtue of such terms or resolutions that other changes occur. Without the fulfillment of changes in the terms, reality indeed would be an endless conflict and man's social movement an incessant revolution. But with the achievement of positive terms it is possible [that change becomes] process, i.e. orderly movement. . . . Finally, we should note that change itself is intelligible in terms of rest, that is accomplishment or fulfillment. Becoming cannot exist nor can it be understood without being. This aspect does not seem sufficiently evident in Sturzo's analysis. . . . The dominant impression from Sturzo's whole analysis of sociological movement in terms of duality and diarchy is that of a somewhat preconceived system of dualistic dynamism" (pp. 523-36).

Sturzo agrees with Oesterle that becoming can neither exist nor be understood without being. But the being of a society is given in the multiplicity of individuals (or perhaps, a multiple individuality) associated to achieve an end. Sturzo could have found a much stronger argument against his opponent: as stated in previous chapters, he often speaks of structures and crystallizations, obviously pointing to rest, achievement, being.

6. Finally, Oesterle attacks Sturzo's treatment of the methods of

liberty and authority. According to the critic, Sturzo views authority as though it were intrinsically disposed to be socially unfavorable. But authority cannot be a constitutive element of society and yet intrinsically antisocial in method. The uncritical and somewhat glowing manner in which he treats the method of liberty [is also faulty]. In fact, "abuses of irresponsible liberty can be just as erroneous and just as fatal to the social body" (p. 526).

Sturzo's reply is very short: He does not believe he has deviated from objectivity; but to avoid further misinterpretation, it would perhaps be better to abandon the terms used in *Inner Laws* and use the terms—method of conviction and method of coercion (M. 105 n.).

Summing up, we might say: We are in presence of two minds, one rather inclined to traditionalism in thought and expression and another inclined to innovations and eager to destroy traditional idols. The former has it easier: one conducts the reader's mind along familiar paths and thus gains confidence and sympathy; the latter must repeat again and again his bold deviation from tradition; doing so, he often does not find the best arguments, because, for him, his innovations seem to be conspicuously better interpretations of facts than the traditional ones. It is another question whether the paths opened by the innovator will or will not prevail.

5. *The Furfey–Pollock papers*

The Furfey–Pollock papers now to be surveyed reproduce two series of lectures delivered in 1943 by the two scholars under the sponsorship of the Luigi Sturzo Foundation for Sociological Studies; one of the sets of the lectures was delivered at the Catholic University of America in Washington, D. C., the other at Fordham University in New York. The lectures were to appear in English in a volume with Sturzo's *On the Method of Sociology* and his *Reply to the Critics*. The volume was planned for publication in 1947, but various obstacles prevented its appearance. Finally, addressed to the American public, the volume appeared in Italy in 1950 as Vol. VII of Sturzo's *Opera Omnia* (First Series). Sturzo wrote an Introduction to the volume, devoting its major part to the Furfey-Pollock papers.

Furfey's article, says Sturzo, expressed the fundamental phases of his sociological theory, namely "Society in the Concrete" and "The

Supernatural Factors of Human Society." His two chapters treat the subject on the sociological level and demonstrate the legitimacy and completeness of his theory as a true sociology, although very different from the current ones.

The paper by Pollock, continues Sturzo, presents the philosophical and historical sides of his sociology with special emphasis on these three topics: man as a social individual; history as a process of rationalization and liberation; and Christianity and the historical and social liberation of men. These three chapters are preceded by a preface which was originally written as an introduction to the whole volume. While Furfey compared Sturzo's sociology with that of the positivists and with the teaching of other Catholic sociologists, Pollock compares his sociology to the naturalistic and pragmatic currents in American sociology, giving references to John Dewey and to the kind of abstract philosophy which holds itself aloof from the study of concrete reality.

The general purpose of Furfey's paper is approximately the same as that of this volume, namely, the conveying of Sturzo's sociology to the American reader. Furfey often proceeds by offering long quotations from Sturzo's work. Taken out of context, these quotations are perhaps even less understandable that Sturzo's work as a whole. But some of Furfey's intervenient statements are illuminating and worthy of being briefly reported. The following are a few cases in point.

A dominant trait of Sturzo's thought is integral realism. All societies are finalistic; therefore, Sturzo's sociology is also finalistic (M. 151).

The sociologist knows that his vision of the study of society is not the same as that of a philosopher or theologian; his talent is primarily applied to the study of the empiric order. But, if he is a believer, he cannot but acknowledge that the supernatural plays a part in human society. Introducing into sociology the study of the impact of the supernatural, Sturzo does not attack empiric sociology; it would have been stupid to do so. What he attacks is not empiric but positivist sociology, which is quite another thing. Positivism is a philosophical system which denies the validity of metaphysics and theology and asserts that natural science is the only valid approach to knowledge. The error of the positivists is not that of applying empiric methods, but that of denying all that is not empiric (M. 154).

He who dedicates himself to "integral sociology" (as Furfey has done) can legitimately study society with empiric methods; this is sociology in the narrow meaning. But he cannot limit himself to that. He must penetrate into the field where sociology is coterminous with philosophy and theology (M. 157).

As shown in Chap. II of this book, another solution is preferable: sociology should be confined to what is knowable empirically, but without asserting itself to be the only type of knowledge about society. Furfey would strongly disagree with this line of thought. "It is difficult to find logical reasons for the identification of sociology with empiric sociology. Of course, there are certain historical reasons for doing so. But, if the term sociology is confined to empiric sociology, then Spencer, Dilthey, Simmel, Max Weber and Vierkandt are not sociologists; and Comte would be a philosopher, and not an empiric scientist" (166).

This of course is an important argument, though Furfey modestly recognizes that arguments from tradition are not telling. The facts referred to by Furfey are true in the sense that the authors he mentions were not exclusively empiric. But these earlier sociologists, by cultivating seeds found in the social philosophies of preceding eras, moved only gradually toward an empiric sociology. More recent sociologists have also derived sociological propositions from philosophical premises. This much is true. But with both of these groups, as with Sturzo, the same task as this volume sets for itself should be performed, namely, the separation of empirically valid propositions from philosophical premises, which commonly appear unnecessary, and the consequent arrangement of the propositions so derived into a consistent system (cf. Chap. II, sec. 5).

Furfey concludes his paper with an eloquent praise of Sturzo's work: "The great contribution of Don Luigi Sturzo has been that of having studied the premises of a sociology which would be really satisfactory. His courage has been too great to be intimidated by the sarcasms of the positivists. His thought has been too profound to be blurred by the materialists. His devotion has been too intensive to remain silent. His works are salutary antidotes to the ideas of the positivists" (M. 168).

Pollock's paper, as enthusiastic as that of Furfey's, is of another kind. Since he is a philosopher, the perspective in which he presents Sturzo's doctrine is significantly at variance with that of this volume. But since the perspective of philosophy is broader than that of any empiric science, and since, in Sturzo's total thought system, the sociological phase forms only a part, a few words about the broader perspective offered by an arduous student of Sturzo's works are not out of place.

For Pollock, the great problem of our day is this: how can values which have formed our Western tradition be brought in contact with what is best in modern culture so that the former would revive and regain strength and the latter be ennobled. To achieve this goal our historico-sociological thought must undergo a radical transformation. In the world of today there is no thinker who could show a better way than Don Sturzo (M. 176). His dynamic or historicist sociology combined with emphasis on social consciousness and the incessant movement toward rationality, is just what we need.

Sturzo's dynamic approach to social phenomena is epitomized by Pollock in the following way: the center of Sturzo's outlook is the notion of the actual process of man. This great illuminating insight, based on historical and sociological research and inspired by philosophical and theological considerations, means this: Underlying the outward succession of events, there is an inward process, which is the human process of the very unfolding of man. . . . What we have, is a real historical process, marked by a growth of human consciousness. . . . History as process confronts us . . . with its unceasing flow of life from which novelty and creativeness are never absent. If there is continuity, there is also the new and unpredictable. . . . The past is kept vital and active only through new achievements and by the development of that which lies implicit within it. In this development, experimentation and risk are indispensable. . . . In turning toward the historical concrete, Sturzo has laid the basis for an integral realism in which thought and event are inseparable.

From among other thoughtful statements, abundant in Pollock's paper, this one is especially worthwhile: "the human community is indeed a mysterious reality exhibiting a wholeness that far transcends a mere atomism, a real oneness which is yet a manyness and which forces us to rethink the very notion of the individual and the way he is related to society. But the fact . . . remains that while society is real *qua* society, it is still a communion of individuals, men in individual-social being" (M. 196).

It is obviously impossible to summarize here a 116-page paper which is vigorous, thoughtful and brilliantly written, but one which, as already stated, emphasizes the philosophical aspects of Sturzo's total doctrine. Their existence is by no means denied in this volume, devoted to the extraction from the total work of those parts which are of sociological relevance. Let us hope for the eventual publication of Pollock's paper in English.

6. The Italian papers

Out of Sturzo's major works on sociology *True Life* came first to the attention of the Italian scholars, since its Italian original was published in 1947, while the Italian version of *Inner Laws* appeared in 1949. After the publication of the former of these works several short articles appeared in Italian presenting, interpreting, and evaluating it to the Italian readers.

In 1949, the publication of the Italian version of the work known in English as *The Inner Laws of Society* in the first volume of Sturzo: *Opera Omnia*, induced Professor G. Marchello, of the University of Torino, to write an article entitled "Historicism and Spiritualism; the Historicist Sociology of Don Luigi Sturzo."[15] It has been reproduced, as an appendix, in Sturzo's volume *On Method*, with the latter's rejoinder.

After having expressed his appreciation of Sturzo's achievement, namely the formulation of the basic lines of a new sociology, that is, historicist sociology on a spiritualistic foundation, and especially Sturzo's vigorous presentation of human possibilities, Marchello raises grave objections against two substantial elements of Sturzo's work.

First, he believes, sociology as presented by Sturzo does not possess scientific autonomy. The [apparently] sociological judgment concerning the "historical resolution of society" is neither autonomous nor scientific, but philosophical, making his sociology a modality of social philosophy. Sturzo acknowledges that the dynamic principle of the concretization of society is rationality. But such a concretization cannot be the object of a merely phenomenal description such as used in science; this concretization must be derived from a principle which would make social experience possible; but the discovery of such a principle can be achieved only on the level of philosophical judgment (M. 293-4). Moreover, there cannot be any doubt that Sturzo's

[15] *Rivista Internazionale di Scienzi Sociali,* vol. 22 (1959), pp. 61-7.

sociology is normative. This is, according to Marchello, inevitable for a sociological theory based on philosophical spiritualism. Such a theory is speculative and after all not scientific (M. 295).

Second, Marchello takes to task Sturzo's thesis of duality-diarchy as one of the fundamental laws of society. "I cannot agree that social monism is conducive to 'statolatry', i.e. deification of the state, or that social pluralism is always atomistic." On the contrary, individual initiative can be better guaranteed "by the simultaneous application of the principle of pluralism of social forms and their tendency to form a kind of hierarchy" (M. 296-7).

In a Postscript to *Del Metodo*, Sturzo refutes Marchello's doubts about the scientific character of his sociology by repeating that, according to him, a science is autonomous if it has a sufficiently individualized object of study and a particular normative value (?). That his sociology complies with the first condition is self-evident; it is the study of society in the concrete, that is, of society in its total configuration, in contrast to sciences which study selected parts of social life. As to the second condition, a purely empiric positivist sociology would not be a normative science (M. 114-5). But the actual object of the social sciences is man and his rational and sensitive nature, his existence, individual and collective, his origin, limitations and destiny (*ibid.* 116). The fact that some philosophical premises or theories are used in a discipline should not deprive it of scientific autonomy. The decisive factors for affirming or denying scientific validity to a discipline are rigorous system and the use of principles and laws drawn from proper objects[16] and by proper methods, and absence of heterogeneous elements and extrapolations (M. 117).

As is often the case, the truth seems to be located midway between the two conflicting assertions: as a whole, Sturzo's thought system transcends the compass of (empiric) science; but it contains a number of empiric propositions which have been presented in Chapters II to VI of this volume.

Marchello's paper was followed by a series of papers devoted mainly to *Società* (the Italian title of *Inner Laws*). One of the most important, by Engenio di Carlo,[17] entitled "the sociology of Luigi Sturzo" can be summarized as follows:

---

[16] Sturzo probably means "proper objects of observation."
[17] *Humanitas*, vol. VI (1951), pp. 509 ff.

Sturzo consistently tries to locate the foundation of social facts on the inner fact of consciousness. The latter appears to be a primary fact, an absolute condition of the social. Consciousness is the constitutive, essential element of society which animates it and renders it effective. Individual–collective consciousness means the consciousness of each of us which reflects itself in those of others through the achievement of common goals. Individual and society claim each other.

Sociality is resolved in terms of *coscienzialità*; here the author uses an untranslatable abstract term designating man's property to possess consciousness. Consequently, social phenomenology is radically psychic. Therefrom a very important theory is derived by Sturzo and this without using any idealistic premises;[18] had he used such premises, he would have gone beyond the frontiers of science.

Sturzo's doctrine is the vision of the whole which precedes any particular research in the realm of social phenomena; in that regard Sturzo's point of view resembles that of Simmel.

On the other hand, Sturzo's sociology is a search for constant normative laws. Thereby it becomes normative as a science of ends and ideals.[19] Sturzo defines his sociology as a normative science, but still holds the view that it is autonomous. But when sociology is treated as an historico-philosophical vision of theological inspiration, is not its autonomy lost? Strictly scientific knowledge is confined to the study of facts and the relations between them (laws); it is not normative, it does not prescribe ends or ideals. Sociology is the study of that irreducible trait of man which is sociality, a theory of the social, a science of general social laws. Sturzo points to the fact that everywhere and at every time religion has influenced human facts. But the problem of the influence of the supernatural as expressed in revelation is different from the problem of the influence of religion as such. Nevertheless, concedes di Carlo, a philosophical aspect is not entirely absent from sociology; such is especially the problem of the particular nature of social reality and autonomy. The problem is rather epistemological; answering it should be the subject matter of a special discipline, introductory to sociology as a concrete and empiric science of social reality. This is a suggestion which has been realized by Paul Furfey in

[18] In this regard, di Carlo is diametrically opposed to Marchello who believes that Sturzo's sociology is spiritualistic.

[19] On this point Sturzo has, without necessity, made a concession to Marchello—after all, his sociology is not normative, but primarily theoretical.

his *Scope and Method of Sociology*[20] the first part of which is devoted to "Metasociology," as a philosophical preface to sociology.

Di Carlo concludes with the statement that, in the United States, Sturzo's sociology has aroused great interest and attention. Alas, the opposite is true, as stated many times in this volume.

In a short but thoughtful paper, "La sociologia come scienza autonoma nel pensiero di Luigi Sturzo,"[21] Franco Leonardi has emphasized the originality of Sturzo's sociology. It stands far away from the two poles of immanentism (dominant in Europe) and rational pragmatism (dominant in Anglo-Saxon countries). He says that Sturzo tries to insert the science of society into a philosophical interpretation of reality, that is a theoretical science, but that it is not derived from *a priori* constructions. But the historical experience which he studies is not a series of facts external to men. Therefore, sociology is the science of the human creation of facts.

In contradistinction to the majority of the authors reported above, Leonardi not only surveys Sturzo's ideas, but also raises certain objections. "Sturzo's insistence on society as a multiple projection of individuals is too drastic. It is true that rationality does not exist outside of individuals, but individual rationality may become rationality of social entities possessing objective reality. Society is not solely interaction and projection; on their foundation there arise social institutions which serve men, receive quasi-autonomous existence and exert influence. On the psychological (not the logical) level one cannot deny the validity of Durkheim's proposition that society presents itself as an *a priori* for individual experience. After all, the process of projection is accompanied and followed by a process of introjection or internalization (p. 250). Therefore, all structural concretizations of society (among them, the institutions) are simultaneously *a priori* and *a posteriori*; from this duality, historical dynamism springs.

Another criticism concerns itself with Sturzo's treatment of social causality. The treatment is said to be one-sided, since it ascribes the prevalent role to religious causation. This does not conform with sociological and historical data. In general, it is undesirable to speak of "prevalent causes" (but Sturzo never does!), since every social fact

[20] *Scope and Method of Sociology* (1953), pp. 1-106.
[21] *Sophia*, vol. 20 (1952), pp. 258-61.

may be causally reconstructed in terms of a network of causes operating in the framework of particular civilizations (p. 251).

It is a pity that Sturzo did not find an opportunity to react to these criticisms. Had he done so, he would probably have said that the influence of institutions on the individuals and the relative independence of the institutions from the existence and consciousness of particular individuals do not destroy his basic thesis that society may be resolved into individual consciousnesses. This is so because the institutions are man-created so that their power over men is human power, so to speak, stored and crystallized. As to religious monism, Sturzo could rightly object that he is not guilty of the error ascribed to him; in his writings, he insists on the indestructible autonomy of religious formations, but not on their dominance in history.

7. A German paper by an Italian

Simultaneously with the Italian papers surveyed, there appeared, in German, a lengthy article, written however by an Italian scholar, F. Battaglia; it is entitled, "Um eine neue Soziologie."[22]

Battaglia begins by stating that, in Italy, sociology has remained on a level already surpassed in other countries. This discipline is looked at with suspicion partly because of its identification with the positivism of Comte and Durkheim, partly because of the dominance of idealistic philosophy in Italy's social sciences. Especially influential have been the views of Benedetto Croce who denied the very possibility of sociology because of the infinite concatenation of causes and the inability of sociology to perceive, in social phenomena, the non-recurring and unique.[23]

In all advanced nations, continues Battaglia, a kind of sociological Renaissance has taken place overcoming the old points of view. Research of a new style has been carried out, with force and enthusiasm: Sturzo's sociology is one of the elements of that movement.

Sturzo's sociology is based on two premises emphasizing the indi-

---

[22] *Archiv fur Rechts- und Sozialphilosophie,* vol. 38 (1949), pp. 25-49. An abridged Italian version has appeared in *Convivium,* vol. 18 (1950), pp. 367-82.

[23] *Teoria e storia dello storigrafo,* 2nd edition, 1920, pp. 53 ff.

vidual and history. For him, society is not a general (abstract?) concept, but is concretized in individual consciousnesses. In individuals who oppose each other and cooperate, there arises, by necessity, collective consciousness which is in fact the soul of society (Sturzo would hardly endorse the term "soul") and which makes a whole out of separate individuals. Society is a process of becoming which coincides with consciousness, namely the socially oriented consciousness of the individuals. This, says Battaglia, is a difficult point. When approaching it, Simmel and von Wiese have made of sociology the study of abstract and conceptual conditions making association possible. The phenomenologists have tried to go beyond chaotic experience, but often submerged what is given in Platonic idealism and intuition.

The assertion that social consciousness is constitutive of society could be traced back to the influence of Petroni and Croce (which is explicitly denied by Sturzo), as well as Gentile.[24] For the idealist, states Battaglia, society is not so much the unity of the multiform, as absolute oneness even when it seems to be dualistic. Along such lines, modern sociology must be built up, if one does not acknowledge that Sturzo has already solved the problem—although he is not an idealist, but a spiritualist (p. 31).

Historicism belongs to the elements of social consciousness, continues Battaglia, which is tantamount to the incessant sequence of present tenses. In that sequence, the moments of causality and finality are realized. But Sturzo's historicism is never flattened to a mere narration of what happened. Light on the sequences of events is thrown by the introduction of the principle of rationality, leaving room however, for irrationality. The realization of rationality cannot lead to the end of history, which can never be terminated.

There follows a survey of Sturzo's doctrine about the fundamental forms of sociality. The denial of the fundamental character of the economic form should be grounded on better reasons than those offered by Sturzo, says Battaglia. Sturzo explicitly denies the primacy of the political form; Battaglia doubts whether this is correct. The Church is treated by Sturzo as a perfect society[25] [it is not so certain

---

[24] Battaglia points to a posthumous work, *Genesi e struttura della società*, which appeared in 1946, i.e. *after* the publication of Sturzo's major works.
[25] Sturzo explicitly affirms the opposite thesis.

that Sturzo does this]. In this way, a bridge to the sociology of the supernatural is being built up.

According to Battaglia, Sturzo's research should be continued in various directions, although it seems impossible to treat the problems more deeply and systematically. But Battaglia refuses to accept Sturzo's view that a genuine international society is impossible; for him, a society consisting of all the particular states and even a perfect unity are possible. That unity could be achieved on the background of the capacity of the States to extend their limits [Sturzo ascribes this property not to the State as such, but only to Empires].

The Italian scholar concludes his painstaking survey of Sturzo's work by saying: "The new sociology is not a principle, but already a structure" (p. 49).

8. Papers in the Scritti

The papers which appeared in 1953 in the Don Luigi Sturzo *Scritti* for obvious reasons do not attempt adverse criticism of the master's work. The paper by Arturo Beccari of the University of Florence, "The sociological doctrine and practical politics of Sturzo,"[26] contains a fine essay on Sturzo's sociology written by a fervent admirer and follower. Here and there some of Sturzo's views are given an interpretation at variance with that offered in this volume. Beccari believes that Sturzo "warns us . . . against aprioristic constructions and the belief in eternal (innate) laws in human society." This is hardly so: Sturzo believes that the movement toward rationality and the cyclic movement culminating in the phases of duality–unification always and everywhere govern human life. These laws are eternal or universal; but they are not the kind of inflexible laws assumed to exist by the physicists and the positivistic sociologists. They represent merely prepotent tendencies from which departures often take place.

"One cannot assert that Sturzo's sociology is unscientific because of the assertion of the omnipresence of religion; this fact is corroborated by ethnology and statistics." One hardly could find corroboration in statistics because statistics of religion cover only a small portion of humanity; moreover, Sturzo is more than sceptical about the validity of statistical findings. The statement is not to the point (as well ob-

---

[26] *Scritti* (*op. cit., supra*) vol. I, pp. 99 ff. If the contrary is not explicitly stated, all the references in this section are to the *Scritti*.

served in the di Carlo paper reported above): doubts about the scientific validity of Sturzo's sociology arise not because of his thesis about the omnipresence of religion (which is probably correct) but because of his assertion that the impact of the supernatural on human society must be studied in sociology.

Beccari well epitomizes Sturzo's doctrine about rationality. For him, rationality is the dynamic principle through which the con-cretization of the process of historical experience is achieved. But Sturzo draws from that proposition the conclusion that there can be no social statics: since man is the subject of this movement, society is by necessity plastic and dynamic. In actuality, Sturzo formulates a long set of propositions which form his statics or social morphology (cf. Chap. V).

Furthermore, Beccari emphasizes that Sturzo does not start with a preconceived spiritualistic conception, but derives his social laws from historical experience. In that regard, he says, the general criticism of Italian sociology by Panunzio[27] cannot be applied to Sturzo.

He concludes by saying that the originality of Sturzo's integral position is superior to all prior partial positions because it expands the content and scientific value of sociology.

"Don Luigi Sturzo's General Theory of State,"[28] by Robert Cap-onigri, Professor at the University of Notre Dame, only partly belongs to the subject matter of this volume. Sturzo's sociology, says the author, is analytical, idealistic and historicist. Of this statement Sturzo would accept only the third part. He could rightly assert that his sociology is not analytical, but synthetic, synthesis preceded by anal-ysis, to which, however, only instrumental value is ascribed. And Sturzo could point to a number of eloquent pages written by him against idealistic sociology understood as an attempt to explain social phenomena as embodiments of ideas existing and developing ac-cording to immanent laws of their own. At this place, Beccari, another contributor to the Scritti, could be appropriately quoted: "Sturzo has high esteem for the action of ideas in social change, but he always looks for confirmation in experience."

Returning to the analytical character of Sturzo's sociology, Caponigri

[27] C. Panunzio, in G. Gurvitch–W. Moore, 20th Century Sociology, (1946), p. 651.
[28] Vol. I, pp. 295 ff.

makes the following statement: "Sturzo dissolves all the substantive character with which positivist sociology has endowed society." Such a characterization of Sturzo's doctrine converts it into one more brand of personalistic, or individualistic sociology. But the greatness of Sturzo is seen in the fact that, despite his acceptance of *liberum arbitrium,* he does not dissolve society into the individuals of which it is composed; he is a sociological synthetist and considers man and society as two faces of the same reality.

Caponigri continues by saying that the diverse social forms have their formal principle,[29] efficient principle and their final principle in individual consciousness. Such a statement is obviously contrary to Sturzo's insistence on the separation of sociology and philosophy. In his *Method* Sturzo explicitly denies the use of the category of formal cause and final cause. Moreover, Caponigri declares these principles to be ideal principles; once again, this is an example of the transfer of Sturzo's sociology onto the philosophical level, which is inevitable only with regard to his views on the impact of the supernatural.

The paper "The sociological theory of Don Luigi Sturzo," by Alessandro Groppoli, Professor at the University of Milano[30] is one of the best summaries of the Italian master's theory. According to Sturzo, says Groppoli, society is identical with the coexistence of a plurality of individuals cooperating for the attainment of common goals; this plurality forms a unity (tutt'uno) with the consciousnesses of the coexisting individuals; each is reflected in the consciousnesses of the others through a complicated play of actions and reactions.

The author continues by quoting Carlo Cattino's *Psicologia delle mente associate* where this statement can be found: "social consciousness is the associated consciousness of cooperating individuals; it forms an entity superior and different from the individual minds; it is an average resulting from the sentiments, ideas and wills of the individual consciousnesses." This is dangerously close to Durkheim's position stated more than 60 years ago and now entirely discarded, and is obviously not Sturzo's position.[31]

Groppoli examines carefully Sturzo's discussion of sociological laws and makes this observation on chance, a concept mentioned by Sturzo

---

[29] Why not cause?
[30] Vol. II, pp. 267 ff.
[31] Cf. Chapter IX, section 2.

only in passing: "Chance actually does not exist; it is only an illness of our minds which, being able to know only the immediate and direct causes of a phenomenon, attributes to them a significance (efficiency) superior to what they mean in reality." This statement is however acceptable only if one adheres to the interpretation of the postulate of order in its absolute meaning asserting necessary and invariant relations between all phenomena. Neither Sturzo nor the present writer believe this to be a correct scientific position.[32]

But Groppoli's thought runs in another direction. "If one does not accept a certain regularity of relations, one precludes all sociology. If neither rationality, nor the complex of environmental forces are determining factors, one cannot understand how Sturzo ascribes to sociology the task to establish laws of social phenomena."

Toward the end of his paper, Groppoli sees more light. "Laws established by sociology, without being absolute and immutable, express merely general tendencies, still presupposing a certain uniformity of relations. Were it not so, Sturzo could not have formulated the law of duality according to which civilization (civiltà) emerges from the struggle of conservative and progressive forces."

Finally, in the paper by Professor Marchello, "Sociology and the ethical judgment,"[33] Sturzo's empiric view is said to contain a reference to reason; a single fact is not understandable if not embedded in a historical and social complex in which it appears as an experience concretely human and rational. Sturzo's views warrant the possibility of an empiric (not to be confused with the physical) but non-deterministic science; on the other hand, it allows an ascent to the ethical and philosophical level. This is very much different from the rather critical views expressed by the same author in 1950 (see above section 6). Only an indirect reference in a footnote is made to that critique which, in Marchello's opinion, explicitly circumscribes the scope of the validity of sociology as an empiric science.

9. In memoriam *papers*

After Don Sturzo's death, several articles appeared in Italy devoted to the activities and works of this prodigious man. But, among the articles, one does not find many on his sociology. The commemorative

[32] N. S. Timasheff, "Order, Causality, Conjuncture" in L. Cross (ed.) *Symposium on Sociology* (1959), pp. 153 ff.

[33] E. Di Carlo, "Luigi Sturzo, sociologo," *Sociologia*, 378-80.

issue of *Sociologia Bollettino dell' Instituto Luigi Sturzo* (July-September, 1959) contains five short papers on the subject, and a similar issue of *Civitas* (April-May, 1960) contains one rather long and substantial article on rationality and history in Sturzo's sociology.

Among the contributors, we find two authors whose treatment of Sturzo's work has been reported in the preceding section, E. di Carlo and F. Battaglia.[34] For Di Carlo, Sturzo's sociological work is an excellent systematization from the historical and psychological points of view. But although historical and psychological, the sociology of the defunct master culminates in integration on the level of spirit. F. Battaglia correctly emphasizes that Sturzo wanted above all to be a sociologist. His sociology is personalistic: every society is derived from individuals, especially from the individual's spiritual essence. But Sturzo has tried to keep up with the demand of objectivity and to demonstrate the actual role of man in history. According to Battaglia, Sturzo insisted on two points, social pluralism and primacy of the individual over society. The last sentence must be read *cum grano salis*: Sturzo rejected any kind of sociological monism; however, his preference was not for plurality, but for duality; and, as shown in Chap. III, a correct reading of Sturzo's sociology results in classifying him among the synthetizing (as opposed to personalistic) sociologists, with some inclination toward personalism.

Marco D'Addio and V. Filippone[35] emphasize the derivation of Sturzo's sociology from experience accumulated through active participation in the social and political life of the Italy of his time. They do not mean that Sturzo's theory is only adapted for a particular political or social program, but that it replaces armchair philosophy and sociology by reasoning on the background of observed facts. According to D'Addio, Sturzo's historicist sociology was born of action and received more and more depth and precision on the background of action; his observations and generalizations have been conducive to the restoration of the primacy of the individual, to the confirmation of the Christian intuitition of the nature of man, and to demonstration of the proposition that religion is the moving spring of social evolution.

V. Filippino emphasizes that the synthesis "liberty-authority" represents the most conspicuous link between Sturzo the sociologist and

---

[34] F. Battaglia, "Luigi Sturzo e il pensiero sociologico," *ibid.*, 375-77.

[35] M. D'Addio, "Sociologia storicista," *Sociologia*, 389-91; V. Filippone, "Razionalità e storia nella sociologia sturziana," *Civitas*, 167-98.

Sturzo the political man. It was through participation in political society that Sturzo reached insights permitting him bluntly to deny the purely economic nature of class struggle and to assert that social crises were first of all crises of liberty. The result was the formulation of a grand style sociological theory in which rationality and history form the two poles treated by the master, not as terms in an irreconciliable opposition, but as elements between which dynamic assimilation is possible.

In G. Palladino's paper,[36] Sturzo's sociology is contemplated more from the sociophilosophical than from the truly sociological point of view. To dialectical materialism and dialectical idealism Sturzo opposed dialectical realism, of which sociological realism is one of the species. Liberty and rationality, struggle and unification constitute the four main pillars of sociological realism. Only on the foundation of such a realism was it possible to affirm the dignity of the human personality and to consider man in his two natures, individual and social.

F. Della Rocca[37] deals with the Church-State problem in the framework of Sturzian sociology. The author correctly states that for Sturzo this was one of the most important problems and ably summarizes Sturzo's main findings.[38] In unison with the majority of the Italian writers on Sturzo's sociology, Della Rocca believes that, in discussing the Church-State problem, Sturzo's historicist integralism was lifted to the level of spirituality. In the present author's opinion, while there is no doubt that although Sturzo's total thought system was eminently spiritualistic, the sociologically relevant parts of that system were not simply derived from a preconceived spiritualistic conception.[39]

10. Summary.

The findings above are not encouraging. There have been quite a few summaries of Sturzo's work, some exact, some not; and quite a few criticisms. But no work in sociology has appeared in which one could

[36] G. Palladino, "Certezze sociologiche di Luigi Sturzo," *Sociologia*, 392-406.

[37] F. Della Rocca, "Chiesa e Stato nella sociologia sturziana," *Sociologia*, 381-88.

[38] A summary of Sturzo's *Church and State* appears in Chap. I, section 4 of this volume.

[39] Cf. Beccari's statement reported in the preceding section.

see even the germ of a Sturzian school.[40] Debate with Sturzo has been conducted mainly with regard to secondary or irrelevant points, irrelevant in the meaning that the respective objections have been raised against something which Sturzo never had said. Nobody has really attempted to translate Sturzo's work into a language understandable to contemporary sociologists and then to establish what in it is actually original and at the same time worthwhile being retained. A tentative answer to the question just posed will be offered in the next chapter. To conclude this chapter, the scope of the debate with Sturzo as appearing in the literature surveyed will be summarized.

1. The most serious objection against Sturzo's treatment of social facts is that it is not sociological, but philosophical. This view has been expressed by F. Mueller, Marchello and di Carlo, while Oesterle believes that Sturzo's sociology is not so much historicist as philosophical. Di Carlo asserts moreover that, in Sturzo's hands, sociology becomes a normative science of ends and ideals.

2. To some authors Sturzo's sociology appears to be nominalist (Mueller) or individualistic (Caponigri).

3. Some authors ignore Sturzo's insistence on the sociological treatment of society and are disappointed because (in this context) Sturzo has no use for such philosophical categories as formal cause, efficient cause, final cause (Mueller, Caponigri).

4. Sturzo's peculiar use of the category of the concrete which stands for what most sociologists would call abstract has provoked attacks from two sides: Mueller believes that Sturzo's treatment of society is unduly abstract while Oesterle holds the view that Sturzo has ignored the possibility of a moderately abstract treatment of his subject matter.

5. The focal point of Sturzo's sociological theory is the identification of society with individual-social consciousness. For doing so he is taken to task by Mueller and Oesterle.

6. Closely connected with the objection above is the reproach addressed to Sturzo on the basis of an alleged overemphasis on "projection" (from the individual onto the social plane) and a correlative omission of its counterpart, "introjection," corresponding, in modern

---

[40] The monograph by Edward Vogt, "Le Leggi sociologiche," despite the fact that it appeared in the journal *Sociologia* (1958), an organ of the Instituto Luigi Sturzo in Rome, deviates from Sturzo's line in that it discusses social phenomena in terms of the four causes, which is explicitly rejected by Sturzo with respect to sociology.

sociological language, to the impact of culture on the individual; this reproach is made by Leonardi.

7. The same Leonardi considers that Sturzo has overemphasized the role of the religious factor in society.

8. Battaglia notes that Sturzo has denied the rank of a fundamental form of sociality to economics on rather weak grounds.

9. The same author disagrees with Sturzo's denial of the primacy of the political factor and with his denial of the very possibility of a true international community.

10. Oesterle has accused Sturzo of overemphasizing dynamics to the extent of ignoring static elements, in other words, of speaking of change without paying attention to that which changes.

11. Oesterle and Marchello have attacked one of Sturzo's predilected ideas, namely his "law of duality" and the exclusion of multinuclear polarization and genuine unity.

12. Sturzo's difficult language (especially the one used by his translators) and his abundant use of rare, even newly invented terms, has been regretfully noted by Kilzer and Mueller.

To almost all these objections and reproaches Sturzo has given answers summarized in this chapter; but relative to some of them, the best answers can be provided by rereading his statements in the major works; quite a few then appear to lack any foundation.

The present author does not feel it useful to recapitulate, at this place, his own statements on the particular subjects made earlier in the book. He would however like to suggest that, of the objections above, he holds more or less warranted those under Nos. 5, 8 and 11, and acknowledges the validity of the one under No. 12.

CHAPTER IX

Sturzo's Place in the General
Stream of Sociological Thought

Sturzo's Place in the General Stream of Sociological Thought

In the preceding chapters, Sturzo's sociological theory has been systematically presented on the background of an analysis of his sociologically relevant works and then confronted with other sociological theories, in two perspectives; first, Sturzo's criticism of the theories of his predecessors and contemporaries, and, second, the interpretation and criticism of his theories by other authors. There remains one last step—to locate Sturzo's sociology in the general stream of sociological thought.

This task may be introduced best by a short summary of the Italian master's sociological views restated whenever possible in terms closer to those used by his fellow sociologists, especially the American ones. The reader might find it interesting to compare this survey with "the sixteen points" in which Sturzo himself summarized his views in 1950 (see Chap. I, section 5), and with the two further summaries he offered several years later (*ibid.*, sect. 6).

1. Sturzo's sociology summarized

For Sturzo, sociology is a science of society as a totality, as given in immediate experience, not yet analyzed into sectors corresponding to the economic, political, religious, domestic and other aspects of social life; this is a translation of Sturzo's often misunderstood statement that sociology is the study of society in the concrete. Thus translated, Sturzo's view largely agrees with those dominant in contemporary sociology.[1]

[1] Cf. N. S. Timasheff, *ST,* p. 20, 23.

But Sturzo's emphasis on the study of society as a totality leads him to the assertion that the study must include the impact of the supernatural on social life. Most sociologists agree that the study of the impact of the *belief* in the supernatural must be included; but with very few exceptions they deny that propositions based on that belief, i.e. *the content of revelation*, would belong to the province of sociology. This seems to be in agreement with the principle of the division of labor in science. Therefore, in the confrontation of Sturzo's sociology with the total stream of sociological thought, Sturzo's presentation of social theory in its totality must be brought down one step, to the exploration of society on the empiric level. As shown in Chapter II, one may find in Sturzo's work a certain number of propositions vindicating this step. After all, he himself does not want to confuse sociology with philosophy. Why, then, should we incorporate elements of theology and thus produce a still greater confusion?

Sturzo's denial of the very possibility of a sociology on a level below "the total social phenomenon" which, for him, includes the impact of the supernatural on human history is based on the postulate that sociology is the only science of society in its totality (in the concrete, according to his somewhat misleading terminology). This is a counterpart of Comte's postulate that sociology, a science built up on the "positive," i.e. empiric level, was the only possible science of society. There is no reason to accept either postulate: sociology, integral for Sturzo or positive for Comte, cannot pretend to be the only science of society. At this place, the problem is not what is true but what is adequate. From this point of view, the most adequate solution is this: sociology is an empiric science of society, but cannot pretend to absorb all knowledge about society. It is more adequate because on that background a universe of discourse can be easily created among the students of society, which is impossible if either the Comtean or the Sturzian postulate is chosen.

After these necessary digressions let us return to the task of offering a summary of Sturzian sociology reduced to the empirical level.

For Sturzo, society is a plurality of individuals durably pursuing common ends and united by social or collective consciousness, which is tantamount to the coalescence of the associative components of their individual consciousnesses. The term collective consciousness is common to Sturzo and Durkheim, the sociologist whom the former treats as "scientific enemy Number One." It continues in use with Gurvitch. However the meaning is different. More about that will be said in the next section.

Sturzo's doctrine of collective consciousness is strategic for his synthetizing conception of the relationship between society and the individual, different both from sociological personalism which asserts the primacy of the individual, and sociological collectivism which ascribes primacy to society. For Sturzo, society and the individual form two aspects of the same reality: society does not exist outside of individuals, and an individual is unthinkable outside society. Today this is probably the prevailing view. It culminates in neo-systematic sociology with which Sturzo's theory will be confronted in section 3.

The individual is treated by Sturzo as a self-determining agent who, while never mechanically compelled to do or not to do something, is nevertheless conditioned in his decisions by his physical and social environment. Thus, although free, man displays a number of uniformities in his social behavior, which may be expressed as sociological laws although they are more flexible than the laws of inorganic nature.

Among the sociological laws, two are basic: 1) the law of motion toward rationality and 2) the law of a cyclic movement of social organizations from pluralism (of social nuclei) through duality toward unification and then back to a pluralism which is intrinsically unstable.

In addition to the two basic laws (Sturzo does not use the term) he formulates a number of secondary laws and sociological constants. The latter cover social phenomena which one may expect to find everywhere and at any time (except perhaps at the primeval stage of human development). Among these constants, there are "the three fundamental forms of sociality," namely the family, the polity, and religion, and an indeterminate number of secondary forms. Sturzo denies the possibility of an exhaustive enumeration because human creativeness is unbounded. Translated into common sociological language, Sturzo's forms of sociality represent *types* of which concrete societies are specimens.

Sturzo uses the concepts of interaction and relation to describe human coexistence in the framework of groups; he emphasizes a few forces, not imposed on men, but generated by them, which keep them close to each other and may therefore be called forces of cohesion;

he prefers the term "synthesis," which is somewhat confusing since it is used by him in other meanings too. The main forces of cohesion form two pairs, liberty–authority, and morality–law. Emphasis on authority, morality and law places Sturzo among the "normativists" in sociology, vs. the relationists and functionalists.[2] In one of his earlier works he unfolded ideas which might have developed into relationism; but he did not pursue this line of thought. As to functionalism, Sturzo comes close to it when he insists on the finality of human action, not simply in the meaning of *finis operantis*, but also in that of *finis operis*. This idea will be followed up in section 5.

But, after all, Sturzo is neither a normativist, nor a relationist, nor a functionalist. He is first of all a subjectivist, or psychologizing sociologist. Interesting similarities could be found between him and Russian subjectivism,[3] a school of sociology silenced and probably killed by the Communist suppression of non-conformist thought. One could also find affinities between Sturzo and Cooley, perhaps even with Lester Ward. But he differs entirely from such psychologizing sociologists as G. Tarde, W. I. Thomas, Max Weber, V. Pareto, or Talcott Parsons.

Syntheses, according to Sturzo, integrate men not only within social groups, but, by mechanisms he only briefly explored, bring about the coalescence of smaller groups into larger units. A majestic pyramid is thus constructed, beginning with small functional groups and their multi-level syntheses, on up through "total societies" (all-inclusive societies like the nation-state) and culminating in civilizations. Syntheses bind such total societies together in different ways, but in the final account they do so on the background of religious affinity. This last idea was recently rediscovered by Arnold Toynbee in volumes VIII and IX of his *Study of History*[4] while in the earlier series (I–VI) "universal religions" were treated as manifestations of the breakdown of civilizations.

The morphological (static) analysis of society is a necessary but not final step in sociological investigation. In Sturzo's words, in addition to the structural dimension, societies possess a processual, or

[2] Cf. N. S. Timasheff, "Basic Concepts of Sociology," *AJS*, vol. 58, (1952), p. 177.
[3] Cf. my *ST*, pp. 119-23.
[4] Cf. Chap. IV, fn. 14.

temporal, or dynamic dimension. This means that society as given in immediate experience cannot be understood as something stable; like everything around ourselves, it is in constant flux; "the present tense" is only a spark between the past and the future. Many elements of the past disappear without a trace; those which do not become instrumental in the structuring of the present. Sturzo never offers a systematic survey of the surviving elements, but uses examples distributed among all the elements of culture—material, ideational, esthetic and behavioral. Recall that this is a translation of Sturzo's ideas into a language not his own.

On the other hand, the future, or, more exactly, the anticipation of the future, affects the present. Man has an irresistible urge to act and to achieve, in order that the future might be better than the present. Moreover, man has to act and does act to preserve "the conquests" already made, in other words, to prevent the deterioration of the *status quo*.

The moving spring of social dynamism is rationality, one of the key concepts in Sturzian sociology. He has so much to say about rationality that to give full value to his statements and simultaneously to forestall the impression of inconsistency (which is not there) one must distinguish three levels. There is, first, personal or subjective rationality, which appears as a human faculty or capability, a faculty found in every human being. The second level is historical or social rationality, which is tantamount to what is deemed rational here and now, and is correlated with the associative aspect of human consciousness. The third level, pure or absolute rationality, is a limit to which men strive without ever being able to attain it. Here again the terminology is not Sturzian except with respect to the third or highest level, but the basis for the distinctions is clearly present in his work.

Rationality as the moving spring of the historical or social process seems at first to set Sturzo's sociology apart from the main stream in current sociology, but it really doesn't. After all, nobody doubts that innovation is reducible to invention, and that invention, though conditioned by a cultural base, is a creative act of a human being whose ability to perform such acts may very well be called rationality. Moreover, Sturzo's theorems about rationality may be easily translated into theorems about values—personal, social and human. We shall return to this idea in section 4.

Sturzo's general view of the trends of social dynamics may be called moderate progressivism. In other words, although there are setbacks and periods of stagnation, man is gradually improving his physical and social environment. Sturzo rightly makes a comparison of the earliest stages of human history on earth (insofar as we can reconstruct it) with man as he is today to be the decisive argument on this point.

Sturzo's cautious and qualified evolutionism, i.e.. the acknowledgment of certain evolutionary tendencies, and of progressivism, i.e. the acknowledgment that, throughout history, there has been a gradual improvement of the social environment in which men have to live and to work, is in full agreement with the partial but conspicuous revival of social evolutionism in our day.[5] It is noteworthy that the bulk of the ideas reported above were expressed by the Italian scholar in the early thirties, so that he could be called an early protagonist of the revival movement.

Sturzo's social dynamics is tantamount to the idea that society has a temporal dimension; just as his social morphology unfolds the idea that society has a structural dimension (this term shows up only in Sturzo's last publications, replacing the "spatial dimensions" of Method and the "three dimensions" of the earlier works). In discussing the temporal dimension, Sturzo succeeds in unifying "the total social phenomenon" (a term he does not use). To the analysis of time into three tenses, there corresponds the analysis of the "total social phenomenon" into the triad culture–social organization–social ends and ideals, in which social organization is taken to mean the organized coexistence of men in the present. And just as the social process is a synthesis of past and future in the present, so human coexistence in social organization is a synthesis of the elements of the past (culture) with elements of the future (social ends and ideals). The new horizons opened by this synthesis were outlined in Chapter III.

To conclude this survey, a few words about Sturzo's methodology must be said. Although he has written a treatise on sociological method, he has never made explicit statements about the consecutive steps leading him to the formulation of sociologically relevant propositions. A careful study of his sociological works permits us to formulate what he really does, although it is common knowledge that

[5] Cf. my ST, pp. 289-94.

statements about methodology found in an author's work may differ substantially from the methods he actually employed. The difference is approximately the same as between ideal and real patterns of behavior.

Sturzo's major field of observation is human history. Surveying it in numerous treatises and monographs, he perceives sociologically relevant facts, i.e. facts which are not strictly economic, political, religious etc., but manifest the structure and the functioning of society *in toto*. The facts do not speak for themselves; they must be interpreted and, naturally, when interpreting them, Sturzo often uses the philosophical foundation which he considers to be true, i.e. the Christian, or, more exactly, the Thomist philosophy, though he almost never makes explicit references to the author of the *Summa Theologica*. Sometimes he looks for inspiration in theology, but the vast majority of his propositions are independent of philosophical or theological premises. Participating actively in social life, he gradually accumulated a number of insights into the structure and functioning of society and masterfully used this knowledge in theory construction. One may say that in addition to the collecting of historical data, his method of gathering facts, was the method of participant observation of the great struggles of our time.

These facts were then accumulated and interpreted and compared, and those constant or recurring were singled out and used to formulate his theorems. This of course is abstraction, a procedure which he explicitly acknowledges, distinguishing it from abstractionism, i.e. the substitution of one-sided abstractions for the wholes from which they have been derived. The individual abstractions are then submitted to synthesis, i.e. unification on the basis of their logical affinity.

Unfortunately, Sturzo does not explain why he chose particular historical facts for classification and interpretation. Most commonly he does not even spell out the facts considered. Sometimes he simply asserts that nobody could mention an historical fact which would contradict his generalization. This is probably true because of the cautious character of his generalizations—his sociological laws are flexible and his sociological constants are declared to be susceptible of exceptions. It remains to be seen whether his generalizations are the best possible or at least the best available ones about human life in society.

2. *Collective consciousness*

In the preceding summary of Sturzo's theory, four points were reserved for further investigation. The first of them is Sturzo's theory of individual-social consciousness, one of the key concepts in Sturzo's sociology. His insistence on it is rather puzzling since, for him, Durkheim with his collective consciousness was scientific enemy No. 1. Of course, the meaning of social consciousness in Durkheim's and Sturzo's works is quite different. To establish in what the difference really consists, we must survey Durkheim's views on the subject. It is well known that Durkheim's conception of collective consciousness varied in time. Out of these conceptions, the earliest one, appearing in *Division du Travail Social* (1893), presents the best term for comparison with Sturzo since the later interpretations express Durkheim's thesis that the interpenetration and fusion of individual minds generates a psychic unit *sui generis*, something like a supermind distinct from the individual minds and exerting on them an almost irresistible pressure. It is true that many of Durkheim's interpreters deny that he was a "sociological realist" (sociological collectivist, in the terminology of this volume). But this denial simply ignores Durkheim's most explicit statements to the contrary, such as the following ones: "Above and outside the conscient being which is 'me' and above and outside conscious beings which are other individuals, there exists only one conscient being, empirical[ly knowable] and observable, which is society."[6] Or else: "In aggregating, interpenetrating, fusing, individual minds engender a psychic being forming a psychic individuality of a new kind. . . . Between individual and collective psychology, there is the same discontinuity as between biology on the one hand and physics and chemistry on the other."[7] Or: "Being placed outside and above the individuals, [the collective consciousness] sees things in their permanent and essential aspects."[8] Sorokin is right when summarizing Durkheim's ideas as being based on the admission of the reality of social mind, collective representations and a society inde-

[6] *Education morale*, course of lectures delivered in 1903-4, published in 1938, p. 68.
[7] *Règles de la methode sociologique*, 1895, English translation, pp. 127-8.
[8] *Les formes élémentaires de la vie religieuse, 1911*, English translation, p. 474.

pendent of, and different from, the reality of individual minds, representations and psychology.[9]

Such ideas are diametrically opposed to those of Sturzo. Sturzo never doubted that there is nothing in society which is not present in, and does not emanate from, individuals.

But Durkheim's doctrine expressed in *Division du Travail Social* can not be so easily dismissed. In that work, collective consciousness is identified with the sum total of beliefs and sentiments common to the average of the members of a society. Although collective consciousness lives in and through individuals, it possesses a distinct reality and is endowed with its proper life. Since collective consciousness is the function of the similarity of the individuals forming a society, it is stronger the greater the similarity. In consequence, it is strongest in primitive society and declines with the division of social labor, i.e. the differentiation of individuals making them less and less similar.

This is of course a more moderate version of the theory of "group mind" which, in different versions, was current in the earlier period of the development of sociological theory. Incidentally, in Eubanks' *Concepts of Sociology*[10] which is a kind of digest of the early American literature on sociological theory, the bibliography on "Group Mind" occupies two pages. At the present time, the theory of group mind, even in the weaker form of collective consciousness, is commonly rejected, except by some followers of Durkheim and Sturzo.

It is noteworthy that in 1938, three years after the appearance of Sturzo's *Essai de sociologie*, G. Gurvitch, though opposing many aspects of Durkheim's doctrine on the subject in a work entitled exactly the same as the French version of Sturzo's work, asserted that the idea of collective consciousness was sound and even basic for sociology.[11] Collective consciousness, he says, is never transcendent, but always immanent, a position which is that of Durkheim in *Division*; he also says that consciousness is founded on "the reciprocity of perspectives between individual and collective mind (psychism) which are merely two abstract expressions of the concrete totality of mental

[9] Sorokin, *CST*, 1928, p. 465.

[10] Eubank, *Concepts of Sociology*, 1931, pp. 493-5.

[11] *Essais de sociologie*, 1938. The major part of the volume is devoted to the discussion of Durkheim's theory; this discussion is the best ever written on Durkheim. The statements cited in the text appear on pp. 24-6.

phenomena," an idea borrowed from Theodor Litt, *Individuum und Gesellschaft* (1919). Collective consciousness forms the deepest and most immediately given level of social reality. Collective consciousness must be distinguished from communication between human minds through symbols which gives rise to inter-mental phenomena, not to collective consciousness. Contrary to the prevailing opinion, human minds are not closed to each other. Through a kind of collective intuition, they can partly fuse. The distinction between collective consciousness and inter-mental phenomena is expressed in the difference between the pronoun "We" and the pronouns "I" and "Thou."

In *La vocation actuelle de la sociologie* (1950) which, to a large extent, is an amplification and improvement of his *Essais*, Gurvitch makes the reciprocity of perspectives trifold, extending between *Me, Thou* and *We*. He continues to insist on collective consciousness but is not quite clear as to whether it extends to phenomena covered by the term We, or also to those covered by the term *Thou*. At any rate, he insists that collective consciousness is in each of us, and each of us is in collective consciousness (pp. 89-90). In the flux of psychic life there is neither purely individual, nor inter-individual, nor collective consciousness, but only accentuation of one of these (p. 30). But collective consciousness is still given the highest importance. Only interpretation in terms of collective symbols and ideas yields true understanding of social phenomena. When a sociologist affirms the collective character of certain ideas and values he simply asserts that these ideas and values cannot be experienced without collective actions. The sociologist does not explore the validity of values. The only fact which interests him is the fact that there is a level of ideas and values which is influenced by the total social phenomenon, which, in its turn, influences the latter (pp. 86, 88). Asserting these reciprocal influences, Gurvitch parts ways with Durkheim.

It is noteworthy that in his latest works (especially *Determinismes sociaux*, 1957) Gurvitch substantially decreases the significance of "the reciprocity of perspectives." According to a fine observation by R. Toulemont,[12] instead of being a key to the depths of the total social phenomenon, the reciprocity of perspectives now connotes only the parallelism of society and the individual.

Now we can explore this problem: What has Sturzo's doctrine

[12] R. Tourlemont, *Sociologie et pluralisme dialectique*, 1955.

(formulated forty years later) in common with Durkheim's master-work, the *Division of Social Labor* and also with Gurvitch's treatment of the subject, begun approximately at the same time as Sturzo's?

In some regards, Sturzo is closer to early Durkheim than to Gurvitch. First of all, both Durkheim and Sturzo lay stress on beliefs and sentiments common to the average members of a society, the common elements in the consciousness of group members essential for their "groupness." Gurvitch does not share this proposition: for him, collective consciousness is not tantamount to common elements in the consciousness as of group members; these are intermental phenomena, while collective consciousness is tantamount to a partial fusion of minds—a statement in the style of Durkheim's later works.

Second, common to early Durkheim and Sturzo is the proposition that the elements common to the group members exist only in the consciousnesses of the individuals forming the group, while the extreme form of the group mind theory[13] considers that common beliefs and sentiments exist independently, whether they are or are not really thought or felt by any individuals. Gurvitch does not go so far, since, in clear contradistinction to Durkheim's later works he asserts that collective consciousness is immanent to individual consciousness (so-to-speak, is inside it) while individual consciousness is immanent to the later. This probably does not differ from Sturzo's views, although they are expressed in different terms.

Third, according both to Sturzo and Durkheim, the common beliefs and sentiments exert a strong influence on the conduct of group members. In Sturzo's theory they do this as part of the social environment of the individual and also as an inseparable part of the consciousness of any particular group member. In his earlier works, Gurvitch ascribed a reality to collective consciousness different from that of the individual minds (despite the mechanism of reciprocal perspectives). In his later works, there is no longer much discussion of collective consciousness in that particular meaning; therefore, he comes closer to Sturzo in these works than he had in his earlier ones.

The most important difference between Sturzo and the earlier position of Durkheim is this: for Sturzo, those elements of individual-social consciousness *common* to the majority or to the totality of a

---

[13] A modality of sociological collectivism (in the terminology of this volume, cf. Chap. III, section 2).

group do not make up a *separate* unit or system endowed with an existence of its own, (although Sturzo is sometimes wont to describe them with the word "essence" [M. 76]). Here we see that the term "individual-social consciousness" is symptomatic of the context of Sturzo's whole doctrine, whereas, for Durkheim, even in his original system, these elements (which live only in and through the individuals) are said, rather inconsistently, to form a system endowed with life of its own. According to Durkheim, this proposition is corroborated by the fact that the elements survive the individuals who have been their bearers. This of course is true, but only in the case of deceased individuals who transmitted their beliefs and sentiments to their survivors. The difference is perhaps not so sharp on the empirical as on the philosophical level. The actual problem is—what is reality? More exactly—does a system consisting of interrelated parts have any reality other than the sum total of its constituent parts?

It is important to note that, when trying to grasp the reality of the collective mind (collective consciousness) Durkheim strove desperately for the solution of the problem of the nature of culture. All his visions of collective mind were proto-visions of culture, a notion well known, but never systematically explored by Durkheim. The same is at least partly true of Sturzo, since the collective component of his individual-social consciousness has approximately the same referent as the term culture. And, finally, the same is true of Gurvitch, the third member of the scholarly trio, who does not submit culture to systematic analysis and synthesis, despite the fact that he has written a number of works devoted to particular aspects of what he calls "the sociology of the spirit" which commonly denotes "cultural sociology," and the sociologies of religion, law or knowledge.

Since the time when Durkheim, Sturzo, and Gurvitch wrote, a great but peaceful revolution has taken place in sociology and cultural anthropology: from it has emerged the view that men are united in societies not by the identity of their *states of consciousness*, but by the identity of their *patterns* of thinking, feeling and acting. These patterns are engendered by interacting men, and, through the process of socialization, are then internalized in the individual group members, becoming part of their personalities, working not from without, but from within.

After this tremendous revolution in the conceptual scheme of soci-

ology, effected through the discovery of culture as one of its root
concepts, shall we discard Sturzo's treatment of individual-social
consciousness? Not at all. An attempt will be made to show that,
in a somewhat modified form and couched in modified terms, Sturzo's
doctrine could contribute greatly to the solution of the difficult problem
of the reality of social groups. Despite all differences in terminology
and emphasis, many authors agree that the reality of a social group
is immediately given and experienced in human interactions. But then
the problem arises: what happens when interaction is discontinued?
Does the group cease to exist altogether? Or is its existence intermittent, flashing on and off like a traffic light? Does a family, for
instance, cease to exist when all its members are asleep, or is a college
non-existent when the students and faculty are off the campus during
vacations?

The questions answer themselves. Clearly we must look beyond
interaction to something that endures even when group members are
not interacting. What remains are attitudes, learned tendencies to
behave in specified ways under specified conditions and values, i.e.
the relatively stable objects of orientation of the attitudes.

Attitudes are relatively stable biopsychic phenomena, while interactions by necessity are intermittent, since at any given moment, men
can carry out only a limited number of actions (ergo, interactions).

The relative stability of attitudes is almost self-evident on the
psychic level; when man acquires an attitude, an infinitesimal change
takes place in his psychic dispositions. Recent advances in the knowledge of brain physiology point in the same direction. According to
Dr. W. Penfield, a leading authority on the subject, a mechanism
seems to exist which permanently records the stream of consciousness,
preserves it in detail and, under certain conditions, especially when
similar impressions are repeated, plays the record at a later time in a
manner analogous to the replaying of a wire or tape recorder.[14] It is
noteworthy that a specialist in brain physiology uses the term "stream
of consciousness" which so many sociologists try to discard. It is
obvious that the mechanism of recording is the foundation upon which
stable behavior tendencies can be built. As shown above, these antici-
patory adjustments of body and mind,—i.e. the attitudes, are not

[14] Communication at a meeting of the National Academy of Science, Nov.
1957; cf. *New York Times*, Nov. 18, p. 38, and Nov. 24, sect. 4, p. 11.

intermittent; the group member is ready to act according to the direction of his attitude until he changes it or loses it.

The continuous reality of the social group is founded, then, not upon intermittent interaction, but upon the lasting possession by its members of interrelated attitudes which initiate, under specific situations, interactions that are appropriate to membership in a particular group.

Attitudes bring us closer than interactions to an understanding of the reality of social groups. Still more understanding can be reached if we apply to the theory of attitudes, especially of interrelated attitudes, some propositions appearing in Sturzo's doctrine on individual-social consciousness.

First of all, attitudes, as bio-psychic phenomena, can be predicated only of individuals: here is individual X and these are his attitudes; there is individual Y and those are his attitudes, maybe similar or even identical with those of X, but nevertheless attitudes of Y.

Second, the attitudes of the individual can be divided into self-oriented (corresponding to the individual component of consciousness in Sturzo's terminology) and other-oriented (corresponding to the associative component); among this second class of attitudes perhaps a subclass of group-oriented attitudes could be formed. The other-oriented attitudes are most specifically expressed in the sentiment of belonging together (the "we-feeling").

Third, these other-oriented attitudes are by necessity externalized and communicated; in other words, they pass from one stream of consciousness to another. This passage is multiform, simultaneous and continuous.

Fourth, the result is an actual convergence of ideas, attitudes and values. A compound is thus formed which Sturzo calls collective consciousness and for which other sociologists have no generic term; relative to larger groups (especially ethnic groups and their divisions and subdivisions) we apply the terms culture and subculture; but we lack any term to designate the concretization of culture on the level of functional groups, such as the family, the school, the parish, the business corporation, the State etc. The Gluecks, in *Unravelling Juvenile Delinquency*,[15] speak of "culture under the roof" to designate the specific content of inter-mental processes crystallized in each

[15] S. and E. Glueck, *Unraveling Juvenile Delinquency*, 1938.

particular family; however, the expression is somewhat cumbersome.

Fifth, the converging other-oriented attitudes do not cease to be parts of the streams of consciousness of the individuals forming the group. They preserve their biopsychic reality and also the double nature predicated by Sturzo of individual-social consciousness. This is only a sketch of a theory of attitudes which could be unfolded on the foundation of Sturzian ideas, an enterprise which seems to be very promising.

A conspicuous advantage of Sturzo's treatment of what we call culture is his insistence on the fact that the collective component of consciousness (= culture) is real both on the individual and collective levels, while for many contemporary sociologists culture is a kind of abstraction, the product of a thought process originating in observation of recurring patterns of actions performed by members of a social group.[16] The incorporation of these Sturzian ideas into the present day theory of culture could liberate it from being a specimen of that abstractionism which Sturzo so justly condemns. Moreover, this would assign to culture a well determined place in the total social phenomenon which thereby would cease to appear as a *mixtum compositum* of reality and abstraction unfit for integration into a theoretical system.

But Sturzo's ideas must be translated into the language of modern sociology to fit the contemporary theory of culture as a system of patterns of thinking, feeling and acting. However, we could abandon the awkward term "pattern," and, following Sorokin, replace it by the term "norm," which better conveys the idea of the oughtness of conforming conduct. These norms are embodied in the attitudes and interactions of the individuals, forming a specified society, large or small, and are therefore "real." Since attitudes and norms are items in the streams of consciousness, one sees that, although the Sturzian terminology could be modified, the quintessence of his thought about the reality of social groups could be maintained and elaborated.

3. Sturzo and neo-systematic sociology

In the preceding discussion the term group has been used and that of system avoided, because Sturzo has explicitly rejected the few speci-

[16] Cf. the mordant remarks of D. Bidney, *Theoretical Anthropology*, 1953, pp. 153.

mens of neo-systematic sociology with which he was familiar. The next problem to be discussed will be this one: is there in neo-systematic sociology anything really incompatible with the Sturzian thought system and, if there is not, could not Sturzo's sociology bring about some refinement in the neo-systematic theory of society?

But a moment's pause. Is this not a preposterous idea? Sturzo studied Pareto, the spiritual father of the trend, but nowhere in his work does he even mention Pareto's famous theorem that society is a system in dynamic equilibrium. He met a modality of the neo-systematic approach to sociology in the work of Hauriou, one of the French institutionalists, and bluntly rejected it because it super-imposed society on the individuals as something distinct from them.

There is in Sturzo's work a passage which, when carefully explored, suggests that Sturzo could easily and profitably have incorporated the notion of system and all that it implies. In *Spiritual Problems* he states: "Our knowledge turns upon reality. . . . But to know is nothing but to systematize. There can be no knowledge of a fact or datum that cannot be brought into a system. . . . Only through finding place in a system does a fact or datum become knowledge" (p. 9).

Had Sturzo spoken of ideas (for example, those forming the Platonic or Hegelian philosophy), this would have been inconsequential. But he speaks of knowledge of facts and does not exclude social facts. He asserts that to be realistic, knowledge of facts must be systematic, or else there is no knowledge. In other words, knowledge must be expressed in terms of concepts and these concepts must form a system.

At this place one may introduce an auxiliary proposition, namely: concepts representing elements of reality (and Sturzo is emphatically a realist, abhorring ideas void of referents in reality) may form a system only if the segments of reality themselves have a systematic structure, i.e. form wholes consisting of interdependent parts. This postulate is the very foundation of the whole procedure of scientific conceptualization: facts are conceptualized according to their nature; the concepts are submitted to logical operations such as comparison, classification, induction, deduction, synthesis and so on. The final result is more or less explicitly reconverted to the level of reality (or of referents).[17] In other words, what has been found to be true by

---

[17] The hypothetical statements about reality are then submitted to verification by confrontation with facts.

manipulating concepts is asserted to be true of reality. Whether this is or is not the case, can and must be verified by confronting theoretical results with facts. What interests us at this place is the proposition: if concepts derived from facts can be submitted to systematic synthesis (and this is what Sturzo means in the quotation above), the segment of reality under study has systematic structure.

In asserting that a plurality of objects forms a system, one does not postulate a reality standing apart from that of the particular objects. The systematic sociologist asserts only that the reality under study is a whole consisting of interdependent parts. We can speak, in systematic terms, of a mechanical system, e.g. of an automobile or of celestial bodies. Thereby we do not assert that we have discovered two realities: one of a car and another tantamount to the sum total of the parts, say, the wheels, the motor, the carburetor and so forth; or one consisting of the central body, the planets and their satellites, and another corresponding to the whole. We assert only that the structure of reality under study is such that it consists of individual parts, plus the relations which make them a whole.

The same is true of the systematic view of organism or society. A systematic sociologist does not discover a substance different from, and superior to, the individuals. He asserts only that the segment of reality chosen for observation and analysis has a systematic structure. The reality of a system differs from the reality of the parts taken one by one in that the former covers not only the reality of the parts but also their relations, without hypostasizing or reifying them.

Sturzo's adverse attitude to neo-systematic sociology seems to be based on the opposite assumption, namely on the assumption that it ascribes to the systems (wholes) a reality independent of the parts. This is not so of the writings of the majority of neo-systematists.

Systematic structure is structure of so high a level that the relationships between the elements[18] may be most diversified, but not so diverse that they go beyond the trait contained in the definition, namely, that the parts observable in a segment of reality chosen for exploration are interrelated or interdependent. What this interdependence of social systems consists of is a problem which has not yet found a commonly accepted solution. Here again Sturzian ideas could

[18] Each part with each other part, or each part with the sum total of the parts which is covered by the term "the whole," although, strictly speaking, the latter includes also the part under comparison.

help. Before unfolding some tentative ideas on the subject, let us state that Sturzo's rejection of the two specimens of that sociology with which he was familiar could be interpreted only as the rejection of these particular specimens. Hauriou's views, based on Platonic idealism, could not appeal to Sturzo because they belong to the "idealistic sociology" which he hated; and MacIver's statement, appearing in a book published in 1933 was in the style of relationism, an approach to the basic concepts of sociology tried by Sturzo in *International Community*, but later on rejected in favor of moderate normativism combined with a psychologizing approach. He never had the opportunity to formulate his opinion about later, more typical specimens of neo-systematic sociology.

In an earlier section of this Chapter we have brought the reality of social groups—we will now use the term "system"—down to the level of norms. Let us dig deeper. The clusters of norms which form culture, subculture, institution, may emerge and endure only on the foundation of definite bonds between group members. The bonds are obviously mental; they are in the minds of the individual members and of outside observers and are tantamount to the awareness and feeling of the individuals of belonging to others, accompanied by the awareness and feeling of the fact that others somehow belong to them. The content of the awareness varies depending on the type of social groups (social forms, in Sturzian terminology). The bond may be marital, or of filiation, or of selective affinity (in friendship groups), of cultural affinity (in ethnic groups), of functional affinity (in economic organizations, schools, and elsewhere), even of compulsion (partly so in the State). The feeling is always the same; it is well expressed in the term "we-feeling" differentiating real social groups (systems) from nominal groups or categories. What is subject to variation, is its intensity, depending on the type of the group and on the personality type of the individuals involved.

If we accept the statements above, we may accomplish a task to which great importance was ascribed by the late Italian master: in place of abstract schemes or perhaps behind these schemes, we perceive living and tangible reality.

But why should we insist on the combination of Sturzian with neo-systematic sociology? Because the advantages of a systematic view of sociology are great. It is instrumental in the unification of sociological knowledge which suffers badly from being scattered, i.e. appearing in unrelated terms. The sociological specialties of which Sturzo is somewhat skeptical may receive full meaning only through systematic synthesis.

There is another, still greater advantage of a systematic treatment of sociology invigorated by the infusion of some Sturzian ideas. If the reasoning above is accepted, culture appears to possess the same kind of reality as the social system: the converging attitudes of group members are manifested both in the identity or similarity of shared norms, and in durably recurring specified interactions. Thus the reality of culture is shown to be of the same kind as the reality of a social system, and the basic triad of modern sociology, society, culture, personality, appears to be homogeneous, whereas in the view of many sociologists and cultural anthropologists culture is an abstraction, a mental construct which obviously cannot form a system together with the concrete social system and the real personality.

As has been mentioned in the preceding section, the inner structure of the great triad is illuminated by another phase of Sturzian sociology, discussed *a propos* of his theory of the temporal dimension of society. According to Sturzo, social organization (manifested in the existence and operation of social systems) may be conceived as a synthesis of culture as a legacy of the past, and man's irresistible urge to act in view of a better future. This urge is an actualization of the creative capacity of the individuals (which corresponds to one of the phases of Sturzian rationality). A complete integration of systematic sociology can be thus achieved.

4. Sturzo's rationality and the theory of values

Let us now shift to Sturzo's doctrine of rationality, one more key concept in his sociology. As explained above, the term rationality (with which Sturzo was never satisfied) connotes three things: on the personal level, a human capacity to discern between good and evil, true and false, and an inclination to act under the impact of this distinction. On the social and historical level, rationality is tantamount to what is rational or deemed rational here and now and is correlated with the associative aspect of human consciousness. On the third level, rationality is a limit toward which men strive without being able to attain it completely.

Explanations in terms of human capacities or faculties—(this is what Sturzo is doing when speaking of rationality on the personal level)—may be understood as a return from the positive (empirical) to the metaphysical stage of knowledge, to use Comte's terminology. Sorokin vigorously attacks such explanations. According to him, they are tantamount to reasoning in a circle. Observing behavior, we infer the existence of specified capacities which we then plant into man, and finally declare that an action under study is fully explained by reference to the capacity.[19] Sorokin's objection is fully valid when addressed to paired or alternative capacities (instincts) which were prominent in social psychology some 50 years ago; then, for every action there was a verbal explanation in terms of one of the alternatives (e.g. love—hatred); but the real question remained unsolved—why just this, and not the antagonistic capacity was operative in the concrete case. But Sorokin's objection is hardly valid with respect to explanations in terms of traits expressing constantly present causal tendencies.

In any case, it is a fact that contemporary sociologists *do* use the procedure just described, modifying it to eliminate the vicious circle. Thus, for instance P. Lazarsfeld[20] mentions as valid such traits as "honesty of men" or "exclusiveness of a school." "We are accustomed," he says, "to distinguish traits as more permanent dispositions in contrast to particular behavioral episodes; on the collective level, the same relation exists. The traits of collectives are more permanent relations and prevailing beliefs as compared with occupational performances, decisions, or movements of a group." Consequently, "the explanation of variations and differences consists of a vaguely conceived underlying or latent property in regard to which people or collectivities differ."

This is exactly what Sturzo is doing: he interprets human behavior by reference to a property common to all men and all actions (rationality in the personal meaning) and explains the variations of behavior by differences between the concrete answers to the question—what is rational. Semi-rationality and pseudo-rationality which Sturzo often

[19] Sorokin, *CST.*, pp. 615, 646.
[20] P. Lazarsfeld, "Problems of Methods," In R. Merton (editor), *Sociology Today*, 1959, pp. 47-8.

mentions, pertain to the levels of rationality which extend beyond the person: an action which cannot but be personally rational may be pseudo-rational when standards beyond the person are applied.

What Sturzo explains in terms of rationality, contemporary sociologists interpret in terms of value. The entrance of that concept into sociology has been almost surreptitious, but now it seems to be generally accepted. W. H. Werkmeister, one of the contributors to a recent symposium on sociology, (edited by L. Gross), says: "Explanation and prediction in the social sciences are impossible without reference to the basic value commitments of those involved" (p. 499).[21] Another contributor to the same symposium, A. Edel, acknowledges the fact of the wide use of the value concept and expresses his regret about the turn in sociological theory in these words: "Norms and values may function as a last refuge or surrogate of spirit, in the sense in which the older dualistic philosophers used it as a mode of explanation" (p. 191). He concedes that it is too late to drop the concept of value,[22] a curious statement indeed: in science, it is never too late to correct an error or to discard an erroneous view. His guess about the "last refuge" corroborates the hypothesis that, in building up the value theory, contemporary sociologists try to restate in empiric terms certain truths which Sturzo has discussed under the label of rationality.

Just as in Sturzo's doctrine of rationality, in the contemporary value theory one may discover a trichotomy. There are, first, personal values which we may establish by observation of an individual's predominant, perhaps even constant choices. We may assume that the recurrence of specified choices is a sufficient ground (reason) for the assumption that there exists a causal tendency of agents of type X to make, under conditions Y, choices of the type Z. The inference may not be fully warranted but still possesses a reasonable degree of probability (plausibility). Logically it is then permissible to assume that it belongs to the nature of agents of type X to effect Z; the particular aspects of the nature of X are however his traits (properties or faculties).

[21] W. H. Werkmeister, "Theory Construction and the problem of objectivity," p. 499.

[22] A. Edel, "The Concept of Level in Social Theory," pp. 191-2.

That constant causal tendency, located in the individual, may be defined as the capacity and inclination to make choices according to more or less stable criteria, which may be utilitarian, logical, ethical or esthetic. This is the trait called personal or inner rationality in Sturzo's work. In contemporary sociology the trait remains nameless while the products of the trait are called values.

Personal traits or capacities interest a sociologist only if they are more or less consistently recurring in individuals forming social groups. On the basis of observation and comparison of the value systems of individuals we are able to establish social values, in the sense of their prevalence in the choices made by the group members. Repeating the reasoning above, we may ascribe to the social group (as a system) the capacity or trait to direct toward uniformity the development of personal value systems. The content of socially and culturally conditioned criteria of choice may be identified with the sum total of behavior patterns which, here and now, are considered most adequate, again, from the utilitarian, logical, ethical or esthetic points of view. Here we meet Sturzo's rationality on the historical or social level.

Since the operation of selection and comparison may be repeated on several levels, social values on different levels could be identified. Again, the systems of social values can be compared. When comparison is carried out on the highest level involving states, ethnic groups, even civilizations (in Toynbee's and Sturzo's meaning of the term) we find a few common elements, mainly among logical and ethical criteria. The values thus selected can be called human values. The concept partly corresponds to Sturzo's absolute rationality. On the purely empiric level, the counterpart to Sturzo's absolute rationality would be the postulate of a hard-core value system, the gradual acceptance of which by men is a functional prerequisite of tolerable conditions of life in society.

Contemporary sociology will hardly accept Sturzo's terminology; the concept of value is there to stay. But a very important idea could and should be borrowed from the Sturzian doctrine on rationality, namely the dynamic aspect of what Sturzo calls rationality (at least on the personal and social levels). As already stated, no ready terminology is available. Tentatively we could speak of the value producing trait of individuals and of the value unifying trait of social groups. Since these traits are dynamic, their products, the values, must be dynamic also. Modern sociology often emphasizes "changing values" but in general is unaware of the fact that values as such are urges to action and consequently to change, statements reducible to Sturzo's doctrine on rationality. In this way, an important link between the theory of values and the theory of sociocultural change could be established.

5. Social finalism

To conclude this survey of those among Sturzo's contributions which may open new perspectives in the development of sociological theory, let us emphasize some aspects of his "social finalism." Of course, the theory of rationality belongs to this, but does not exhaust the subject.

First of all, let us locate the place of the doctrine of finality in his sociological theory. The finalistic aspect of society is expressed in the formula "society is organico-finalistic." The first attribute mentioned in this formula points to the fact that society is essentially organized—Sturzo uses the term organization in a rather broad meaning and does not distinguish between organized and unorganized groups. What is denoted as organization in a formula appearing in an earlier work, *The Inner Laws*, appears in one of the last works of the master as society's structural dimension juxtaposed with the temporal dimension. Consequently, society is asserted to possess three dimensions—temporal, structural-organizational and finalistic. If, considering the temporal dimension, we concentrate on the past, or more exactly, on the impact of the past on the present and, through it, on the future, we encounter culture. The triad culture—organization—finalism (i.e. ends and ideals) reappears once again; as we know, this is the triad into which, according to the present author's interpretation of Sturzo's theory, the total social phenomenon may be analyzed *prima facie*. Consequently, the study of social finalism must form one of the main divisions of sociological theory.

Relative to man's activity, Sturzo, like the functionalists, poses the question "what for"—a question badly neglected by many earlier sociologists and still considered non-scientific by large groups of our contemporaries. Sturzo poses this question because, for him, human nature, by inner necessity, involves finality (this is hardly ever denied by anyone except perhaps extreme behaviorists), and finality is an expression of rationality belonging to the central core of human nature. Projected onto the social plane, this finality becomes social finality which, in accordance with Sturzo's sociological synthetism, does not make it independent of, or imposed on, individuals in the pursuit of their ends: social ends are the interrelated and shared ends of individuals forming a society.

On the contrary, for the functionalists, social finalism (in the meaning of *finis operis*) is completely detached from the personal ends of the group members; there may or may not be conformity between personal ends and the social function. Their finalism is expressed in sets of empirically grounded propositions answering the question—what does this or that activity (carried out in the framework of a group) contribute to the survival and eventually the development of the group, or of society-at-large? The sociologists have taken over this procedure from biology and cultural anthropology, two fields where it proved to be very fruitful; however imitation is not tantamount to logical derivation; the sociologists could have arrived at functionalism even if it were not used in biology and anthropology.

The functionalists do not ascribe value to survival—their sociology is, of course, "value-less." Survival is taken for granted, as a convenient starting point of explication. The individual propositions thus arrived at may be logically constructed as hypothetical propositions reading as follows: If a group is to survive and develop, conditions A, B, and C must be met."[23] Just as functionalists in biology may discuss *sine ira e studio* the survival conditions of mosquitoes, parasites and other nuisances, functional sociologists may, and actually do, discuss the survival conditions of criminal gangs, party machines, subversive groups and so on. Sturzo would not follow suit. For him the postulate of survival has meaning only relative to "true societies"[24]; only those societies must survive which ought to. Pseudo-societies, i.e. pluralities of men pursuing specified and common ends incompatible with the common ends of "total society" must not and should not survive.

It is obvious that the functional sociologists do not believe that "pseudo-societies" (in the meaning just defined) ought to exist; they

[23] These conditions are usually denoted as functional prerequisites.
[24] In the meaning explained in Chapter III, section 1.

simply do not pose the question of oughtness. It is also obvious that it is worthwhile to explore the conditions of survival even relative to "pseudo-societies," since knowledge of such conditions is essential for drawing up programs aimed at their removal; e.g., knowledge of the conditions fostering the survival of organized crime is necessary for the purpose of rationally combating it. It is also obvious that the conditions of survival of social groups whose members indulge in deviant behavior (from the point of view of society-at-large) may differ from those of social groups integrated into the total social order. In consequence, Sturzo's distinction between societies and pseudo-societies (perhaps with change in terminology) could lead to a fruitful line of exploration in the functional style.

Summing up, we can say: Sturzo invites us to resolve an objective function into a composition of forces represented by a multitude of activities each of which may be interpreted according to the scheme of individual means and ends. Whenever we do so, we are on the level of meaningful interpretation, of Max Weber's *verstehen*.

Recently, Karl Mannheim has suggested that the functional approach could replace the Weberian *verstehen*.[25] Sturzo's work allows us to offer another more satisfactory solution because he discusses social phenomena from three points of view: 1) causality (rather probability, since his sociological laws are "flexible"); 2) the meaning of human actions in society for the actors (*finis operantis*, Weberian *verstehen*); and 3) the significance of human actions in society for the survival and development of the latter (*finis operis*).

Since the major part of Sturzo's functional statements have appeared in *Essai de sociologie* (1935), while, in the main stream of sociology, works in the functional style (at least on the level of theory) belong rather to the 40's and 50's, Sturzo can be considered as one of the early protagonists, or perhaps, "revivers"[26] of functionalism.

6. Conclusions

In conclusion, one may say: A survey of Sturzo's sociological theory and the confrontation of some parts of the theory with modern socio-

[25] K. Mannheim, *Essays on the Sociology of Culture*, 1956, pp. 75-77 and my *ST*, p. 275.

[26] The term "reviver" is used because, after all, the program of functionalism was traced by Durkheim in 1893.

logical thought allows one to contend that he has made important contributions to sociological theory on the highest level. He has masterfully unfolded that particularly difficult approach to the understanding of society which has been here called sociological synthetism or harmonism. His theory of individual-social consciousness was an anticipation of the modern theory of culture as one of the elements of the triad society–culture–personality, forming "the total social phenomenon," and offering a solid background for the integration of the elements of the triad. Another triad, culture–social organization–social finalism, presents great advantages for the construction of a theoretical system of Sociology on the highest level. Sturzo's theory of rationality was an anticipation of the later development of the value theory. His presentation of the historical process under the impact of rationality was an anticipation of the revival of moderate evolutionism.

Of course, a fair judgment about the significance of Sturzo's contributions can be made only if they are confronted with the state of sociology in the middle thirties when his meditations were objectified in *Essai de sociologie*. But even if one compares Sturzo's masterwork in sociology with the state of sociology today, the judgment should not be that it is obsolete and superseded by more recent theories. As shown in this Chapter, some of Sturzo's contributions may be appraised as anticipations of many recent and important developments in sociology and as indicators for ways of further refinement and integration.

Nevertheless, it cannot be expected that a new Sturzian school of sociology would ever emerge. Our time is no longer propitious to the formation of new schools. The present and the immediate future belong to a movement of convergence in sociological theory.[27] The admirers of Sturzo's work should not stay apart. They should join the mainstream and, by their contributions, prove that it is worth while to know and to use the ideas of the great Italian master. In this way, they might help those who are not satisfied with the superficial propositions, so abundant in sociology, which often put information in the place of knowledge and understanding.

Recently, in a thoughtful paper,[28] John Donovan has expressed the idea that modern sociology is split between two trends, the natural

[27] Cf. my *ST*, pp. 192, 303-8.
[28] John Donovan, "New Directions in Sociology," *ACSR*, vol. 20, (1959), pp. 2-14.

science trend and the humanistic. Of course, the difference is only in emphasis; both recognize the necessity of understanding social phenomena on the levels both of causality and of meaning. Sturzo's work is one of the noblest and most brilliant contributions to humanistic sociology. The great master is dead; but his legacy could and should inspire many among the younger generation of sociologists to formulate a really humanistic theory of society, incorporating all the progress made in our science during the past two decades.

Table of Concordance

Between the English version (E) and
Italian version (I) of Sturzo's *Società*

E	I	E	I	E	I	E	I
XI	3	15	42–43	53	80	91	117–18
XII	4	16	43–44	54	80–81	92	118–19
XIII	4–5	17	44–45	55	81–82	93	119–20
XIV	5–6	18	45–46	56	82–83	94	120–21
XV	6–7	19	46–47	57	83–84	95	122–23
XVI	7–8	20	47–48	58	84–85	96	123–24
XVII	8–9	21	48–49	59	85–86	97	124
XVIII	9–10	22	49–50	60	86–87	98	125
XIX	10–11	23	50–51	61	87–88	99	125–26
XX	11–12	24	51	62	88–89	100	126–27
XXI	12–13	25	51–52	63	89–90	101	127–28
XXII	13–14	26	52–53	64	90–91	102	128–29
XXIII	14–15	27	53–54	65	91–92	103	129–30
XXIV	15–16	28	54–55	66	93–94	104	130–31
XXV	16–17	29	55–56	67	94–95	105	131–32
XXVI	17–18	30	57–58	68	95–96	106	132–33
XXVII	18–19	31	58	69	96	107	133–34
XXVIII	19–20	32	58–59	70	96–97	108	134–35
XXIX	20–21	33	59–60	71	97–98	109	135–36
XXX	21–22	34	60–61	72	98–99	110	136–37
XXXI	22–23	35	61–62	73	99–100	111	137–38
XXXII	23–24	36	62–63	74	100–01	112	138–39
XXXIII	24–25	37	63–64	75	101–02	113	139–40
XXXIV	25–26	38	64–65	76	102–03	114	140–41
XXXV	26–27	39	65–66	77	103–04	115	141–42
XXXVI	27–28	40	66–67	78	104–05	116	142–43
3	31	41	67–68	79	105–06	117	143–44
4	32	42	68–69	80	106–07	118	144–45
5	32–33	43	69–70	81	108	119	145–46
6	33–34	44	70–71	82	109	120	146–47
7	34–35	45	71–72	83	109–10	121	147–48
8	35–36	46	72–73	84	110–11	122	148–49
9	36–37	47	73–74	85	111–12	123	149–50
10	37–38	48	74–75	86	112–13	124	150–51
11	38–39	49	75–76	87	113–14	125	151–52
12	39–40	50	77–78	88	114–15	126	152–53
13	40–41	51	78–79	89	115–16	127	153–54
14	41–42	52	79–80	90	116–17	128	154

(Continued)

TABLE OF CONCORDANCE (cont'd)

E	I	E	I	E	I	E	I
129	155	178	205–06	227	252–53	276	300–01
130	156–57	179	206–07	228	253–54	277	301–02
131	157–58	180	207–08	229	254–55	278	302–03
132	158	181	208–09	230	255–56	279	303–04
133	158–59	182	209–10	231	256–57	280	304–05
134	159–60	183	210–11	232	257–58	281	305–06
135	161–62	184	211–12	233	258–59	282	306
136	162	185	212–13	234	259–60	283	306–07
137	163	186	213–14	235	260–61	284	307–08
138	164	187	214–15	236	261–62	285	308–09
139	165	188	215–16	237	262–63	286	309–10
140	165–66	189	216–17	238	263–64	287	310–11
141	167	190	217–18	239	264–65	288	311–12
142	168	191	218–19	240	266–67	289	312–13
143	169	192	219–20	241	267	290	313–14
144	169–70	193	220–21	242	268	291	314–15
145	170–71	194	221–22	243	268–69	292	315–16
146	171–72	195	222	244	269–70	293	316–17
147	172–73	196	223	245	270–71	294	317
148	173–74	197	223–24	246	271–72	295	318
149	174–75	198	224–25	247	272–73	296	318–19
150	175–76	199	225–26	248	273–74	297	319–20
151	176–77	200	226–27	249	274–75	298	320
152	177–78	201	227–28	250	275–76	299	321–22
153	179–80	202	228–29	251	276–77	300	322–23
154	181–82	203	229	252	277–78	301	323–24
155	182–83	204	230–31	253	278–79	302	324–25
156	183–84	205	231–32	254	279–80	303	325
157	184–85	206	232–33	255	280–81	304	326
158	186	207	233–34	256	281–82	305	326–27
159	—*	208	234–35	257	282–83	306	327–28
160	—*	209	235–36	258	283–84	307	328–29
161	189–90	210	236–37	259	284–85	308	330
162	190–91	211	237–38	260	285	309	330–31
163	191–92	212	238–39	261	286	310	331–32
164	192–93	213	239–40	262	286–87	311	332–33
165	193–94	214	240	263	287–88	312	333–34
166	194–95	215	240–41	264	288–89	313	334–35
167	195	216	241–42	265	289–90	314	335
168	196	217	242–43	266	290–91		
169	196–97	218	243–44	267	291–92		
170	197–98	219	244–45	268	292–93		
171	198–99	220	245–46	269	294–95		
172	199–200	221	246–47	270	295		
173	200–01	222	247–48	271	296		
174	201–02	223	248–49	272	296–97		
175	202–03	224	249–50	273	297–98		
176	203–04	225	250–51	274	298–99		
177	204–05	226	251–52	275	299–30		

* These pages carrying only the title of Part II of *Società* are not numbered in the Italian version.

Index

243